new home builder

builder

THE SELF-BUILDER'S GUIDE TO DESIGNING AND BUILDING YOUR OWN HOME

PAUL HYMERS

NEW
HOLLAND

Dedication

For my Mum, Dorothy – the best home-builder I know.

This edition published in 2008
First published in 2004 by New Holland Publishers (UK) Ltd
Garfield House, 86–88 Edgware Road
London W2 2EA
London • Cape Town • Sydney • Auckland
www.newhollandpublishers.com

ISBN 978 1 84773 107 4

Senior Editor: Clare Hubbard
Editor: Ian Kearey
Designer: Casebourne Rose Design Associates
Illustrator: Sue Rose
Cover photograph: Scandia Hus Ltd (www.scandia-hus.co.uk)

Printed and bound by Kyodo Printing Co (Singapore) Pte Ltd

ACKNOWLEDGEMENTS
As always, many thanks to Melanie, Karina and Rochelle for their
help and advice. When I told Rochelle I needed to cut 12,000 words at the end, she
instantly suggested I change all the 'ands' to commas, which I thought was inspired.
A big thank you to my Building and Development Control Colleagues, past and
present, for sharing with me their knowledge and expertise and attempting to fill the massive
gaps in mine; in particular, Planners Maxine, Mike, Rachel and Peter, and Highways Officer Gill.
Page 23 – image reproduced from 1907 Ordnance Survey map.
Pages 38–39 – images reproduced by kind permission of Potton Limited
(timber frame package company, www.potton.co.uk)

Contents

Introduction

S OME 20,000 TO 25,000 people have been busy building
their own homes in Britain each year, and the figure seems
to rise steadily. In spite of this often proving a daunting, if
not traumatic experience, the rewards from self-building are so
great as to overcome all the fears and drive more and more of
us towards it.

The oldest remains of buildings date from 12,000BC in the
late Stone Age, but home building didn't really take off until
the beginning of agriculture some 2,000 years later, when we
gave up chasing our food around and decided to stay put and
grow it. Still, it appears that since we first came down from the
trees and started foraging around on the ground, hunting and
gathering and generally striving against all odds to develop a
straight backbone, we have sought shelter from danger and the
elements. If your home offers you nothing else, it offers you
protection from the adversities of life and the weather.

I mention this because, deep down, I think we all still have a
primeval urge to build our own shelters. Many of us settle it by
erecting a garden shed, but not all. The desire to build our own
home is a common dream, and one which an ever-increasing
number of us are realizing. As a result, more and more banks
and building societies are offering specialized mortgages to
cater for self-builders, and companies from pipe manufacturers
to plot-finding specialists are springing up to serve this ever-
growing market.

Given the scale of the challenge, you might be forgiven for
thinking self-builders mad, but the rewards are too great to
resist. Financially, most do extremely well, leaping up the
property ladder several rungs at a time.

But there are so many other advantages, not least the
overwhelming sense of achievement and the ability to control

the quality of both the materials and the labour. You don't have to settle for some developer's idea of what standards you expect, which should come as a tremendous relief, because all the evidence suggests that most of the large housing developers believe you are prepared to pay considerable amounts for very low standards and still be happy. History has proved them right. Their profits have been escalating for years, and they don't seem to be able to charge too much or deliver too low as far as the house-buying public is concerned.

Not only that, but when problems do come to light with new homes, developers have not proved themselves to be overly keen in resolving them. One company that was revealed as building 10 per cent of its homes on a new estate with very soft mortar (you could rake the brick joints out with your fingers) claimed that it wasn't a structural problem. The new owners thought differently; with their properties built from bricks and soft mortar, they could imagine what the weather would do to them over the years. Even so, the developers refused to compensate them.

When you self-build you can check the work as it proceeds, or have your own surveyor check it and be assured that the workmanship is to the industry standard and to your standard. You can also take delight in choosing to buy what quality of materials you like – and what a tremendous range there is to discover, for almost everything from bathtaps to bricks.

Information is still scarce for the self-builder with little or no experience in the building industry, and you will need all the help you can get. This book will, I hope, prove an invaluable companion along the way, helping you to understand the complexities and challenges of each stage of the project, from financing and plot-finding to landscaping and street numbering.

CHAPTER 1

Finance

SELF-BUILDING **your own home is as much about planning your finances as it is about planning your building. And before you can begin on your plans you have to establish your budget.**

How much you can spend on the enterprise is dependent upon three factors:

◆ SAVINGS How much, if any, savings you have set aside for the self-build project.
◆ EQUITY How much, if any, equity you have in your existing home. Remember that you should deduct the cost of topping up any underperforming endowments on that type of mortgage, together with legal fees and fees for estate agents involved in selling your existing home.
◆ MORTGAGE The amount of any new mortgage you will be taking out for your new home.

If most of your budget is coming from a mortgage, a thorough investigation of what types of mortgage are available to you should make a good place to start. With this done, you will need to establish your limits for the mortgage.

When money is cheap and interests rates are low, banks are happy to lend sums up to three or four times your annual income – however, these loans all come with repayments to match, and you need to bear in mind the consequences of not being able to keep up with the repayments.

Some banks will want you to sell your existing home before building the new one, which means finding accommodation to rent, or living in a site caravan during the build. Many will expect you to find a quarter of the land cost and a smaller fraction of the building costs as a deposit. Very few will lend you all but 5 per cent of the costs.

Mortgages
Traditional mortgages are available to us because of the security of the property we are buying. Its value has been assessed to make sure it is worth at least, if not more than, the sum we are

borrowing to purchase it. Lenders can then be confident that their asset, should they ever need to repossess it, will cover the loan. All of this is possible when borrowing to buy an existing property, but when borrowing to build a home from scratch, things are a little different. The lenders don't have the luxury of security from a building that is yet to exist, and the way they deal with this fact varies tremendously from one to another. Self-build mortgages are not available from all banks and building societies, and even the largest may only deal with a few hundred such mortgages a year, representing a tiny proportion of their business.

Some that do offer self-build mortgages won't lend a penny until the first-floor structure is reached, which can make life a bit difficult if you have no savings, or have expensive foundations to install. Most require that you put up enough money towards the plot, or actually buy the plot outright before they will entertain a mortgage on the rest.

How much towards the total sum they are prepared to lend you is known as the LTV (loan to value) ratio. Normally this is somewhere between 75 per cent and 95 per cent, but since this represents a huge variation it is important that you shop around to find one that meets your needs.

 The usual checks on your ability to meet the repayments are made based on your and your partner's income.

Of course you will need to check out their interest rates, together with the timing of instalments or stage payments and how much they will be prepared to release at each stage. In providing the mortgage in this way, their level of commitment in the project increases with the level of the building: foundations, ground floor, first floor, roof level, etc, keeping your head just above water – but only just.

This can cause problems, particularly if you run over budget or hit unforeseen problems, and self-builders are occasionally scuppered by the restricted cash flow of these arrangements. What troubles mortgage lenders more than anything is the risk of your contractor going bankrupt – taking their money with them before it has been built into the home and leaving a negative equity.

These situations where more cash is needed upfront than they would normally dare risk are sometimes dealt with by insurance. You may be offered an indemnity scheme, for which you will, of course, have to pay a premium in advance, that allows the lender to provide a higher percentage of the build cost ahead of the stage reached. This type of mortgage could be particularly beneficial if you are building a package-kit home that requires full payment in advance of delivery, followed instantly by the labour costs incurred in erecting it. These indemnities are becoming common place for anyone wishing to receive more than 75 per cent on the LTV ratio.

Needless to say, all lenders will require copies of your Planning and Building Regulation Approvals before funds will be provided, as well as some evidence that you are proceeding productively. That might seem like an obvious thing to say, but in the past, when the building industry was booming, such checks were overlooked. Some large detached homes that were built in the 1990s reached the plastering stage without having made a Building Regulations application, before the owner ran out of the lender's funds and left them to inherit the mess.

With some banks caught in a loss of equity situation like this in years gone by, they have become less confident about funding self-build projects and require that you at least have sufficient capital to buy the land and materials as security. They may also require an independent surveyor's valuation of the work executed before stage payments are made now.

There are quite a few different mortgages available now to self-builders from a variety of lenders. In 2002 there were, as far as I can tell, 30 different lenders offering self-build mortgages. It was not so many years ago when none of the banks really had anything tailored for this purpose. The self-builder's problem, of course, is one of cash flow. Previously, if you didn't have a huge lump sum saved up to buy the plot and some materials, you couldn't even contemplate it.

To overcome this problem, self-builders have resorted to living in caravans or mobile homes on the site or renting accommodation elsewhere, since only by selling their existing homes could they raise the capital to start building the new one. Mobile homes are pretty comfortable these days, with fitted kitchens and separate bedrooms, so this may not be such a hardship, but renting them isn't cheap and Temporary Planning Permission is usually required to install them on site.

You need to think long and hard about whether you are prepared to live in rented accommodation with the security of knowing your existing home is sold and you have the money to build, or whether you are looking for some kind of bridging mortgage. In the past, bridging loans have crippled people before the new home was completed. The interest they had to pay on two mortgages caused tremendous damage.

 Having some funds is pretty much essential, since 100 per cent mortgages to both buy land and build are unheard-of.

Some of the specialist product suppliers have gone as far as lending 95 per cent in advance on the land and major purchases, however, and in many cases there is a system of stage payments based on a surveyor's inspection.

Perhaps the best way forward is to find yourself a mortgage broker to whom you can explain your requirements, and let them do the searching. Just make sure that they are registered with the Mortgage Code Register of Intermediaries. Some mortgage lenders themselves have also set themselves up as brokers, offering independent fee-charging services. Note the words 'fee-charging' because if, like me, you have ever in the past been given 'independent' financial advice you may have wondered how independent it was, given the fact that you weren't actually paying for it. Instead, the adviser took a cut from the product he sold you. I was always troubled by this arrangement, and I would strongly advise you to look for commission-free advice that you have to pay for on completion of the mortgage. Most brokers won't charge until then, by which time you have should have received their services in finding the mortgage that suits you, rather than one that suited their commission.

The cost of borrowing

Interest rates vary with the economic climate and, to a lesser extent, between lenders. Interest is only charged on the amount you have drawn down from the date it is released. You should check out each lender you consider and compare rates and products available. Some may charge an application fee of a few hundred pounds, but others may waive this.

The valuation fees that you pay when buying a new house and the ones which invoke a surveyor's valuation survey to check if the home is worth what you're borrowing both apply to borrowing for self-builds as well, even on the value of the plot. The cost of this survey may be another few hundred pounds, and must be borne in mind.

With stage payment mortgages, a separate fee may also be

charged with the release of each payment. Although this charge by itself is usually not high, when you add all of the lender's charges up it amounts to a considerable sum. Never believe anyone who tells you that borrowing is cheap!

Buying a plot

The price of land varies with the region and the state of the housing market, but clearly the cost of land must have a limit given its potential, and generally you should consider 40 per cent as the maximum element of your budget for the land purchase, including stamp duty and legal fees. If it becomes greater than this – and at times and in some places it does – then you need to carry out your calculations carefully and make sure that the value of your finished home will make the enterprise worthwhile. As with any venture, if the market drops while you are building, thus devaluing your home before it is finished, your financial rewards may be eaten up before you move in. Speculative builders tend to reduce this risk by building quickly and getting the finished home on the market fast.

Finding the right balance between what you're building and the cost of the land is important. It means not building too small or too cheaply on a large, expensive plot, or too large and too costly on a small, badly located plot. Look for a balance.

Buying an option

It is amazing how many 'building' plots are advertized for sale without planning permission for development. Many of them are new rural plots, agricultural land split up into varying sized plots, where even the faintest suspicion of planning permission is absent – and likely to stay that way. I've seen plots like these advertized from a few thousand pounds upwards, but buying them at any price in the hope that planning permission will be forthcoming is gambling beyond the National Lottery odds.

The only safe way to buy land without any Planning Approval on it is to buy the option.

This is the right to buy it if approval is forthcoming. You are buying a place in the queue with the choice of buying or not. How much you pay for the option is for you to negotiate with the landowner, but people have been known to pay as little as £1 or as much as 10 per cent of the selling price, should consent be given. You need to have agreed a selling price if consent is given for your design in order to make buying an option worthwhile.

It makes sense for you to apply for consent, if not in full then in outline, and the fact that you don't own the land is no hindrance. Part of the application form involves you signing a certificate to that effect and notifying the landowner of your application. If you are successful, the cost of the option should be deducted from the agreed price. It is not unusual for options to be time-limited, perhaps to one or two years.

Buying a plot at auction

This can be an excellent way of buying land or a property to redevelop, so long as you are blessed with self-control. You should have set in your mind the bidding limit you are prepared to go to before entering an auction – and be able to stop when you reach it.

Anything at an auction has a guide price and a minimum reserve price below which it will not be sold. You will need to have done your homework on the plot before the auction and be in full possession of the facts regarding its approvals and any potential problems, because invariably auction catalogue details are no different from estate agents' windows when it comes to disclosing information.

Do not think about bidding without having sight of the local authority approvals, land search results and covenants that exist. This should be the bare information that you need, and most auction companies provide it as a matter of course, but you should consider it as only the beginning of your research.

Inspect the site and see for yourself any potential problems with trees, ground conditions or neighbouring land and buildings. Visit the council offices and check out the approvals and their conditions, discuss any changes you were thinking of making with the officers, and find out whether it lies within a designated area of any kind with special restrictions.

Information that is held on public registers, like the local plan, is treated to be in possession of the bidders without them actually being told about it specifically by the sellers or auctioneers. So it is very much a case of 'bidder beware'.

The completion of a sale and final payment will usually take place at the seller's solicitor's office, not the auction house, and you should expect to receive the details regarding to whom, and by when, you must pay. If you have any doubts about the details of the contract and the parties' rights, you could do worse than refer to the Contracts (Rights of Third Parties) Act 1999. The reference section of your local library should be able to help you with this.

Auction sale memorandum

Lot number
Date
Seller's name and address
Buyer's name and address
Lot description
The price (excluding any VAT)
Deposit paid

The seller agrees to sell and the buyer agrees to buy the lot for the price. This agreement is subject to the conditions so far as they apply for the lot.

We acknowledge receipt of the deposit.

Signed by the buyer

Signed by the agent for the seller (auctioneers)

Buyer's solicitor's details (name and address, contact details, etc)

You will likely be required to sign a sale memorandum on paying the deposit, and if you fail to do so, the contract between you and the auctioneers is considered failed. The memorandum requires along with it some proof of your identity along with payment, which could be accepted by cheque, bankers draft or any other forms of payment set out in the catalogue. If, for whatever reason, you fail to meet these requirements, apart from losing the sale and it being re-auctioned, you may be liable to a claim against you for breach of contract from the seller. An example of a sale memorandum is shown left.

A percentage of the selling price must be paid once your bid is accepted, that is to say at the auction. Finding 10 per cent on the day with the remainder a month or two later, or whatever, is not meant to come as a surprise to you once the bidding is finished. Some mortgage lenders will provide finance even before a plot is found and issue certificates that will enable you to buy land at auction, but you will need the upfront funds to be instantly available.

A point worth remembering on reserve prices on lots is that the seller can usually be allowed to bid up to the reserve price, knowing that they can't actually buy it at this, in order to get things going. They must stop before the reserve has been reached.

Auctioneers themselves often impose considerable powers relating to the conduct of the auction. They can sell lots in any order they like, they may chose to split or combine lots, withdraw them or cancel the auction altogether. The details they are given to describe the lots are taken from the seller, and so they claim no responsibility for errors.

Buying by sealed tender

This system is perhaps more common in Scotland than the rest of the UK, but it is wonderfully simplistic and often favoured by landowners such as local authorities and statutory undertakers selling off land. Anyone wishing to take part must deliver a fixed offer in a sealed envelope, clearly labelled to prevent premature opening. The highest bidder wins. A guide price is given, as with auctions, but the downside is that you have no idea what competition you have, as you do at auction, and what they are offering. Your bid or tender could be well in excess of everybody else's, or indeed well below. Contracts for building work are won and lost on this basis as a matter of practice. Sealed bids are the same: they have to be delivered by a set time and date, and must be opened together.

How much is the building work going to cost?

This is the single most common of all questions relating to self-build. The only safe answer is, 'More than you think.'

I don't believe many of us will sit down and work out to the penny what the total cost of any project will be. We all tend to price out the major elements and then, when it comes to the finishings and the bits and bobs, our estimating runs a little vague or stops altogether.

My advice is to price the fabric of the building through to the plastered walls and sanitaryware fittings, then allow reasonable sums for the tiling and carpets – but stop there.

Kitchens, of course, can be priced as an item in themselves by a specialist supplier and fitter, and they tend to include everything right down to the under-cupboard lights. Because of this and the fact that they have a bare room to work with, kitchen installation firms are able to produce a CAD drawing and priced design of unswerving accuracy (so long as they measure the room properly and don't rely on your building plans). Bathrooms can be done in the same way by specialist companies. Set your budget for these rooms, though, because you can more or less pay what you like, such is the range and quality of products available.

The only accurate way to estimate the cost of your self-build and monitor it as work proceeds is to have a bill of quantities produced. Contractors working on medium- to large-sized jobs (and a new home usually comes into the category of medium) will prepare bills of quantities for just this purpose.

A standardized method of measuring building work has been in existence in the industry for decades now, whereby each element of a construction has a set way of being measured. Because of this standardization, some books are available as annuals with examples of what the current prices are for these elements. They are only examples, of course, but they will give you a guide to what costs you are likely to incur. In the same publications rates per square metre of floor area provide a rough guide to costing. The most notable of these publications is produced by Spon, but there are others, and some more advanced estimating systems are now available on computer program.

If you are committed to keeping a very close eye on the costs and knowing what they are, then only a bill of quantities will do it for you, and possibly a quantity surveyor to go with them. I personally don't see many self-builders employing a quantity surveyor to monitor their projects, but it isn't unusual to engage one at the start to 'take off' the measurements from the architect's plans and create a bill of quantities. If you can persuade one to produce the bill on a computer program (a basic spreadsheet software that you both can run will do), then you can make adjustments to it yourself as work proceeds.

Supplying the plans to a few general contractors to price in total is another way of costing the job, but their quotes may vary tremendously due to exclusions, prime cost and provisional sums aimed at protecting themselves against underpricing and unforeseen problems. Of course, builders who are desperate for work may actively seek to underprice on an estimate basis, knowing they can bump things up as the work goes.

Finding a builder who will give you a firm quotation (a fixed price, as opposed to a best guess) could prove difficult, and they might want some assurances that you are genuinely interested in employing them. A quotation based on a full bill of quantities is an expensive thing for any builder to produce, and some will decline to tender on this basis. Those that do will usually be the larger firms with overheads of perhaps 10 per cent to add in.

The best place to start for an approximate estimate of the build cost is with reference to the published rates of cost per square metre of floor area.

As well as Spon, the RICS (Royal Institute of Chartered Surveyors) and other professional associations issue these annually as guide prices, but there can be a wide difference between the lower and upper rates banded about. If you do use them, work around them as if they were bandings to give you a minimum and maximum cost, rather than one you could hang a hat on, but they at least give you a rough idea.

Insurance and warranty

Remember to include in the cost of the project all the necessary insurances and warranties. Lenders will normally want to see evidence of both public liability cover and contract works cover, if not employers' liability insurance as well.

Public liability insurance will cover you against claims made by third parties who are injured or have property damaged by your works. Contracts works insurance will protect you from your self-build becoming damaged by fire, storm, theft or vandalism during its construction. There may well be excesses to pay here for each loss that is incurred.

Employers' liability cover is required where you are employing tradesmen or sub-contractors, and covers you for claims resulting from their employment on your site. Optional cover can always be obtained for plant and tools that can have a habit of disappearing from a site. Mobile home insurance can also be purchased if you wish, regardless of whether it is being used for a site hut or living accommodation.

Many insurance companies offer self-build insurance packages that gather some or all of these elements together under one policy. Premiums are based on the cover, which usually means the value of the construction, although you may be eligible to claim some discount if you live on the site or pay higher excesses.

House-building warranties are unique products essential to all new homes, because without them, potential buyers are unable to acquire a mortgage on the property. There are only two major insurance companies providing warranties on a national basis: the NHBC (National House Building Council) and Zurich. Both have self-build products and a nationwide team of inspectors who carry out spot checks throughout the construction process.

On successful completion of your project the insurance company will issue a ten-year warranty against defects for the new home. If you find them to be too expensive or not right for your particular situation, you may be able to find a package of insurances that include the same cover or a private surveyor who is able to offer such a warranty backed by regular inspections.

VAT refunds

DIY home building has benefited from VAT refunds for many years, and hopefully will continue to do so. The tax refund applies to the VAT you have been paying for materials, but not to plant hire or labour used in the building of the home and the site. However, this can still add up to a significant sum of money, which is precious to any self-builder.

To qualify for the refund you will need to have kept detailed receipts and full and accurate records of your purchases. Incidentally, the system also applies to conversions of buildings into dwellings and, more recently, the renovation of derelict homes, where VAT on labour services can also be claimed back. (The latter was first announced in the 2001 Budget in an attempt to encourage the re-use of the many empty and abandoned homes we have at a time when we are also suffering from a chronic shortage of housing.)

These concessions relate to self-builders building homes for themselves, and not to property developers, building to sell. This doesn't mean you can never sell the place without having to pay the cash back, but it does mean that you are expected to live in it for a period of time. To my knowledge nothing has been published in the form of an exact time-scale saying for how long you must occupy your home before selling up, but if you do so within a year, questions may be asked. There are part-time developers around, building one property perhaps every year or two, who seek to masquerade as self-builders to obtain the tax benefits, and the system tries to keep an eye out for them. The tax benefits, of course, extend to Capital Gains Tax as well as VAT recovery if you are not building to make a living.

The scheme doesn't apply to attached annexes for dependent relatives, for example, but only to self-contained dwellings that can be sold separately. It may be possible to claim on detached self-contained annexes, which have independent access, such as a front door, but there is a tie-up here with the planning department of the local authority, who will be aware of the potential of such applications to be sold off in the future as separate dwellings.

In addition to covering the building of the home itself, any detached garages, conservatories and so on, serving the property can also be included in the VAT recovery.

You can obtain forms, known as Notice 719, from HM Customs and Excise offices or as downloads from their website. Copies of your plans, Planning Permission and Completion Certificate are needed to accompany the application – the latter being proof that the building is finished.

What isn't included?

Professional fees are not covered by the claim structure, so the various services supplied by your architect, structural engineer, and even the Planning and Building Control surveyors, are all subject to VAT. Plant hire equipment, such as scaffolding, power tools and mechanical plant are not covered either.

If the property you are building is intended for sale on completion, you cannot make a claim. If the property is intended for business use rather than purely residential, you cannot make a claim. If only a proportion of the home is intended for business use, you should enquire with your region's Customs and Excise office as to whether this will affect a claim.

You can only make the one claim on completion of your self-build; if you miss some receipts and elements out, you cannot make a second claim.

Payments to contractors

The Construction Act 1996 (aka the Housing Grants, Construction and Regeneration Act 1996) invokes a code of practice on matters of payment in the contract or agreement between you and any contractor, which includes the following:

◆ It should be specified how much is to be paid and when it is to be paid, the latter being best described as a stage in the works, rather than a time which might not be achieved.
◆ Get a receipt for all payments made to your contractor.
◆ If it is your intention, when this stage arrives, to withhold payment due to problems, for example with the workmanship or materials, then you should notify the contractor immediately in writing of the amount you are withholding, stating the reasons why.
◆ If you fail to do this but still withhold the payment, the contractor can give you no less than seven days notice of his intention to stop work. This right to 'pull off' ceases once payment is made, and the final completion date should be extended to allow for the time lost.
◆ In the case of most self-build projects, stage payments arranged at certain stages are appropriate – all structural work complete, electricity and plumbing first fix complete – and these may, of course, coincide with the payments made to you by your mortgage lender.
◆ The final payment should be due within 30 days of practical completion.
◆ All payments should be made within 17 days of the date they are due (the billing date).

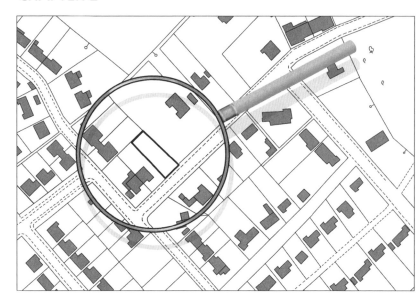

CHAPTER 2

PLOT

Plot

ONE **of the good things about building your own house is that you get to choose the location for where you are going to live. Instead of looking around for your dream home wherever it may be located, you get to find the location and bring your dream home to it. You decide on exactly where your home will be located – in the suburbs, in the town, close to work, or amidst the character of a village or the splendour of the beautiful countryside. At least in theory.**

You may be lucky enough to find a building plot exactly where you want it. My wife often remarks on passing a remote clover meadow or primrosed valley side, 'Now why couldn't we build a home right there?'

Maybe there was a time when you could (the Iron Age perhaps), and maybe there are still some countries where you can. But not now and not here in Britain. If anyone gets to build on green land it's the mass house-builders – when the Government lifts planning restrictions to make up some ground on the national housing shortfall, not when a self-builder wants to take up the good life. As a rule, and apart from homes built with agricultural restrictions, new homes in the countryside are restricted to replacement dwellings.

And there in lies the issue. Building plots are not simply pieces of land that have yet to be built on. More often than not, they are pieces of land that have already been built on and require something to be demolished before being redeveloped. At other times they are pieces of land carved off from large gardens, infilling a gap along a street. Sometimes in urban areas, they are brownfield sites of abandoned factories, or leftover plots on small developments where the builders have gone broke. Mostly they are found where they are found, rather than ideally where you would want them to be.

Serial self-builders are perhaps those who aren't too fussed about the location, since their chances of finding a good plot at a fair price are greatly enhanced. Often they build several homes, staying long enough in each to avoid taxation.

Having said all that, the location is everything when it comes to property value and desirability. It can also be everything when it comes to quality of life, and if your self-build is the one chance you have to find a home for life, then finding the right location is everything. And these days, more than ever before, there is a wealth of services of all types available to help you search for the plot you want.

There are Internet-based plot-finder services that offer a database of thousands of building plots throughout the land, where you can enter the area of your choice and be notified by e-mail whenever a new one comes on to the market; and there are estate agents with whom you can register, and auctions whose catalogues you can peruse.

The length and breadth of it

Parcels of land have been bought and sold – and hence measured – for millennia, and along the way they have attracted a variety of units of measurement. Instead of replacing and rationalising them as time has gone by, we seem to have added to them indiscriminately. Thus today in the UK we refer to, and buy and sell land areas in terms that nobody, except possibly farmers, can make any sense of whatsoever.

To add to the confusion, overleaf is a table of just what equates to what.

1sq y = 9sq ft
4,840sq y = 1 acre = 43,560sq ft = 0.405 hectares = 4,047sq m
1sq mile = 640 acres = 259 hectares
2,420sq y = 0.5 (half) acre = 21,780sq ft = 0.202 hectares = 2,023.5sq m
1,210sq y = 0.25 (quarter) acre = 10,890sq ft = 0.101 hectares = 1,012sq m
1,613sq y = 0.33 (third) acre = 14,517sq ft = 0.135 hectares = 1,349sq m
968sq y = 0.2 (fifth) acre = 8,712sq ft = 0.081 hectares = 809sq m
484sq y = 0.1 (tenth) acre = 4,356sq ft = 0.04 hectares = 405sq m

You should already know the size of home you want to build, or at least the number of rooms. Expanding that through a bit to include what hard landscaping and the extent of garden you are looking for, should be all that is required to estimate the minimum size of building plot you will need. Armed with this information, you can start looking for plots that fit the bill. There is little point in looking at all plots or possible plots, if half of them are the wrong size or shape to satisfy your needs.

As a guide, the average-sized building plot of a tenth of an acre will take a two-storey, four-bedroom detached house, which would cover perhaps a quarter of it and leave the rest for garden.

What to look for in a plot

Put in as much effort as you can researching the location of your site, once you have found one that fits the bill. By that I mean, check out everything that is important to you, whether it be the public transport serving the area, the proximity of local shops and schools, or the crime rate in the area and what surrounds the site to a radius of a mile. You might discover some elements that will surprise you – a chemical factory three-quarters of a mile away that delivers a hideous odour with a north-easterly wind, or a local plan to develop the field behind the site into a business park.

Site investigation

Site investigation work can be split into two types, desk study and site study. They are both important, and you should aim to complete as much of both before buying the plot, or at least before starting to build.

The reason for carrying out a site investigation survey is to discover the nature of the land you are to going to build your home on, and in particular what possible problems, if any, are in store for you. With new-home building, it is an essential process that may enable you to decide whether or not to go ahead with the project on this site.

If the land was built on before, it is likely that services, if not foundations, are still in the ground. Your investigation may reveal where the water main runs, or if there are any live drainage pipes or soakaways, come to that. These things needn't come as a surprise waiting to be discovered when the foundation trenches are dug, and indeed, if you have more than one possible location for siting your home, it may help you to decide where exactly you are going to position it on the plot.

Desk study

◆ RESTRICTIVE COVENANTS

Restrictive Covenants are clauses in a contract which was drawn up for the sale of the land previously, and are binding on all future purchasers. They may require, for example, land-owners to seek permission from previous owners (estate developers) for any new buildings on the land, and in so doing seek to control the character of the area as a whole. The Land Registry will declare their existence on a search of the plot. Covenants may be removed by application to the Lands Tribunal under Section 84 of the Property Act 1925.

◆ GEOLOGY

The United Kingdom has a good deal of geological diversity. The highly shrinkable clays that cause so much trouble in the south-east of England are unheard-of in Scotland, where metamorphic rocks prevail.

In some counties, such as Kent, the type of ground conditions changes from one town to another. Rock chalk, found nowhere else in the world, sits alongside Wealden clay, clay alongside green sand or gravel beds or sand. Large-scale geological survey maps are produced for regions throughout the country, and they provide a good guide which can be extremely useful. However, they do only provide us with a generalized assessment of the situation, and you may need to make further investigations.

◆ FLOOD RISK

The Environment Agency has drawn up plans of the areas at risk of flooding, and you should check these against your site. Look for any signs of past flooding or a high water table in evidence on nearby buildings. Are you near to a river or on the coast? Consult with the neighbours to find out the history of the area. Is the water table high? Flood damage to your home has to be one of the most destructive and disheartening things, and if you need to raise your floor level a few extra courses and build in a floodwater storage chamber to be on the safe side, it must be well worth it.

◆ LOCAL KNOWLEDGE

If you are new to the area, ask the neighbours what experience they have with the ground conditions; for example, does the soil dry out quickly in summer, shrinking and cracking? If they've lived there for some time, their knowledge will be invaluable, particularly if they are keen gardeners, so check out the neighbours with the best gardens first.

◆ MAPS

The very first Ordnance Survey maps were produced in 1872, but earlier maps are sometimes found in local libraries. Consulting large-scale maps of the area may reveal previous buildings on the site, the foundations of which could still exist underground, for example, likewise, the presence of an old pond or pit that may since have been backfilled.

Copies of 1:2500- or 1:1250-scale OS maps are only obtainable from certain outlets licensed by Ordnance Survey to sell them, and most local authorities fit the bill. They are digitally reproduced now. If there is any doubt as to where exactly the boundary of your plot lies, then the Land Registry will provide a marked-up map on application with a fee.

Each county or district has a geological survey map that details the ground conditions in the area. They are surprisingly accurate, but are small-scale and hence only able to offer general advice. They should tell you what the naturally occurring ground conditions are for your locality, and whether or not slip planes, for example, are present between colliding materials.

◆ RIGHTS OF WAY

If you have recently purchased the land, a Local Land Search should already have been carried out by now. If it revealed nothing else, it should have told you whether or not there are any public footpaths or private rights of way across your land. They need not be obvious on site, since they may be unused and therefore forgotten.

Even so, all public footpaths are recorded on 'statutory conclusive' record maps that are maintained at your local council offices and may be viewed by any member of the public. So if you are in any doubt, go and check.

Private rights of way, if obstructed, are enforceable through civil law, so if you were to build across one, quite apart from rendering your property subsequently unmortgageable or unsaleable, you may be fined and required to pull the obstructing building down. The fact that you may have obtained Planning Permission for the dwelling would be no defence.

If a right of way does exist that you are unhappy with, you can apply for an order to do away with or divert the path. (The planning authority, on receiving an application for such an order, is required to advertise the fact for 28 days to allow people to register any objections.)

◆ EXISTING FOUNDATIONS

If there are existing foundations on site, their depth and scope need to be established. Most domestic buildings prior to 1976 were built from shallow foundations, and it may be an easy matter to pull them out as you excavate your new foundation trenches. Others, from industrial buildings or more recent dwellings, may have deeper foundations that you may prefer to bridge over with a reinforced ground-beam design.

Site study

◆ SUBSOIL

To help you investigate the subsoil, a trial hole can be dug between 1 and 4m deep. If positioned at 5m away from any building, including any new extensions, it could later be used as a soakaway for rainwater disposal. If the hole reveals nothing else, it will tell you what the subsoil conditions are, whether they be clay or chalk, and so on.

◆ TREES

Are there any trees or large woody shrubs nearby? If so, note their position, size and species. In some situations, trees up to 30m away from the building can have an effect on the design of the foundations. See pages 105–108 for advice.

If your plot is located in a Conservation Area, you cannot lop or fell any trees without the consent of the local authority. Six weeks' notice is required.

If you wish to fell a tree that is in the way of your development, you must check beforehand to make sure that it does not have a preservation order placed upon it. Most local authority planning departments have a tree or landscape officer who can advise you if this is the case.

◆ VEGETATION

Note the vegetation on the site and be aware of any sudden changes in its appearance which may give a clue towards ground conditions – for example, in summer a strip of dead grass across a lawn will show where a shallow drain, usually bedded and covered with pea-shingle, runs below ground.

◆ SERVICES

If your site was built on before, services are likely to still be in the ground. That isn't a problem if they are inactive and waiting to be removed. If they are live or you want to re-employ them, you are going to need to trace them.

The relevant service companies will be able to give you the location of their pipes and ducts either by an on-site survey or plan. Gas, electricity, water and telephone now offer a free site survey to determine the exact position of their service pipes. They are able to do this by using sensitive detection equipment – in the past, they were only able to issue marked-up location plans, which were often inaccurate. If you can't get a site survey done and have to settle for a plan or nothing at all, then beware and dig carefully.

Drainage should also be investigated. Local authorities hold records of public sewers but not private drains. Although previous plans can be of some help in this matter, the only sure way to find out where private drainage runs is to lift manhole covers and measure depths from the bottom of the channel to the cover. Only site surveys can trace them accurately, and coloured vegetable dyes mixed with water are useful in finding out what goes where.

If you are hoping to connect into the existing drains on site and avoid a new public sewer connection, you need to ensure that they are deep enough. Apart from an adequate fall, the connection needs to be made in the general direction of the flow.

Building on a site where the sewers are higher or level with your new drains will mean installing a pump to connect into them. However, it is important that pumps are regularly maintained, and they run on electricity, so there is a cost and a risk of losing the supply.

◆ GROUND LEVELS

Is the plot level or does the ground slope? If it has a steep slope, then you may have to employ the services of a structural engineer to ensure that it will not become unstable when developed. If your home is to be built at the base of a slope, the excavations must not cause the ground to become unstable by removing the slope's support. The nature of the subsoil and the angle of the slope determine slope stability – chalk can have an almost vertical angle of repose, whereas gravel or sand has a shallow angle.

◆ TRIAL HOLES

To discover the secrets of the ground beneath your garden, you must dig. A few well-placed trial holes can reveal a great deal. Among some of the most common findings are wells, old soakaways, backfilled ground, redundant water tanks and the foundations of long-demolished buildings. Old wells and soakaways are best filled up with hardcore and bridged over. If they lie within the footprint of your home, this can invoke some structural design work. If they aren't too deep and are dry, it may be better to fill them with concrete and be done with it.

If the hole is of indeterminate depth, it may be wiser to fill it with hardcore, topping it off with some suitably level material and reinforcing the foundation concrete with steel bars.

You will need to find some good loadbearing ground on

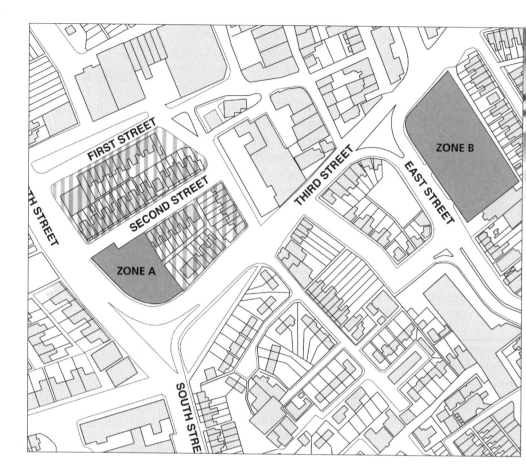

FIRST STREET

SECOND STREET

THIRD STREET

EAST STREET

ZONE B

ZONE A

SOUTH STREET

H STREET

▲ Modern maps are digitally stored and overlaid with information known as the G.I.S. (Geographical Information System). For example – the hatched areas denote conservation areas and the shaded areas are redevelopment sites.

either side of such a hole, if you are going to bridge over it like this. You should bear in mind that a brick-built well or tank may have some backfilled ground around the outside (for working space during its construction), and a more generous bearing is thus required to overcome it. Be aware that the soil around wells or soakaways may be softer, due to water seeping out over a long period of time. You may have to divert old pipes away or break them out entirely before work proceeds further.

Old foul-water tanks may represent a bigger problem – while they may have been backfilled, they often weren't treated or properly capped off. It is advisable to have any redundant septic tank or cesspool thoroughly emptied, doused with lime to settle the gases, and filled with hardcore before capping it off with reinforced concrete. The actual foundation or ground floor above an object of this size will need a structural engineer's ground-beam design to bridge over.

Apart from man-made obstacles, nature can also throw up some problems: you may, for example, be unfortunate enough to have a fissure in the ground or swallow holes. Faults in sedimentary rock or relics from the last Ice Age, and even underground watercourses can affect your foundation design, and are unlikely to be covered by the district's geological survey map.

Perhaps the worst situation is to find backfilled ground. Apart from being a little softer and perhaps variable in colour, backfilled ground is sometimes only recognizable by the presence of tiny fragments of unnatural material in the sides and bottom of the trench. Look for pieces of house brick or china – they do not occur naturally anywhere, and are proof that the ground is backfill; consolidated backfill maybe, but backfill nonetheless.

This dilemma is made worse by the uncertainty of how deep the backfill is. It could be extremely deep, making traditional foundations impossible or uneconomical, but on the other hand it may be that the natural undisturbed ground is just beneath it, waiting to be discovered. You can build on consolidated backfill, but wider foundations or a raft foundation may be appropriate over conventional footings. Digging trial holes in the corners of the foundations will prove to be a cautious way forward.

Brownfield plots

Until you became a developer you might have been forgiven – though not by me – for thinking that brownfields are simply those that have recently been ploughed, or possibly that have been left uncultivated by virtue of some bizarre European Union ruling that pays farmers for setting aside one field to stubble. You'd be wrong. It is much worse than that.

Brownfield sites are those that have been developed before, often by industry, and are now in need of redevelopment if only a developer with enough enthusiasm to clean them up can be found. Every town has brownfield sites: they are the places where long-forgotten factories once stood, where gasworks had gasometers scarring the skyline, and where coal yards had coal stacked in great heaps. The industries that once occupied these sites may have left years ago, but their legacy remains in the soil; and before anyone can build on them, these pollutants have to be removed and carefully disposed of. Even small sites like timber yards or village garages are polluted.

Soil reports for brownfield sites read like an inventory for chemical warfare. Where once an industry stood, its legacy is a list of contaminants in the ground that sounds frightening – mercury, arsenic, lead – every kind of poison known to man seems to be traceable.

🏠 Nowadays it is almost unheard-of to find a brownfield site that hasn't been contaminated.

A timber yard may be rich in copper-chrome-arsenic (CCA) from timber preservative spilled over years of wood treatment. A landfill site may be engulfed with methane gas percolating through the ground from decaying vegetable matter. Even a green site used for agriculture may contain polluted soil from years of being sprayed with insecticides.

The Government produced a national database, the first of its kind, of brownfield sites that existed, but when they counted up the number of new homes you could get on them the total fell sadly short of the 2,000,000 needed – 710,000, to be exact – and guess where the biggest shortages of brownfield sites were? Right where the demand for new homes is at the greatest.

When this database was published, house builders were quick to point this out, and indeed they nearly fell over each other in the rush to make derisory comments about the cost and the problems of developing on these sites, making comments about 'how it was all very well having a database, but those jolly local council planners often wanted trade-offs in public facilities for granting Planning Permission, which was rather putting them off building anything...'.

With national house builders shying away from small brownfield developments, it could be that these are left as urban infill plots for self-builders like you to snap up at a bargain price. But beware, if the plot doesn't come with an accepted survey you will be taking a significant risk in buying it blind.

Almost certainly in days gone by, we didn't look too closely at the ground we built our homes on. Times change, and these days all manner of possible risks are analyzed and legislated for.

The UK needs new homes in huge numbers, although the Government is frequently moving the target figure – once declaring that 4,400,000 homes were needed by 2016, then soon after revising that to 3,800,000 by 2021 – the message is the same, 'we need to get building'. They also added that 60 per cent of these new homes should be built upon brownfield sites, following the subsequent uproar about where they planned to build them, which was largely on our countryside. The Council for the Protection of Rural England would like to see that percentage increased – and who can blame them, for the green bits of our environment are shrinking quite rapidly, particularly in the south-east.

Flooding

It used to be the case that differing environmental problems were the responsibility of differing bodies – the National Rivers Authority for flooding and water aquifer management, the Waste Management Authority (often the County Council) for landfill sites, and so on. All this changed in 1996 when the Environment Agency was set up to deal with them all, thus allowing the Government and the public the opportunity to blame one body for all environmental disasters, rather than, somewhat inconveniently, several bodies.

This change works well and, if you watch the news, every time, say, a section of the Norfolk coastline floods, the EA gets blamed for not doing enough to prevent it or warn people. This has led to it getting into a bit of a froth about issues like flooding, and having now been accused of not doing enough to protect people's homes once too often, the EA enthusiastically objects to any new ground-level accommodation in flood-risk areas. A map has been produced, with great swathes of low-lying country around the coast and watercourses being marked as 'at risk'.

House builders have spent some considerable time scratching their heads in meetings where some of these 'flood escape' conditions are attached to the Planning Permission. Tiny, one-bedroom bungalows tucked away in a coastal town centre, for example, have been forced to have ladders that go up to the roof, whereupon they coincide with a rooflight opening out, permitting the occupants to scramble out onto the roof and await rescue.

Sounds sensible until you consider the facts. The building can be located miles from the sea. It is a back land development on a very small scale and likely to be occupied by an elderly person, the rooms are so small that there isn't the room for a full staircase and so a very steep, fixed-ladder-type stair has to be installed (the EA insists that it must be built-in and not removable, and that it must be inside the bungalow to be a means of flood escape), and there is a church across the road with a 30m-high bell tower.

Now if I'm wrong about this I apologise, but the towns and areas they select for such treatment are chosen only by virtue of their geography. Every year in Britain we see flash floods damage our buildings and threaten our lives, and the result is a knee-jerk reaction about the homes we build, because nothing can be done with the existing ones. Even if the estimated time for the sea to advance this far would be four or five hours (but only if it was a record high spring tide combined with heavy rain and a strong inshore gale), there would be plenty of time for an old lady to get up, get into some thermals and cross the road to the church.

The EA is seldom willing to compromise on these issues, only repeating that there wouldn't be enough time to warn everybody. From a Building Regulations point of view, stairways are dangerous places and every year people die or are seriously injured from falls on stairs, so there are certain design features that mean they have to be safe – and running at a vicious angle up to a sloping ceiling with a rooflight in it so you can climb out onto the tiles isn't one of them. If you're faced in your design with planning conditions like this, check out all the other possibilities first.

I am not deriding the problem they face: it is huge, and flooding is a terrible thing, but so are fire, radon, methane and carbon dioxide, and we have electronic detectors to warn us of those. Is it impossible to have a ground detector warning of rising ground water? A well with a ball-float alarm would probably work. On parts of our coastline where the ground is actually lower than sea level there are local bylaws requiring the storage of inflatable dinghies in bungalows along the shore. Bylaws are a sensible way of dealing with this, and draw attention to the fact that you are residing in a high-risk area and one day you may have mackerel swimming through your lounge.

Perhaps as you read this the EA has rationalized its advice and realized that unless a shed-size meteorite hits the North Sea a tsunami-like killer wave is unlikely to swamp us. But sea levels are predicted to rise gradually from global warming at a considerable rate, and that alone is ruling out bungalow developments in parts of the country.

Landfill

Pollution control is a science of its own these days, and I'm pleased about that – it can only lead to a cleaner and healthier world for us to live in. One day, perhaps, the only risk to our health will come from the fatal stress of knowing just how much pollution and contamination we have caused to the planet and how hard we have had to work to control it.

Nobody really bothered about landfill until fairly recently. Out of sight really does mean out of mind, and burying our rubbish in dirty great holes meant that we would never have to see it again. It wasn't until the 1990s that we became aware that the vast quantities of methane gas emanating from these sites as organic material decomposed could become a problem if it was ever trapped and built up.

If left to dissipate in the open air, then it presented no harm at all, but this gas has a tendency to migrate through the ground and turn up where you least expect it. If it does turn up beneath buildings and is left to build up beneath a floor, for example, then it could reach the state where it becomes highly explosive.

 With growing awareness of this potentially serious situation, waste disposal units began to look at their landfill sites, the soil around them and the distances between them and buildings.

When the first alarm calls for methane gas contamination were sounded in the early 1990s, the waste management authorities acted swiftly but silently. They produced landfill site atlases, which identified where the ground tips were or had been and what possible risks of methane gas in the ground there were to the people living in the vicinity. They decided upon a radius of 250m around the sites where the gas could migrate from and form a potentially explosive mixture in the floor void to any house. They could equally have chosen 10 or 1,000m, but they settled on 250 – as a kind of average, I suppose.

In producing these maps, at a stroke they blighted many homes. It didn't help that they endeavoured to conceal the risks from the public by making the atlases strictly confidential. Under no circumstances were the public allowed to see them, for the very sight of landfill site atlases would cause mass hysteria and property blight, even when there might not be a problem at all. Instead, they required planners and building control officers to carry out on-site monitoring of old landfill areas that had already been developed or were being developed nearby. Chaps in white coats turning up with electronic warning meters and sinking long tubes into the ground in people's gardens had a remarkable effect on property value itself – people who had bought homes without any problems found they couldn't sell them.

A similar thing happened around coal-mining towns all over the country when the 'safe' distance from a shaft to a house was suddenly reduced and people who had bought homes with nothing declared on the land search suddenly found they were too close to a mine when they came to sell. Hundreds, if not thousands, of homes were blighted.

Discovering new risks to our health is something we seem to do well, and spreading wide panic and confusion is something we do even better, whether it is Belgian chocolates, factory-farmed eggs, genetically modified wheat or ground contamination.

Traditionally, what can only make it worse is an active policy of concealment. Suspicion always leads to panic and blight.

With landfill tax fuelling recycling of materials and new technology in landfill site construction, things are improving now. Instead of relying upon little more than a clay liner to the holes, black plastic geomembranes are used now to line the sides before they are filled.

Plastic technology has meant that ridiculously strong sheets of plastic can be made and welded together in vast sheets up to a kilometre square.

These plastic sheets, once removed from the effects of UV light by being buried underground, have life expectancies that are frankly indecent. Accelerated ageing tests indicate 2,500 years before they degrade. Personally, I find it a little scary that we have invented plastics that will last for millennia. Naturally the companies that manufacture this stuff sell it on the basis that the rubbish, once contained in a site lined with this stuff, is going to stay there, and no amount of gas will ever migrate out through the ground.

One side effect of plastic liners you may be familiar with in your kitchen pedal bin: leachates – the liquid that seeps out of organic material and is retained by the plastic liner. If this isn't drained away from a landfill site, the garbage is going to start to float one day. To take care of it, leachate collection layers are provided at the bottom with drainage taking them to soakaways outside the liner. Fascinating stuff.

When methane does arrive beneath our buildings, if they haven't been built with protection from it, the end result can be disastrous. One national house builder found to their cost on one of their new developments that once methane gets in to the home's cavities, it really isn't possible to do much about it. The homeowners had to be moved out into hotels, and the homes ultimately had to be demolished and rebuilt further up the road, where the gas wasn't present.

Contamination

When the Environment Agency took to the problem and a new Environmental Protection Act was introduced, a more open policy of risk assessment was adopted, including the inspection of all sites and the publication of any contaminants found.

As you might imagine, the chemical analysis of the soil on

brownfield sites usually reveals a multitude of contaminants, but often the levels are extremely low, and we have without question been living with them for many, many years already without growing third eyes in our foreheads and glowing in the dark. Because of this, specific action levels for each contaminant are now set at which they are a risk to our health – for instance, just how much cyanide can there be in the soil before we grip our throats and roll to the ground, eyes bulging, or how much radiation before we can read at night without having to switch the light on, and so on.

Some chemicals and metals present may not be directly harmful, but they could be damaging to ecosystems or the groundwater and therefore affect us indirectly. The controls must therefore allow for a surprisingly wide range of circumstances: people growing their own food on a garden vegetable plot, aquifer areas where ground water is collected for our water supplies and even – and this absolutely astounds me – soil digestion. Yes, people eating the soil. It has never occurred to me to do this, but apparently it is quite common among children under two. These pathological soil-eating habits run a massive risk in that small traces of some things are still a threat.

In different soils, the risk of methane migration varies tremendously.

In wet, sticky clay it may scarcely travel a metre or two, whereas in a fissured chalk or gravel it could migrate for up to 10 miles. The risk of anyone being killed seems to be very small, but the threat remains and the potential to blight property from the merest suggestion of methane gas in the ground is frightening, to say the least. To date there have been around 15 cases of methane gas explosions, and so it remains the least life-threatening of gases. Carbon-monoxide poisoning kills more people in buildings every year when faulty gas appliances fail to ignite and gas leaks silently around the occupants.

The Victorian age of industry and the pollution of the last century has led to most redevelopment sites being contaminated by chemicals of one form or another. Sulphuric acid from the oil industry, arsenic from shoe factories, lead from iron and steel works – the list goes on, with many sites having a long list of contaminants present in the soil.

Contaminants can have an effect on our health if the levels are significant, but they can cause damage to buildings by attacking concrete foundations. In addition to physical risks, there is also the matter of blight that can't be ignored. Pollution is an emotive issue, and the talk of contamination can destroy property values, even when the actual presence of it is negligible.

If you've bought a brownfield plot, you can expect to see a condition of Planning Permission being a soil investigation survey, carried out in advance of any building works (including reducing levels) since any movement or excavation on the site can spread the contamination around. The report will need to identify what contaminants are present and what the concentration levels of individual chemicals are, and whether they are inert or mobile. In the case of mobile contaminants, some will have definite paths, such as radon gas or methane, which as a vapour will be heading to the surface. Other chemicals, such as leachates, can sink to pollute the groundwater and so on.

All chemicals have different action levels at which their measured concentrations are too high to ignore, and they must be dealt with. The levels also depend on the proposed use of the site, residential use being one of the more onerous. Your garden surrounding the home is the main problem: soil will be valuable at the surface as a growing medium for vegetables and is exposed for children to come into contact with, and for these reasons alone, contaminated land has to be dealt with effectively.

Treating contamination

This is a specialist contractor's job with British Standard documentation setting out the practice of how it should be done. Samples will need to be taken for laboratory analysis from the soil and any water or gas present.

The report needs to conclude with any remedial treatment necessary and – most importantly – an analysis of the cost. If there are particular hotspots on the plot, then there may be options; for example, they could be removed by bulk excavation of the area and refilling with topsoil, or they may be covered over by a hard-surface driveway and parking area, or they may even be diluted or biotreated.

It is also possible that continual long-term monitoring of the soil is needed, particularly where contamination of groundwater is a risk. Given the 'perceived risk' generated by such monitoring exercises and the threat of them devaluing or blighting the home, you might want to think long and hard about building on a plot where long-term monitoring is required. Removing contaminated soil is the commonest solution, but a licence for transporting it to another site will be needed.

Biochemical or fungal treatment to stabilize the contaminants may be an option as a form of natural treatment, but this is only available for certain chemicals. Metals like lead and iron can't be treated in this way.

Flushing contaminants out with water or other chemicals as a method of washing the soil can also be done in some cases, and indeed even vacuum suction treatment can deal with petrol and other volatile pollutants, if you intend to build on a former garage site, for example.

If the nasties can't be taken out of the soil economically, maybe they can be contained within it by an impervious layer that prevents them from surfacing. Clay is a natural containing material that is often used to line landfill sites, since at a particular thickness it prevents any gases from migrating through. Plastic linings have also been developed for the same purpose that have life expectancies beyond comprehension. Archaeologists will be digging them up in future millennia, wondering why we buried vast sheets of plastic beneath our homes.

 Retesting of contaminated soil after treatment is inevitable, since only proving that the plot has been effectively cleansed will ensure its authorized development and your safe occupation.

Radon

In parts of the country the geology is such that a natural radiation called radon is present. Background radiation, as you may already have heard, is emitted from quite a few different sources, ranging from your TV to your mobile phone or, for the more adventurous, cosmic rays. So why single out radon as a major threat to our health, and then why take precautions in our house-building against it?

Well, first because those who have been exposed to high levels of radon run a higher risk of developing lung cancer, and since radon is a gas, it is possible to trap it in parts of our homes where it could build up to a dangerous level. The precautions to avoid this happening aren't complicated or particularly expensive.

The geology where radon is present is generally granite and other rock, but not clay, so parts of the south-west of England have the highest levels, as the build-up of radon results from uranium decaying in all soils and rocks.

Radon levels that could enter your home will vary depending on the inside and outside temperatures, but are normally higher at night.

Ventilation can help to disperse radon, but the best precaution is to stop it getting in through the ground floor by using a gas-resistant membrane in the floor construction.

The particles of this radioactive gas can be inhaled and attach to the tissues of our lungs, irradiating them, and of course the higher the levels of radiation, the higher the risk of radon causing us harm. The Government has set an 'action level', and from studies have prepared an atlas of the country indicating the areas where radon prevention is needed in all new homes. This atlas should be available at your local authority, but you should also be advised by your local building control office if measures are required to your self-build under the Building Regulations.

Essentially, the survey has been conducted on the 103 postcode areas in the country and identifies the number of homes found in the survey (a spot check survey, of course) within the area that were above the action level.

CHAPTER 3

Design

IF **you haven't spent ages thinking about the design of your home and trying to work out the best possible layout, then you aren't doing it right. Either that, or you've just borrowed somebody else's layout plans because they looked OK. Nothing wrong with that; as homebuyers we are always buying somebody else's layout plan for the same reason, but then we don't have the option of changing it.**

Here is the one chance you have of arranging everything the way you want it, so give yourself some time to really think about it, and put aside the instinct to conform with what you've seen in other homes.

The best way to tackle design is with a lot of scrap paper. Later on you may be able to have it drawn up into true illustrations, or even walk-through computer graphics to help you visualize the space you'll have in three dimensions.

Family homes often lend themselves to a basic layout on the ground floor, annexed to the kitchen and/or dining room plus an entrance hall that is furnished with a small WC mysteriously labelled as a cloakroom. On the first floor, things are a lot more cellular, with three or four bedrooms and a bathroom arranged around a landing.

Getting the layout right

This must be difficult, because the vast majority of homes seem to be laid out wrong. I'm not suggesting anyone is to blame here – national house-builders are working to very limited floor spaces and are still trying to convince us that the house is a four-bedroom executive one, even if they do have to leave the internal doors off in the show house to do it.

Once you know what rooms and spaces you need (want), you have to find a way of putting them in a layout that works. Because we are mobile creatures that are continually on the move about our homes, we need a layout that facilitates our movements. A layout that flows. Like a garden that leads you from one place to another with purpose but also with pleasure, your home should be designed around the same ethos.

Start with the front door – your point of arrival. The plot and its orientation will help you decide on which elevation it should be.

If it's exposed to the south-west, for example, the rain could be driving into you as you grapple with the locks, so maybe it will need some shelter – an extended porch roof canopy or an open porch. Enclosed porches are fine, but they do have the effect of moving the front door position out a bit and hence moving the problem of getting into the house out a bit. Open porches or canopies give you some protection from the elements and the chance to work out how you are going to get your things through the door now you've arrived home. The front door is in itself a design decision; whether you choose PVCu, leaded light glass or solid wood, it should reflect the character of your home and be wide enough to let you, and everything else that might come with you, in. It's amazing how many houses are built with the logistical

▾ An example of a layout for a five-bedroom house.

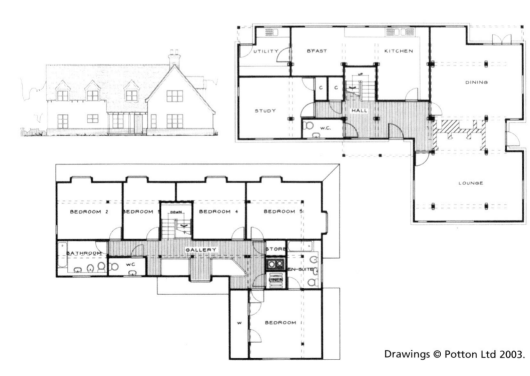

Drawings © Potton Ltd 2003.

impossibility of bringing a sofa in.

Many of us prefer not to be standing in the lounge at this point, but would rather be in a hall or entrance room. One that is warm and welcomes you in to your home by virtue of its size, decor and ambience is a bonus. If you draw some good light to this area it would help, but essentially warmth and the feeling of a safe harbour are what most of us look for. A corner fireplace will do this wonderfully, even if it is only decorative.

Moving on into the home is where things can get really difficult. The staircase to the other floor or floors must be located for easy access and escape, but at the same time you might not want it to lead straight up from the front door. The kitchen needs some relationship with the utility room and dining room if you have one, even if it's only a casual one, so long as they aren't too remote from each other.

You might want to avoid too long a corridor or passage, or indeed, avoid any corridor or passage if you can. They have a habit of finding their way into any design, particularly bungalows, where the bedrooms and other private rooms can't be reached via other habitable rooms. If you have to have a corridor, look toward making it brightly lit with glazed walls or roofs, or at the very least large windows. To house rabbits it would be fine, but the 800mm–1m-wide corridor running through the house is dysfunctional at best and institutional at worst.

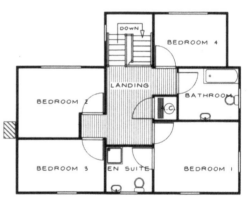

▲ These diagrams show the layout of a four-bedroom house.

Drawings © Potton Ltd 2003.

Consider where you might vault the ceiling up to the rafters to create space, because this works tremendously well, even in small rooms. To increase the space in smaller or children's bedrooms, a gallery can be constructed where the bed is somewhere between the floor and the roof-line ceiling, allowing some desk space or play space beneath it. If you aren't going to raise the ceiling in here to the rafters, then you must accept that the layout has a time dependency based on the growth of your children. They may not want to sleep so near to the ceiling as they get older, and may not physically be able to get beneath the bed to use the space there either. Even so, the camp or galley bed approach is practical and great fun for young children.

I know nothing about Feng Shui, but I can empathize with the point; to create a layout within your home, room or garden that you can live with – one that doesn't annoy, irritate, depress or generally wind you up. Homes can do all of these things simply by having their walls or doorways in the wrong place. The way in which you get there is the bit about Feng Shui that confuses me, in other words everything other than its objectives, which probably rules me out from ever becoming a consultant. Once I learnt that you had to imagine a dragon roaming through your home and seeing whether it felt comfortable, and realized my first question was, 'What size dragon?' I knew it was beyond me.

So I'm guessing here when I say that the dragon, mythical beast though it is, is perceived as an ungainly creature prone to knocking things over and setting things alight accidentally. Not entirely unlike myself. The point is that if it can find its way around your home without getting stuck or stressed out, then you and I should. We should be able to glide about the place like ballerinas, in total harmony with our environment.

I'll be the first to apologise if I've completely got hold of the wrong end of the Feng Shui stick, because I'm sure there is a lot more than space involved in it. But creating a layout in which you can move freely from room to room is a good place to start with your home design. So think like a dragon (or any other clumsy author-type creature) and imagine how it might feel living in your dream home, and you might realize that you couldn't.

Curves

Curves look great, everybody appreciates nice curves – but for some reason we don't think in curves when we design our homes. Corners and straight lines are what we think in. This may have stemmed from the fact that achieving perfectly square corners and perfectly straight walls was something to aim for and not often achieved – so why not deliberately fail at it and try to bend the wall into a curve?

Curves are a lot more achievable now than they used to be, with the advent of flexible materials like roof sheeting, plywood and even plasterboard, all of which are available now in flexi-form for bending into bespoke curves. Think of the opportunities inside your home where you once were going to create hard-edged, shoulder-jabbing corners; in those tight spaces you can now have smooth rounded corners that flow into the walls.

All it's going to take is a bit of extra time and cost, setting out the internal stud partitions or cutting up blocks, and you could transform your home.

Light

 Light is a multi-directional force, so don't stop at the window sizes for working out how it will illuminate your life.

Think about reflected light as well as direct light – about how it will bounce around inside the rooms. A glass-block partition or plate-glass screen can transform an inner room, and a roof light above a staircase will brighten the climbing, making it safer as well as more engaging.

If you've ever stood at the bottom of a staircase that ascends up into gloom, you will know how immeasurably better it would be to have one bathed in beams of sunlight before you.

The size of rooms

The only problem is of course, people aren't all the same. An agoraphobic would find the idea of open space living a frightening prospect. Small rooms with small windows and solid doors would, for them, be far less stressful. I think we may all be partly agoraphobic, as we like the idea of having a sanctuary – our cave – to retreat to, and in any case, some rooms are best kept small: bathrooms, for example. Overly large bathrooms are simply wrong, they give you a feeling of, well, vulnerability. You need some space to move safely and easily between appliances, but anything more and the feelings of comfort and privacy disappear. Bedrooms are similar, but since we can occupy so much of them with furniture and fittings, they can be quite big before they reach the same stage.

Kitchens need to be a practical shape as well as the right size. They are workshops, and as such things have to be readily accessible. If you plan your kitchen on such a scale that you have to continually cross a 5m void to bring saucepans to the cooker or fetch things from the fridge, then you are soon going to become tired of it and physically tired in general. The triangle rule should apply to all kitchens, the triangle being formed by the points of kitchen sink, fridge and cooker joined together on a plan. Ask yourself: do you need an island breakfast bar if it means you have to circumnavigate it to get from the cooker to the sink?

Architectural design

We are generally, as a nation, keen on architecture – we must be, as I have seen so many new homes built on architectural themes. Some have several mixed together. Apart from architects and conservationists, nobody cares whether it's a pseudo-Georgian portico made of PVCu stuck over the front door – if it helps to make our built landscape look a bit more interesting, then it's fine by me.

A lot of standard timber-frame house kits are based on the appearance of a half-timbered Elizabethan house without the fancy chimney stacks or tiny leaded windows.

They are popular. If the Elizabethans had had access to large panes of double-glazing they wouldn't have made such tiny windows themselves, so unless there is some overriding (I could say overbearing) conservation issue that requires you to follow authenticity in the design, feel free to mix and match architecture to achieve your design.

I have seen the occasional self-build home designed with some loyalty towards a particular theme. One was a 17th-century cottage complete with low ceilings, cut-down doorways that you had to stoop to pass through (and I mean every single doorway, including the front entrance door) and unevenly plastered walls. But of course the authenticity stopped at the kitchen door, where the 21st-century technology began, because the owners didn't want to actually live like 17th-century people.

I wondered what made them choose to build a brand new home without doors you could walk upright through, because I'd always imagined this to be one of the drawbacks of living in such an old place – there have been cases where people have died after clocking their heads so frequently in old cottages – and I was told it was part of the character. Without the insensitive controls of the Building Regulations they would of course have built in an impracticably steep staircase or ridiculously small window openings. And therein lies the problem, because you are building a brand-spanking-new home it will have to comply with the brand-spanking-new Building Regulations of its time and not the building codes introduced just after the Great Fire of London! A design that reflects a period of history will always be a compromised one, but that doesn't mean to say it is bad design.

In addition to the more commonly mimicked periods of architecture, there are those of the last century that are worth a look at, for no other reason than that they might inspire you in one particular aspect. The most frequently referred to example of modern domestic architecture is the house known as 'Fallingwater', designed by Frank Lloyd Wright. With wide, impossibly cantilevered balconies projecting out over a waterfall, the building still manages to be contemporary and yet blend in quite well with the landscape. Those impossible cantilevered bits are now regarded as impossible, since they pushed the laws of structural design a tad too far and are now failing. Wright was a brilliant designer, but a poor technologist.

Even before 'Fallingwater', the American architect had created the 'Robie House'. This Chicago home was truly ahead of its time in 1910, with great rectangular planes oversailing on a low level and the world's first-ever integral garage. Sixty-seven years later, architect Seth Stein took the integral garage one step further in his 'Garage House', which made the car a focal point in the living room. Located in Knightsbridge, London, where parking was a bit tight, this tiny house is laid out around a lift that raises the car up into the living room, where you can sit and gaze at it instead of the TV. If that is too cluttered an icon for you, the 'Stein House' in Highgate, London, built at the same time, is a statement in minimalism. Formed in simple uncluttered lines from glass and white-rendered walls, the light floods through.

Of course for this style of home to work, you have to be able to see pretty much all of the surfaces – walls, ceilings and floors –

▾ Exterior house features determine whether your build will fit with its neighbours.

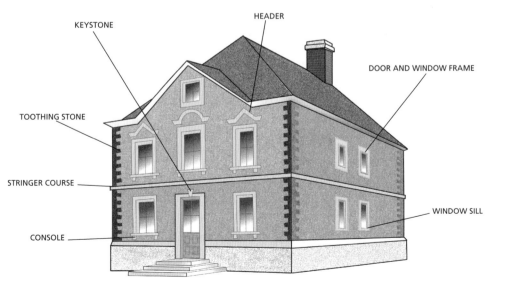

KEYSTONE

HEADER

DOOR AND WINDOW FRAME

TOOTHING STONE

STRINGER COURSE

CONSOLE

WINDOW SILL

which in most family homes is considered impossible. When it can be achieved and punctuated with the very occasional item of furniture, it takes on an ethereal quality. To go the whole way with this architectural theme would be too much for most of us, but there may be certain aspects that you can employ in your design, the glass balustrading to the stairs, for example.

Your dream home

If you've dreamed of building your own home for a while now, you probably have a well-developed idea of what it will look like, the rooms you want and their size. You might have seen homes that you like the look of – the shape of the roof, the roof tiles and bricks, and so on. But if you haven't already done so, start to put a file together of pictures and notes on your favourite designs, down to clippings from magazines of a chimney style you like or a style of window. Do not at this stage trouble yourself with the notion that they don't fit together.

Prepare a few sketches of floor layouts, indicating the use of rooms and their approximate sizes.

This is easier if you have already bought the plot. If you haven't, your plans may need to be a little more flexible and accommodate what land is available, rather than dictate what you need.

There are one or two books of standard house plans that are always worth browsing through at your local library, and you have the option of viewing other people's plans on deposit with the local planning authority.

Some of the basic design points below might seem a little too specific or detailed for this stage, but they have been chosen because they have a dramatic affect on the design.

Rooms and layout

How many bedrooms, and of what size?

The answer to this question pretty much determines the size of your home. But, as most of us can count our family members without any help and know instinctively whether we want to accommodate guests or not, the only thing to think about here is what size bedrooms. The minimum comfortable width of room for a double bed with space down the sides is 4m, and for single bedrooms 3m. The smallest of bedrooms, as national house-builders will tell you, become implausible below about 6sq m in floor area (2.45 x 2.45m).

How many WCs?

I think the record I've seen in an average family-sized home is six. I didn't at the time, and still don't, believe that six toilets are necessary in one house. We do seem to want a lot of WCs as home-buying consumers, however, and most new homes are built today with three or four – one in the bathroom, one en-suite off the master bedroom, and one in the cloakroom downstairs.

How many bathrooms/en-suites?

This is linked with the toilet question, but the number of showers or baths is the issue here. It isn't uncommon for people to locate a shower in a cloakroom if they are the outdoors type. Where it becomes harder is the eternal dilemma – bath or shower? Invariably developers are prone to provide both, if not as separate appliances then as a bath with a screen and mixer shower at the taps. But here you are building your dream home for yourself, and if that means installing baths in the en-suites instead of shower cubicles, then so be it. The only possible thing I can think of that might restrict your choice is the hot-water supply – if you choose mixer showers, possibly the flow rate from your boiler or vessel might not be able to cope with more than one at a time.

Is a separate dining room necessary?

So many people I've met have built in the obligatory dining room separate to the lounge and to the kitchen, only to find that they never actually use it. They either eat in the spacious kitchen they created or in the lounge watching TV, or possibly in the conservatory – but never in the dining room. Think carefully about your eating habits, and try not to waste valuable space by conforming to out-of-date tradition.

Utility room or an appliance-fitted kitchen?

Whether you choose to build in a utility room or not is often a matter of space. They are popular for housing those noisy appliances like tumble-dryers, washing machines and boilers if you have the room, but you might not consider one essential. Kitchens can be designed to house all of the above and more within the cupboard units.

Where utility rooms become essential is as a dividing space between back door and garage. In this way they have an added bonus as a space to remove muddy boots and keep out the car smells or the wet cat – a buffer zone between the inside of your home and the outside.

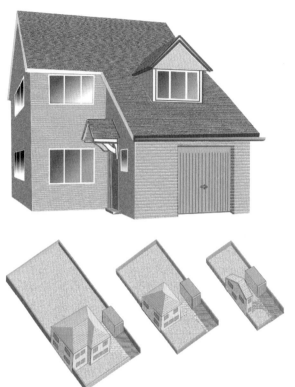

Attached or detached garaging?

Attached garages tend to be undersized in mass-house developments. They are invariably 2.4m wide and 5.5m long. You may want to expand on these dimensions if you actually want to put the car in it and get out of it afterwards.

Space for study or play?

I've seen studies crammed into what I thought were understair cupboards, and I've seen them settled on landings or in hallways. Anywhere there is a plug point, new house builders are prone to label a space 'Study'. I might be alone here, but a study surely has to be more than somewhere to plug in the computer, doesn't it? What about room for bookshelves, cupboards and natural light?

▲ Car storage dominates this house (top). The smaller the site, the more intrusive the on-site car storage and access become (below).

If you plan on working from home or have children who will need at some time a TV-less zone to do their homework, then you probably want a study; it needn't be huge, but it will need to be functional.

Playrooms are for those of us with more floor space than we know what to do with. If you fall into this category, I envy you.

Entrance halls

Entrance halls are about first impressions. Does your home layout welcome you in or leave you out in the porch? Every home needs an entrance – I mean beyond the door: a space that says you may not have walked straight into an inhabited room, but you are welcome to.

For most homes the stairs rise from this space; whether you call it the hallway or the foyer room is irrelevant (just don't call it the study), you will want it to be warm and uncluttered, but inviting. Many people choose a galleried landing at the top of the stairs specifically so the hall at the bottom of them can be ceiling-less, well-lit, spacious and airy – as well as, of course, offering a nice view of the feature staircase.

Roofs

Design

Roof design can transform a home. Whether with a series of high gables, long sloping catslides that almost reach the ground or hip ends, the roof is the icing on the cake of your new home.

The appearance of the roof is, and should be, its most important consideration, but it is your shelter from the elements and must be designed and built to resist the worst of them. Long valley gutters can become a maintenance nightmare in the future. High winds can rip up oversailing verge tiles, and rain can wash the granular face of concrete tiles into the gutters for years to come. Snow can also build up in valleys and at abutments between roof and walls, adding extra loads in winter.

Where roofs are often underused is in sun shading. A wide overhanging roof at the eaves can reduce solar overheating from the south-facing windows below, making the room temperature more constant and comfortable. In fact it is south-east and south-west elevations that fare the worst from sun power, because of the lower position of the sun at these orientations.

The space for up to 6m behind a window can be heated by the sun's energy, and some shading will help you to control the worst of that heat in summer. If you don't fancy an overhanging roof you are left with using solar-reflective glass or installing blinds. Curtains are not so effective, and frankly, who wants to draw them in summer, when for once the sun has broken the cloud bank we call 'the sky' and is brightening the place up a bit? Blinds can be fitted within the cavity of double-glazed panels and

▲ Wind is deflected around and over the building, creating areas of negative pressure or suction that can cause damage.

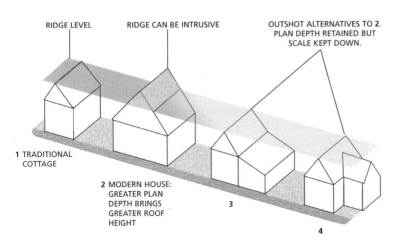

RIDGE LEVEL   RIDGE CAN BE INTRUSIVE   OUTSHOT ALTERNATIVES TO 2. PLAN DEPTH RETAINED BUT SCALE KEPT DOWN.

1 TRADITIONAL COTTAGE

2 MODERN HOUSE: GREATER PLAN DEPTH BRINGS GREATER ROOF HEIGHT

3

4

◀ Whilst maintaining the size on plan, reducing the roof volume will reduce the visual impact of the building as a whole.

TOP HUNG
REVERSIBLE

TOP HUNG

SIDE HUNG
REVERSIBLE

SIDE HUNG

TOP HUNG
PROJECTING

SIDE HUNG
PROJECTING

▲ The choice of window opening affects ventilation, security, cleaning access and escape from fire.

operated electrically, but at considerable expense. Fitting them inside will help to a lesser degree when it comes to keeping the heat out of your home. For most of the year you will want to let what heat you can in and prevent it from escaping, and glass has never been a good insulant.

Roof coverings

Choosing your roof covering is as important as choosing your bricks or wall finish. The material you cover your roof with has a profound effect on the appearance of your home.

Having seen examples of where the wrong tile has been chosen, perhaps from a sample of one or two individual tiles, I would strongly recommend that you look around at existing houses or scan magazines with a view to finding a tile or slate that looks good in situ. Most manufacturers will have brochures and websites with pictures of their tiles installed. Some materials suit particular shapes of roof and not others, and the pitch of the roof slope will determine the range of your choice – the shallower the angle of the roof, the less choice you will have. All roof tile manufacturers specify the minimum pitch required to ensure weather resistance for each type of tile they produce.

If you live in a Conservation Area or a Special Landscape Area, the planning authority may impose specific requirements on your Planning Permission for the type of roof covering, to ensure it blends in with the existing built environment.

Windows and glazing

In April 2002 the Government bumped up the Building Regulations standard for the insulation qualities of windows and doors by a huge amount, which relied on using wider cavities between panes and low-emission coatings to bounce some of the heat back into the house. It isn't easy to increase the thermal efficiency of glass much more without using argon-filled cavities or fitting triple-glazing.

So, apart from letting in solar heat and letting out manufactured heat, what have windows ever done for us? Views. Ah yes, views – this goes without saying.

The Department of Education now give advice on window areas to designers of new schools to ensure they are big enough to afford a view. The number of times I was cautioned for looking out the window instead of getting on with my work, and yet now views out are an important feature of classroom design. If window areas should be at least 20 per cent of the wall area for a school classroom, they need to be at least that for your home.

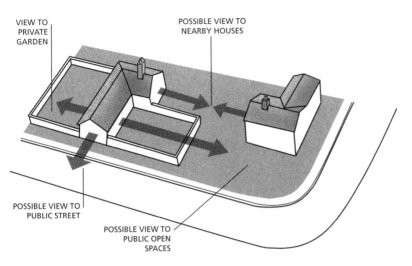

VIEW TO PRIVATE GARDEN

POSSIBLE VIEW TO NEARBY HOUSES

POSSIBLE VIEW TO PUBLIC STREET

POSSIBLE VIEW TO PUBLIC OPEN SPACES

◄ How your home relates to other buildings from the inside, in respect of privacy and overlooking, is a key part of successful design.

So, apart from letting in solar heat, letting out manufactured heat, and giving us views of our surroundings, what have windows ever done for us? Ventilation. Right, fresh air, of course – can't live without it – but how much do we need? At least 3L every second, apparently, to maintain our good health. Or, to put it another way, 5 per cent of the floor area of each room is an absolute minimum for the openable area of a window. One-twentieth. And if you install trickle vents into the frames you can meet the background ventilation standards at the same time, the standards that were mysteriously doubled a few short years after they were introduced.

Have people been asphyxiating in their new hermetically sealed homes, or was this aimed at preventing some other problem? I can't say. Either way, window manufacturers, to a man, now produce crack-vent positions on all their window openings that mean they can be locked in the slightly ajar position for security and air. Just how secure they would be on the ground floor rear elevation is questionable, since the gap they create is just enough for a jemmy bar to fit in.

Noise

Good double-glazing or triple-glazing and well-fitted casements will reduce noise levels from the outside world. If your plot is near a busy road or railway line, you will want to choose and position your windows carefully. It is never going to be silent, but how much background noise can we tolerate? Apparently about 50 decibels (dBA) is normal, but you should aim for 30dBA, which is basically as much as we can stand in the background.

Daylight

Natural light is priceless. We don't seem to be able to reproduce it, and it is free; all we need do is design our homes to let it in. Can't be that hard; can it? How much light is necessary? 500 lux is considered to be good light for studying or reading, which is actually about 500 times brighter than what we can physically just about see in. In plain terms, a window at least 10 per cent in area of the floor to a room is regarded as the absolute minimum, although controls don't exist in England and Wales under the Building Regulations. In the darkest part of your home try to avoid dropping below 80 lux, for the very good reason that accidents are likely to happen beneath this level of illumination – on staircases for example.

Fire escapes

It's not a nice thought, but one day or, more likely, one night, you might be trapped in your home by a fire and unable to get to the door. The windows are your only hope, and if you haven't designed the openings big enough to climb out through, your chances of escape are severely hampered. For most of us, and again I'm talking about averages that you might want to expand upon, a casement that opens up 800mm high and 550mm wide is a size we can comfortably get through. Fanlights by themselves are to be avoided, and narrow casements that are impeded by the standard scissor-hinges of the frame are defeating the point. With PVCu windows, you usually have to specify a fire-escape hinge if you don't want to fit the scissors type that slide in as they open.

What is needed is a figure that meets all of these elements, which seem at once to contradict each other. I have come up with 25 per cent of floor area for each room translated into window area. This figure is round, it is easily converted to a fraction, and mostly it meets the requirements, but it is only a suggestion. Glass can be designed in to cover whole walls or tiny windows – it is just a case of how much maths you want to throw at it.

Your new home will need some maths anyway for its carbon index figure. This measure of how many tonnes of carbon it will emit each year is calculated for every new home. You can use the calculation as a way of demonstrating compliance with the ever-stricter energy-efficiency standards of the Building Regulations, and in so doing, you can also open up the design possibilities. For example, a highly efficient boiler and heating system can compensate in this calculation for larger areas of glass than would otherwise be allowed.

Front entrance doors

We used to pay a good deal of attention to the front doors of our homes. I think in recent years its importance has become lost, perhaps at the same time as we starting replacing our solid wood with PVCu. Plastic doors are weathertight, they don't shrink or warp and don't need decorating, but finding one with a design you can live with and at a price you think it's worth, is a challenge. The frames are much larger than with wooden alternatives, and the moulded panels tend to be too small in proportion to the rest of the door.

In Britain today, new homes have to be built with a degree of accessibility for people with disabilities, and a key part of this consideration is the front door.

The doorstep has become a thing of the past, and it is now necessary to incorporate a level or near-level threshold. Even if you or your family members aren't disabled, it will prove an asset to children, mums with buggies and elderly relatives who visit, not to mention you in your old age. Standard PVCu doors presented a

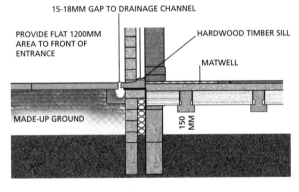

15-18MM GAP TO DRAINAGE CHANNEL

PROVIDE FLAT 1200MM AREA TO FRONT OF ENTRANCE

HARDWOOD TIMBER SILL

MATWELL

MADE-UP GROUND

150 MM

◄ Level access should be provided to main entrance door.

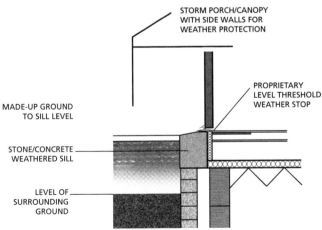

STORM PORCH/CANOPY WITH SIDE WALLS FOR WEATHER PROTECTION

PROPRIETARY LEVEL THRESHOLD WEATHER STOP

MADE-UP GROUND TO SILL LEVEL

STONE/CONCRETE WEATHERED SILL

LEVEL OF SURROUNDING GROUND

◄ Level threshold with porch or canopy protection.

formidable trip hazard with a threshold, but they can be designed out and replaced with a level threshold. To prevent wind-driven rain from coming in beneath the door, a drainage channel in front of the threshold must be included. In exposed areas you should also consider sheltering the door by an open porch or canopy roof, if not locating it on the protected side of the building.

Site gradients

Variation in levels on the plot can have a bearing on the design. If nothing else, the drainage is affected (and hence the position of bathrooms) and maybe the foundation depths and ground floor level. Steep gradients can affect the potential for making the home accessible for disabled visitors and residents: over 1:20 when relating the floor level to the road level or driveway may be too steep for a ramped approach, making steps the only way of getting up to the front door. If the driveway itself is too steep, it may not be possible to construct a suitable rollover for cars.

The only way to be sure of the gradients is to undertake a levelling survey of your plot with spot levels marked out at strategic points around it.

When this is transferred to the block plan your designer will be able to check out the relationship with the existing drains or public sewer and form an appropriate ground-floor slab level.

Viciously sloping sites have advantages as well as disadvantages, so don't be disheartened if you have one. They are excellent for devising sub-ground or split-floor levels. They can be set into the bank, with garages or utility rooms at the lower level, and built over with habitable rooms that relate in the rear elevation to the ground level there, but have a first-floor aspect at the front. The same applies for setting a basic two-storey home into a bank, where access can be formed at the upper level out onto the ground behind, opening up the exciting possibilities of first-floor conservatories and garden rooms.

In this way the home may be three storeys for the living accommodation. Split-level homes like this aren't always covered by regulations, so you may have to discuss with your architect and building control surveyor how you think your home will work in terms of its layout for fire safety. In general, it is better to work with the lie of the land, rather than try to level it.

Architects and structural engineers

Once you have some ammunition for the design of your new home, you can approach an architect or architectural designer. Most will want to spend some time talking to you about your needs from your new home, how it will appear externally, and how the rooms will relate to each other and the garden before they draft basic sketch proposals for you to consider. Having an architect draw up your ideas into professional working plans will bring them to life. Well-drafted plans will sell the design and enable you to tweak it to perfection. On a practical basis, without full design drawings, you will find it impossible to get any firm quotes from contractors and difficult to engage them in building it. Not only that, but you have no assurance that your proposed home is achievable and complies with Building Regulations and other standards until it has been reproduced on paper and approved. Good plans are essential – don't leave your home without them.

Whether you decide to take an architect's services beyond the design stage into project management is entirely up to you. Most self-builders find organizing the project extremely time-consuming at best and extremely stressful at worst. It can be both, and rewarding at the same time, because you get the satisfaction of making the important decisions about your home, and decisions will have to be made continuously as work proceeds.

First of all, you need to be available, if not actually on site then by phone, because having workmen stopping for hours or a whole day every time a problem occurs will be hopeless. Arranging for materials to be estimated, ordered and checked on delivery can itself be an uphill struggle, and for this reason some self-builder companies have established themselves as a design and supply of materials service.

This takes the headache out of measuring everything, quantifying it and getting it to site, all of which they arrange for you. On the downside, you might have been able to get materials a little cheaper by shopping around, but you have to weigh this against the time you would spend doing this.

You will, of course, be receiving an inspection service from your warranty insurers and Building Control Surveyor. Although they are both beneficial to you, they have their own interests of insurance and Building Regulations to look after, and they should not be confused with your own needs for managing the work and controlling its quality. In this respect, you or your own project manager should be on site regularly – if not actually each day – during the build. Not all designers offer a project management service, so before appointing anyone you need to decide whether or not you are going to fulfil the role yourself.

Architect or architectural designer?

As with builders, designers do not have to be registered or licensed with anyone to trade, and only those individuals who are registered with the Architects Registration Board are entitled to use the name 'architect' – which may explain why there are so many 'architectural technicians' and 'design consultants' around. They may voluntarily belong to a professional institution, but there are a whole host of different ones for them to choose from. All these institutes require their members to have relevant academic and technical qualifications, but you should be aware that they all have varying levels of membership designed to suit individual qualifications.

They are therefore, in effect, trade organizations for white-collar professionals, and should not be used as a measuring stick to judge the quality or otherwise of a designer. Having said that, most encourage their members to at least follow a basic 'code of conduct' in their professional activities and undertake continuing professional development.

Structural design work

Most architects and architectural designers are neither insured nor competent to carry out bespoke structural design work, and a structural engineer will need to be employed for this element of your self-build. Their design calculations will resolve any structural beams and elements, fixing details and sometimes procedural information for the architectural designer to transfer onto the plans. It is vitally important that the structural engineer's design conclusions are transferred on to the plans, as a builder will rely on these first.

So often, abortive work is carried out because the builder has relied solely upon the architectural plans and not followed the engineer's calculations. To be fair, structural calculations are not always easy to understand, and unless they have been translated onto the drawings or spelt out in the written specification, builders will often overlook them.

The only sure way to prevent this from happening is to check for yourself that your engineer is happy that the structural design is represented on the final plans as well as in the calculations. Make both designer and engineer aware that you want a comprehensive and clear drawing indicating all of the structural work and the sequence in which it is to be carried out. Relevant professional bodies for engineers are the Chartered Institute of Structural Engineers and the Institute of Civil Engineers.

Design consultations

 Most designers will offer a limited free consultation period, when they will discuss the feasibility of your project, but it helps if you have some ideas or rough sketch plans to show them.

When making this appointment, ask them to bring to the meeting some examples of new homes designed for their previous clients. You should always view their design work before agreeing the terms of their engagement.

Agreeing terms of engagement

Some designers prefer to use their own institute's standard forms of engagement, but if they don't, make sure that a written contract of some sort is established between you. If you can, agree on a fixed fee for each stage of the design – feasibility and sketch plans, outline consent, full Planning Consent, working plans and Building Regulations. Your agreement should make clear whether their fee includes any structural calculations or details that may be required by Building Control in the final stage.

Calculations may well be an expensive 'extra' in the design process, since the designer may have to engage the services of a structural engineer on your behalf and you need to know this in advance. Are the planning and building control fees included or to be added on?

Many disputes have arisen between clients and their agents over who was due to pay the council's fees. It is worth remembering that in the eyes of the local authority the responsibility lies with you, the applicant, and it would be to the applicant that they would look in the event of a bad debt. If you do agree for your designer to pay the fees on your behalf, make it a condition of the contract between the two of you. Building control fees are split into two separate charges, one for the plan's submission, and the other for the inspection service. The latter is usually charged to you, the self-builder, after the first inspection of the work.

CHAPTER 4

Consents and Building Laws

THERE are two types of planning permission that you may apply for, Full and Outline. The latter may already have been acquired to sell the plot as a bona fide building plot.

Planning Permission

The form of application

With an application for Outline Permission the applicant has had the choice of deciding which issues are to be considered and which are to be left out until later. The choice can be made from five categories:-

- ◆ External appearance
- ◆ Means of access
- ◆ Siting
- ◆ Landscaping
- ◆ Design

Any one or more of these can be included within the application, leaving the remainder to be dealt with by a subsequent application as 'reserved matters'.

These issues will form the conditions of an Outline Permission. If you've bought a plot with this type of approval on it, you need to know what the implications of the conditions or reserved matters are, and a discussion with your local planning officer to review them is the best way forward.

If you are thinking of applying for Outline Permission yourself, as a way of determining whether 'your' plot has development potential, then you should check with the planning officer first to ensure that it's appropriate to leave the issues you have in mind as 'reserved matters'. Highway safety and access may be fundamental to the site, and it may be unwise to leave them for later if your self-build depends on their approval. If your plot lies within a Conservation Area or within the curtilage of a Listed Building, design and an outline application may not be appropriate on these terms.

Full applications leave nothing to be dealt with later, except what lies within the conditions attached to the permission. Those conditions may include materials approval by requiring the submission of samples of bricks and roof tile samples, or even a window, for example, but fundamentally the holistic design of the home is considered in the full application, and hence drawings of reasonable detail are required.

The plans necessary for full planning consent should include:

◆ The scale to which they are drawn – 1:50 is standard for most floor layouts and elevations, but as small as 1:100 may still be acceptable.
◆ Duplications on A1 or A2 size paper – but not A0 or A3, which are usually too large and too small respectively.
◆ Dated and numbered plans, with the numbers cross-referenced onto the application form.
◆ A site location plan of 1:1250 scale with the plot outlined in red, and any adjoining land that you control outlined in blue. If there are any rights of way nearby, you should show them edged in brown. Ordnance Survey extracts are available, usually as print-offs from the digital mapping system; under copyright protection law, they may be for personal use but not sold on – effectively this can mean that you, the self-building owner of the land, can buy a copy from a licensed outlet, but an agent or architect working on your behalf couldn't.
◆ Floor layout plans, labelled to show the use of each room, and with the home dimensioned externally to enable the floor area to be calculated.
◆ Elevations of all sides of the home, illustrating the type and colour of facing materials and the design. If other buildings are close by (adjoining), it may be appropriate to show the new dwelling in context to them and the overall street scene. A clear and well-drawn architectural plan will help, because presentation of any proposal enhances it, and the use of colour in elevations is beneficial if it can be accurately reproduced. Blendable or watercolour crayon pencils are ideal for this kind of illustrating, because they can be used with subtlety to define true colours.

Site block plan

In addition to the location plan, a zoom-in on the plot itself must be included, and a scale of 1:500 or 1:100 is what's needed, depending on the size of the plot and the plan. This is the drawing that will show the siting of your home on the plot and its immediate environs: trees, driveway, parking areas and paths.

All boundaries need to be clearly marked and the building's distance from them, as well as the boundary treatment proposed or existing – such as chainlink fence, hedging, 1.8m brick wall, for example – should be included.

Existing trees that are affected by the proposed dwelling need to be identified, along with their species and crown-spread. A survey and advice may have to be undertaken later on their pruning or removal. Most authorities have a policy that seeks to keep existing trees in place wherever it is possible, and part of your planning application form will ask you this very question. If your site lies within the confines of a Conservation Area, it is an offence to lop or fell any trees at all without the expressed consent of the council, to whom you must give at least six weeks notice.

▾ Typical planning application form (see below and on page 63).

Something that also has to be considered with new homes is where the refuse is being collected from, in the sense that a collection point near the highway is needed, as opposed to one hundreds of metres away up two flights of steps. Refuse doesn't need a bin store as such for the one-off home, just space enough for it to be deposited on a weekly basis for collection, and this should also be shown on the block plan.

Planning Application Form 1

FOR OFFICE USE ONLY
APPLICATION NO

PLEASE READ ACCOMPANYING NOTES FIRST
AND COMPLETE IN BLOCK LETTERS

1A. NAME AND ADDRESS OF APPLICANT	1B. NAME AND ADDRESS OF AGENT
Telephone No.	Name for contact Telephone No.

2. ADDRESS OF THE APPLICATION SITE

3. DESCRIPTION OF PROPOSED DEVELOPMENT

4. TYPE OF APPLICATION   (PLEASE TICK ONE BOX)

A ☐ AN APPLICATION FOR NEW BUILDING WORKS

B ☐ A FULL APPLICATION FOR A CHANGE OF USE ONLY WHICH DOES NOT INVOLVE ANY BUILDING WORKS

C ☐ A FULL APPLICATION FOR CHANGE OF USE AND NEW BUILDING WORKS

D ☐ AN OUTLINE APPLICATION (ANSWER QUESTION 5)

E ☐ AN APPLICATION FOR APPROVAL OF RESERVED MATTERS OF PERMISSION
(ANSWER QUESTION 6) .... REF.NO._____

F ☐ AN APPLICATION FOR REMOVAL/VARIATION OF CONDITION OF PLANNING PERMISSION
.... REF.NO._____

G ☐ AN APPLICATION FOR RENEWAL OF TEMPORARY PERMISSION ..... REF.NO._____

WOULD YOU BE PREPARED TO ACCEPT A TEMPORARY PERMISSION? .... YES ☐ NO ☐

5. OUTLINE APPLICATION   (IF YOU TICKED D IN QUESTION 4 PLEASE TICK ONE OR MORE BOXES)

THE FOLLOWING MATTERS ARE RESERVED FOR FUTURE CONSIDERATION

External Appearance ☐   Means of Access ☐   Siting ☐   Landscaping ☐   Design ☐

6. RESERVED MATTERS   (IF YOU TICKED E IN QUESTION 4 PLEASE STATE WHICH RESERVED MATTERS ARE DEALT WITH IN THIS APPLICATION)

Of the two types of application, outline planning is usually applied for by land owners exploring the principle of building, and often they are simply trying to maximise the value of the plot with a broad permission to develop it. However, the system was overhauled in 2006 to increase the information needed for outline applications and now these have to be far more detailed. For new homes, design drawings and statements are necessary. Outline planning permission can still have some reserved matters that can be deferred until later in the full application, but design and access statements are now required and they in themselves must contain some detail. It is possible to refer to some of these details as 'indicative' of the final design and still change it later and to some extent this may be unavoidable. It is a bit of a flaw in this new system that a design, scale and layout plan is needed perhaps long before you know yourself what these will look like when the final design appears.

Design Statements

Included with your planning application you may be required to submit a design statement. In written form, these statements set your stall out and provide a summary of your proposals and the considerations you have made part of them.

Although the 'development' of an existing dwelling by extending it does not require them (unless you are in the grounds of a listed building, a conservation area or other designated area such as a National Park, Area of Outstanding Natural Beauty, Site of Special Scientific Interest, etc.), new homes will always need supporting statements that explain and 'justify' the proposal.

There are six elements to the content of design statements (seven when you include access) according to the 'Town and Country Planning (General Development Procedure) (Amendment) (no.2) (England) Order 2005'.

◆ PROPOSED USE
A fairly brief description of the use should head up your design statement, but do be overly specific about the use – e.g. the construction of a two-storey detached four bedroom dwelling with associated car parking and double garage.

◆ QUANTUM
This is a posh way of saying 'how many' units (homes) are proposed and as well as spelling it out in the statement, that your proposal is for 'x' number of self-contained dwellings, you should also mark on the plans the unit numbers if you are building more than one. Ground floor plans need clearly marking with plot

(unit) numbers. When the development is complete these can be converted into postal addresses on application for street numbering, without causing too much confusion.

◆ LAYOUT

Although your plans should illustrate the layout clearly, the statement should also describe it in words. The approach to the building, its position, the routes to access and egress, the open spaces and the relationship to other buildings and spaces outside of the development.

◆ SCALE

The new home must be broadly dimensioned to illustrate the mass of the building and the effect its presence will have on the site. Height, width and length of the proposed new build should be stated along with the resulting volume. For re-development projects, this could also be expressed as the increase in the cubic volume from any existing building on the site that it replaces. You may also want to state this increase as a percentage in context with the scale of the existing building to illustrate statistically the size of the development. If they care to, planning authorities can ask for axonometric drawings to illustrate the scale of the proposed home.

◆ APPEARANCE

More than a simple description of the materials used externally, this should also cover those aspects of the building which determine the impression it makes. With conversions, it may be unaffected by the proposal but, quite often, new windows and doors may be necessary and these will have a bearing on its appearance. Sometimes, one aspect of a building can be improved by cladding treatments that break up large expanses of one material, such as brickwork. A single panel of vertical hanging tiles or timber boards, for example, would do the trick.

Along with hard surfacing for car parking and access, landscaping is often an essential part of the scheme and also considered in with appearance.

◆ RESPONSE TO CONTEXT

This might best be described as a reference to those policies in force that surround your proposal. The local planning policies and national guidance notes are available (on the internet but also in libraries and local council offices) which will be used in judging your application and, together with its context in physical, social and economic terms, they will determine whether it is given permission or not. The statement should be a rationale of how the proposal came about.

Access Statements

What used to be described as 'access for the disabled', then 'access for people with disabilities', has now finally being referred to as just plain but politically correct 'access'. Applicable to the same proposals as design statements, access today is about inclusive design for people and it should be approached in that vain. Instead of making special features for access that are separated and unique, look for an all inclusive design approach. In this, minority groups like children, senior citizens and people with disabilities will all be able to get into and use your new homes, just as easily as able-bodied adults.

These statements are typically needed where there is a significant increase in the number of dwellings on the site and should cover five principals that set out:

1 How the occupiers and visitors will be able to access the homes from the existing transport network and what the access routes and points to the site are.

2 Whether any consultation has taken place with local access groups or other bodies, and what, if any, aspects of the outcome of that consultation have been included in the proposal.

3 It will explain the policy and approach adopted to access, and how the policies relating to access on relevant developments have been taken into account in the design.

4 How any specific issues which might restrict access to the proposals have been addressed.

5 How in the future the features of access to the homes will be maintained.

Flood Risk Assessment Statement

If you thought that the design statement and the access statement were enough, you may not be quite finished yet. If you fall (as many of us do in the UK) in or near to a flood zone, a flooding risk assessment statement is now also required. Introduced in 2007, these statements should also form part of your outline or full application.

Flooding has become prevalent in recent times, not least of all in the June 2007, the wettest since records began, which saw more than 28,000 homes in the Midlands and North of England flooded at a cost of some £1.5 billion.

The Environment Agency Flood Maps are available online so you can check whether you fall within the higher risk zones 2 or 3, by entering your postcode or address.

Unfortunately, there is also a third zone, zone 1, which still necessitates drawing up a statement. These exist where the Environment Agency have notified local planning authorities of areas (settlement, usually) where development could cause additional run-off of surface water which won't help the flood risk. The three zones are defined by probability – the probability, that is, of an annual flooding event in any given year. The odds are of course based on historical data, which may not actually count for much in a changing climate; nonetheless here they are:

Zone 1 – Low Probability (<1:1000)
Zone 2 – Medium Probability (1:100 – 1:1000)
Zone 3 – High Probability (>1:100)

Just as the design and access statements, the flood risk assessment should be a site specific appraisal.

The risk of increasing the flood water in areas surrounding the site by run-off from hard surfaces could be negated by the installation of French drains or channel drainage across driveways that discharge rainwater to an attenuation tank or to a soakaway. Attenuation tanks act as buffers in periods of high rainfall to prevent a sudden discharge of water into the drains (which are often overburdened at these times) or into a soakaway causing them to overflow. Soakaways need careful design and the guidance contained in BRE digest 365 is always useful to follow.

The Policy Statement PPS25 (published by Communities & Local Government Planning) does advise planning authorities to adopt a sequential approach to developing new land. Thus priority is given to locating new development areas in flood zone 1 first and then zone 2, following an assessment of the flood vulnerability in this zone (using table D.2 Annex D of the PPS25 document) and then finally flood zone 3. All of which means, you should do the same when submitting your statement.

Submitting your application

Planning applications have to be made in multiple copies, commonly six sets of plans and six sets of forms (signed twice on each). Local planning authorities have a great deal of consulting to do on applications, and copies are required to be forwarded around to consultees and made available for interested parties to come and view.

Those who are likely to be consulted on your planning application include:

◆ The local parish and town councils
◆ The Highways Authority
◆ The Environment Agency
◆ The Council for the Protection of Rural England
◆ Neighbours (public representations)
◆ Conservation officers
◆ Tree preservation officers
◆ Environmental health officers
◆ County archaeologists
◆ Local water authority

Neighbour notification

In England and Wales, the local planning authority will notify your neighbours of your proposals, either by letter, advertisement in the local press or by a notice displayed nearby. In Scotland it is your responsibility to consult with your new neighbours and submit their signed

7. ACCESS AND PUBLIC RIGHTS OF WAY
WILL THE PROPOSAL INVOLVE THE CONSTRUCTION OF A NEW VEHICULAR ACCESS?..... YES ☐ NO ☐
OR ALTERATION OF AN EXISTING VEHICULAR ACCESS? .... YES ☐ NO ☐
AND/OR THE CREATION OR ALTERATION OF A PEDESTRIAN ACCESS? .... YES ☐ NO ☐
ARE THERE ANY PUBLIC RIGHTS OF WAY WITHIN THE SITE? .... YES ☐ NO ☐

8. TREES
DOES THE PROPOSAL INVOLVE THE FELLING OF ANY TREES? .... YES ☐ NO ☐

9. DRAINAGE
HOW WILL THE FOUL SEWAGE BE DEALT WITH?
HOW WILL THE SURFACE WATER BE DISPOSED OF?

10. SPOIL
HOW MUCH SPOIL/DEMOLITION RUBBLE (IF ANY) WOULD RESULT FROM THE PROPOSAL?   NONE/_____ M³
WHERE WOULD THE SPOIL/DEMOLITION RUBBLE BE DISPOSED OF?

11. EXISTING USES
PLEASE STATE EXISTING USE OR, IF VACANT, THE LAST USE(S) OF SITE
IF RESIDENTIAL, STATE EXISTING NUMBER OF DWELLINGS _____

12. SITE AREA
WHAT IS THE SITE AREA? _____ Hectares

13. OTHER LAND
DO YOU OWN OR CONTROL ANY ADJOINING LAND .... YES ☐ NO ☐
(If yes, please show this land on the submitted plans edged in blue)

14. TO BE COMPLETED BY ALL APPLICANTS
I submit a site plan and the following plans
and enclose the fee of £ _____ by cheque/P.O. No. _____/cash
Signed _____ Date _____

15. OWNERS CERTIFICATE
UNDER SECTION 66 OF THE TOWN AND COUNTRY PLANNING ACT 1990.   **CERTIFICATE A**
I, hereby certify that:
1. No person other than the applicant was an owner of any part of the land to which the application relates at the beginning of the period of 21 days before the date of the accompanying application.
2. None of the land to which the application relates constitutes or forms part of an agricultural holding.
Signed _____ Date _____
On behalf of _____

16. ADDITIONAL INFORMATION
DOES THE PROPOSAL INCLUDE INDUSTRY, OFFICES, WAREHOUSING, STORAGE, SHOPS? ..... YES ☐ NO ☐
IS THE PROPOSAL FOR AN AGRICULTURAL DWELLING OR FOR EXTRACTING MINERALS? ..... YES ☐ NO ☐
(IF YES, PLEASE COMPLETE THE APPROPRIATE ADDITIONAL FORM)
July 2000/WP paf1

comments. Forms for this purpose are usually acquired with the planning application forms and should be returned completed when the application is made. In the former, interested parties have a couple of weeks to lodge their objections, if any. It is therefore sometimes beneficial to show them your plans and consult with them beforehand.

Many people and organizations are consulted in the planning process – parish councils, environmental groups, etc – and it takes some time for all comments to be collected. If there are any objections, it does not necessarily mean that your scheme will be refused. It usually means that it will be presented at a planning committee or sub-committee meeting and will thus be decided by councillors rather than by delegated powers (planning officers).

In most local authorities applications can be made and tracked electronically via the internet. Many architects can submit plans as 'computer-aided designs' through this service via the government's 'planning portal' site (see Useful contacts page 262).

Your application

If you are in any doubt over the questions contained on the application forms for planning and Building Regulations – and some of them look pretty odd – it is wise to ask for assistance at the council offices, rather than guessing. Incomplete or incorrect submissions might delay your application, and this is a bureaucratic process when it's running smoothly!

You should receive a letter of receipt for the application and fee paid, together with a date (eight weeks or thirteen weeks for sites over 1 hectare) which is the statutory date by which the application should be decided. Be warned, though, that the date can be extended, but only with your consent. For planning applications the extension of time can be lengthy, and you have little choice but to agree because it is deemed to be refused if consent hasn't been granted.

A programme of the planning committee meeting dates should also be available, and agendas for these can be sought a few days in advance of each meeting. These are public meetings, and you are able to attend and have your say.

It should be possible to find out in advance whether your application is recommended for approval by the planning case officer, and what the objections are.

If you do decide to attend the meeting, you may need to give notice in advance that you're coming, and be aware that you are not allowed normally to question the committee or indeed enter into a debate with them. There may even be a time limit of a few minutes imposed on your speech. As with appeals against planning decisions, you should restrict your commendation of the proposals to planning issues, but note that the committee may elect to postpone the decision to visit the site, for example. Usually it is considered inappropriate for you to invite them to a visit the site, even if you feel that it may help, but your recommendation for the proposal might lead them towards thinking it was essential.

Planning issues

Not everything is considered to be a planning issue. Loss of view and devaluing neighbouring properties, for example, aren't, and objections on these grounds to your application are irrelevant. To have a bearing on the decision, they must be planning issues.

◆ OVERSHADING

If your new home is proposed on the south side of a neighbouring building, then it may be judged unsatisfactory because of excessive overshading. This would only happen if your proposal was close to the building next door.

◆ OVERLOOKING

If your design includes side elevation windows which overlook a neighbouring property, the planning officer may consider that in doing so they encroach upon the privacy of the people living there. It is usually not sufficient to suggest glazing the offending window with obscure-glass unless it is a bathroom and would normally be so glazed, since it is relatively simple for future owners to replace the glass with a clear pane.

Apart from removing the window and re-positioning it on another elevation which doesn't overlook, the only acceptable solution is to design it as a high-level window with the bottom cill height at least 1.78m above the finished floor level. If you have a roof directly over the room served by this window, a rooflight will achieve the same.

◆ APPEARANCE

The visual appearance of the conversion is a prime consideration and one which is often the cause of much disagreement. Clearly 'good design' is a matter of opinion and, believe it or not, some planning officers have been known to disagree with self-builders as to what constitutes 'good design'.

▸ Lines of visibility at drive entrances.

▾ Turning space on drive-ways.

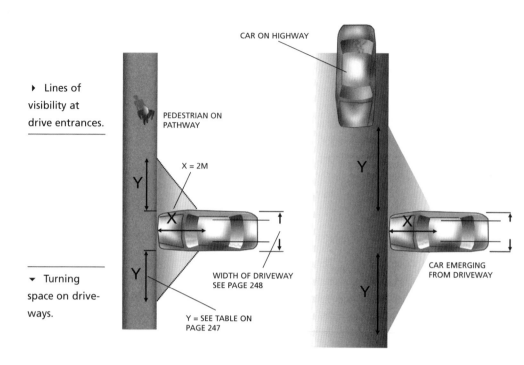

CAR ON HIGHWAY

PEDESTRIAN ON PATHWAY

X = 2M

WIDTH OF DRIVEWAY
SEE PAGE 248

Y = SEE TABLE ON
PAGE 247

CAR EMERGING
FROM DRIVEWAY

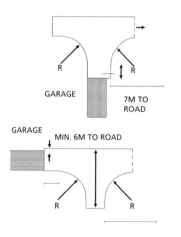

GARAGE

7M TO ROAD

GARAGE

MIN. 6M TO ROAD

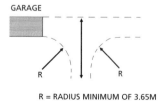

GARAGE

R = RADIUS MINIMUM OF 3.65M

The only advice I can give you is that your new home should not adversely affect the character or appearance of the area in its choice of materials and architectural style. In Conservation Areas or in the environs of a listed building, this is of prime importance. Consideration may have to be given to the style of windows employed locally, the shape of roofs and so on.

◆ SCALE

The volume of your new home, or, to put it another way, the bulk of it is important when it comes to considering its impact on the environment. This becomes more critical in rural settings, special landscape areas, etc, where the effect of a building on the setting is a prime consideration.

◆ HIGHWAY SAFETY AND OFF-STREET CAR PARKING

Safe access for vehicles coming on and off your property is essential. Clear lines of visibility must be provided, and to this end, your plans will need to be detailed and

Bad design   Good design

▲ With infill plots it is particularly important to consider the effect on the street scene (*see also overleaf*).

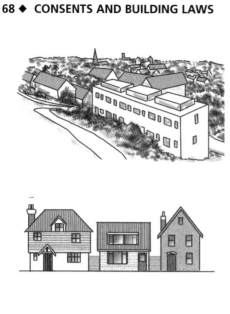

Bad design   Good design

dimensioned to demonstrate this. Parking space, either in garages or on hard-standings and drives should also be specified.

Your local planning guidelines might require a four-bedroom property to have at least three car spaces. These spaces have to be a given size and agreed with the Highways Officer, who will be consulted on your planning application. More advice on parking and safety is given on pages 246–249.

◆ DRAINAGE

Although drainage is covered by the Building Regulations in much detail, it is also necessary to demonstrate that your new home will have a means of drainage to get Planning Permission. More relevant is the issue of flooding, and whether your proposal is sited on a flood plain can have an adverse effect on surrounding property.

Conditions of Planning Permission

A few conditions come with every Planning Permission. Here are some of the more common ones that may occur in your case.

Commencement period

Permissions are only valid for a set period of time: three years from the decision date. To comply you have to start work within that time, and by 'start work' they normally mean at least completing the ground works to the floor slab stage. It is usually not sufficient to simply dig and concrete the foundations or reduce the site levels, but to be sure what is needed to meet this requirement check with your planning officer.

Materials approval

A sample of external materials should be submitted for approval. This normally means a brick and a roof tile, but could extend to a window or door in Conservation Areas, where visual appearance is more onerous.

Archaeological matters

Something relatively new to the planning system provides for the excavations of new buildings to be subjected to archaeological inspection in areas of particular importance. 'At the developer's expense' is the key phrase here. The authority may impose a condition relating to the supply of a report on archaeological inspection, but it will be up to you to appoint an archaeologist, perhaps from an approved list or through contact with the county archaeologist, and take it from there.

The excavations will either be allowed to proceed by an agreed method, or the sitework will need to be suspended for a period of time whilst the history guys do the digging for you. I have known people not be too upset by the delay caused by this process, particularly as the archaeologists, many of whom are students or volunteers, render trench bottoms perfectly level with their trowels – far better than you could ever expect from a groundworker.

But it pays to know in advance if your application will have such a condition attached, and since this is usually only as a result of its location, it isn't too difficult to find out in advance.

Agricultural conditions

These apply where the proposed home is tied to a farm or agricultural holding, and cannot be sold separately from it. These conditions permit a limited amount of use from the land in which the new home relates. Farmhouses are not usually considered as domestic dwellings for planning purposes, as they tend to come with agricultural restrictions that tie them to the business of farming and the holding of the farmland surrounding them.

Boundary treatment

Before works start, a plan must be drawn up indicating the design, position, materials and type of boundary treatment to be erected. The treatment may have to be completed before the property is occupied, or within some other prescribed timetable.

Sight lines

Before works start, the details of the sight lines at the junction of the drive and existing road should be submitted and approved. The height of any planting within the visibility splays formed by sight lines should not exceed 1.05m.

Parking

The home must not be occupied until the parking spaces or garaging have been laid out, surfaced or formed in accordance with the approved details. Car spaces must not be used for any other purpose other than the parking of vehicles.

Demolition of existing dwellings

Any existing dwellings must be demolished and all materials arising from the demolition removed from site within three months of the occupation of the new dwelling.

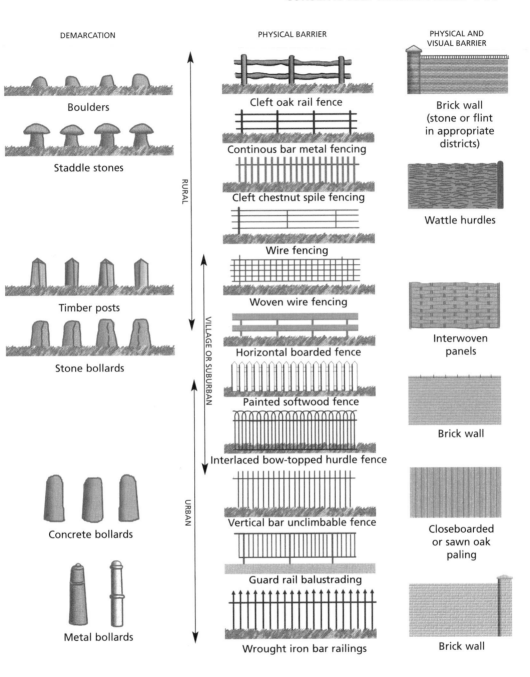

DEMARCATION

Boulders

Staddle stones

RURAL

Timber posts

Stone bollards

VILLAGE OR SUBURBAN

Concrete bollards

URBAN

Metal bollards

PHYSICAL BARRIER

Cleft oak rail fence

Continous bar metal fencing

Cleft chestnut spile fencing

Wire fencing

Woven wire fencing

Horizontal boarded fence

Painted softwood fence

Interlaced bow-topped hurdle fence

Vertical bar unclimbable fence

Guard rail balustrading

Wrought iron bar railings

PHYSICAL AND VISUAL BARRIER

Brick wall
(stone or flint
in appropriate
districts)

Wattle hurdles

Interwoven
panels

Brick wall

Closeboarded
or sawn oak
paling

Brick wall

Permitted development rights and special areas

Check to see if you have a condition removing your permitted development rights, which are sometimes used in Conservation Areas or rural areas where greater control is wanted over the scale or appearance of the property. Such a condition will mean you have to apply for all future additions that would otherwise

▲ Boundary treatment should reflect the area in which you are building.

be exempt, although in these cases the fee is often waived. Whilst conditions like this can occur anywhere, 'Article 4' areas can be designated by planning authorities (with Government approval) across a wider area. They achieve the same thing by removing permitted development, and greater control is exercised on development within a designated locality. Often they are unique locations within an area already labelled as a Conservation Area.

Conservation Areas are defined as 'areas of special architectural or historic interest, the character or appearance of which it is desirable to preserve or enhance.' They are designated by the controlling local authority in consultation with parish councils, local amenity societies and the general public. Areas of Special Control exist in some parts of the UK; although too small to be considered as Conservation Areas, they have been designated so to protect their architectural or historical value. Permitted development will be affected.

Refused planning permission

In the unfortunate event of your application being refused Planning Permission, try to find out from your planning department what the reasons for rejection were. While these will be stated on the refusal notice, they are likely to be in planning jargon with policy references, so some clarification may be needed. Try to discuss ways with your planning officer as to how they could be overcome by revising the scheme. If this isn't possible, you have one other recourse – to submit a Planning Appeal to the Planning Inspectorate agency of the Communities and Local Government (CLG) or the Welsh or Scottish Offices, or DOE for Northern Ireland as appropriate.

Planning appeals

Currently appeals are a lengthy and time-consuming process. Often after the appeal is submitted it takes four to five months before the inspector visits the site, and then another two to three months after the visit before a decision is issued. The CLG do not currently charge for appeals, and so an appeal can be entirely free if you do it yourself. Many people engage their solicitors in this process but if they are not fully conversant with local planning policies and CLG advice circulars (and most won't be), they are likely to be only of administrative help. Planning consultants who specialize in planning applications and appeals are the best choice, and some might offer you an appraisal of your chances from an initial review.

You can appeal against the planning authority failure to give you a decision on your planning application within eight weeks. Not many people do, because it can take the best part of a year to get a planning appeal decided, by which time you might as well have waited for the council to make a decision. Appeals may also be made against conditions of approval.

If you decide to appeal you must lodge the appeal within six months of the refusal date – and not just the forms, but all the accompanying documents that go with them.

Appeals are normally dealt with on the basis of a written statement in which you may quote the case for your application to be approved and request that the council's decision is overturned. Although the written procedure is essentially about preparing a text argument, you can illustrate it with photographs and drawings if you think it will help to illustrate your point.

As with committee representations, you should focus your argument on planning issues, particularly those listed on the grounds for refusal. They will be code-referenced on your refusal notice, as they refer to policies from the local or regional plan. To fight an appeal effectively, it is important to know what those policies are, and you can visit the planning authority's offices and view them within the structure plan.

It is important to know what the grounds for refusal were before deciding whether or not to appeal.

It may have been refused on a design basis, or it may be a fundamental refusal against the principle of developing the site; either way, you will need to know what it is you are appealing against.

Anyone who objected to your planning application will be notified regarding the appeal by the local authority and they will have an opportunity to further comment directly to the Inspectorate if they wish.

Appeals run to a timetable: after two weeks of receiving an application, the council will send you a questionnaire they have completed, and they will notify those who objected before. After six weeks, written reports will be submitted to the Inspectorate by yourself and the local authority, giving your reasons for appealing and theirs for the refusal.

The Inspectorate will forward copies to all involved parties, so you don't have to notify them. After nine weeks, you can comment on their report and contest any new issues or points that have been raised that weren't covered before.

You then wait for the Inspectorate to notify you of a site visit date. At the visit, you are able to point out features raised in the appeal so that they aren't missed, but you are not permitted to discuss the reason for appealing or argue over the reasons for refusal. If the site can be seen from public land (the road, for example) the inspector may visit unaccompanied.

Building Regulations

The two systems of building control

You can choose where you go for your building control service – your local authority or an approved inspector. Local authority building control sections tend to be based in planning departments or technical service departments at your local council, and they should offer a competitive local service. Approved inspectors are nationally based for the most part, and their inspectors tend to operate regionally. Some, like the NHBC (National House Building Council), are primarily interested in new-home building and can run the service alongside a warranty guarantee. Generally, however, they find one-off self-build projects less than lucrative, and as profit-making businesses they prefer to concentrate on larger commercial projects or housing estate developments. Self-builders often need a lot of advice from their building control surveyor, and since the building control fees are fixed for each project they may be unwilling to entertain your questions for too long.

Local authority building control services do not have to make a profit, but should be self-financing. They also provide other services that are not fee-related and hence not subjected to self-financing controls.

In building your new home you are required to comply with Building Regulations.

These regulations impose health and safety, energy conservation and accessibility requirements onto the built environment, and providing you meet these minimum standards in the design and construction, you will receive Building Regulation Approval. In Scotland this is referred to as a Building Warrant.

Full plans approval

Building Regulation approval has to be applied for, but it is a significantly different process. The control service has two elements to it, a plans check and inspections on site. With a full plans check you can expect them to write to you, setting out a list of defects or amendments to the plans required before approval. Alternatively, they may simply make these points the subject of a Conditional Approval. Either way, they should be addressed before work starts to avoid problems on site.

It is best to submit a full plans submission because you will then have the advantage of working from plans that you know comply with the requirements. If you follow the specification you can avoid problems and even abortive work. But you do have a choice because you are eligible to submit a Building Notice instead of full plans, which relies solely on the inspection service to establish whether the work complies.

Building notice

This is simply a statement form which basically says that you will be complying with the Regulations in executing the work, and gives the building control surveyor 48 hours notice of your intention to start the self-build. They will inspect the work at various stages on notification by you and advise you of any problems. A big element of risk goes with the Building Notice method, because you do not have the benefit of an approved plan to work to, and hence no assurance that your 'design' meets the current regulations. Your building control surveyor will only know if you have contravened a regulation requirement after you've done it.

It is normally considered unwise to tackle a new-home build in this way, but if you do, make sure you have at least some basic layout plans and a lot of prior discussion with your building control service before each stage is started. That way they can agree on the details beforehand. You will in any case need a block plan, with the drainage proposals indicated and the siting of your home on the plot. The notice procedure is not available in Scotland.

Refusal of plans and determinations

Because the requirements of the regulations are functional requirements, there is some scope for deciding what constitutes compliance and what doesn't. The scope is reduced by the Approved Documents, which give detailed advice on all the requirements, but they aren't intended to be the sole means of showing compliance. If you feel your designer's work has been unjustly refused approval based on these or any other standards or accepted guides then you can appeal to the CLG for a determination. Like a planning appeal, the CLG will consider both sides of the argument and make an informed decision on which to support – a judgement as a referee, and a legally binding one.

You can only use this procedure at the design stage on refused full plans applications. It is not possible to use it where work is in progress. As with planning appeals, it can be a long, long time before the determination is given, so you need to really care enough about your design to leave it for a year or so before starting work.

Advice on Building Regulations

If you need any advice on particular requirements of the Building Regulations, the Building Control Section of your local authority will be only too pleased to help. In England and Wales the requirements are contained in 15 'Approved Documents' lettered A to P and issued by the CLG as guides to compliance. The Scottish Building Standards have been arranged into a handbook of six parts. (Parts I and O, like in car registrations, don't exist.)

Each one deals with separate issues, e.g. Part A – Structure, Part B – Fire Spread, Part C – Resistance to Weather and Ground Moisture. Approved Document L comes in two parts, the first, L1, for dwellings – the second, L2, is for buildings other than dwellings and hence won't apply. These documents are the guides for energy conservation, and they are thick.

The Approved Documents can be purchased from the HMSO or any good bookshop, and have recently been published on CD-ROM.

You are not going to need to buy them for one new house, but if you do need to refer to them, they are usually found in the free download pages of the CLG, and also of course at your local authority building control office.

Building near public sewers

Not all public sewers are recognizable on site – some may be only 150mm in diameter and serving just a few properties in your locality – but if they are recorded on the map of public sewers, then they are the property of the water authority.

Because of this it is important that you do some research and check the maps of public sewers yourself in your area before you start work, if not actually before you design in the exact position of your home. Wherever possible, you want to keep some separation between your new home and the adopted drain – at least 3m is good. This should be enough to avoid you attracting special conditions in relation to building over or near the sewer. In 2002 this issue was made a little easier to deal with by the Government when it was included in the Building Regulations in some detail. As a result, you may well be able to resolve the matter with your building control officer instead of the water authority.

This largely depends on the size and importance of the sewer. Anything over 225mm in diameter is likely to be judged important enough to warrant their attention and a legal agreement between you, setting out protection and rights of access to it. Any smaller a diameter and, so long as your foundations are deep enough not to load it, you should be able to resolve protection measures with building control.

It is entirely possible that some assessment of its condition will have to be made before you go too far down the line. This could simply be a matter of exposing it and cleaning it off for a look-see, or if it is too deep or inaccessible, a camera survey might have to be done. CCTV surveys by video cameras designed like rats to run along inside the drains are very effective. The video image can be played back on TV in glorious sharp colour to show the state of the pipework, with a measurement displayed to tell you where along the pipe any cracks or holes occur. If you're planning on connecting your drains into this sewer, and I suspect you will be, then knowing it is in sound condition will be welcome. Alas, needless to say the CCTV surveys aren't cheap and would have to be executed by specialists – at your expense, of course.

Making sure you protect the sewer from future damage is the aim here, and this applies to any private drains you want to keep alive just the same as it does to public ones. The basic principles are to make sure the foundations extend to the same depth as their invert if they are that close, and if they actually pass through your building that they are encased appropriately and protected by lintels over the top.

Site inspections

It is a requirement of the Building Regulations that the builder notifies the building control officer at various stages of the work, and leaves the work at these stages exposed for inspection before covering it up and continuing. Failure to give such notice may mean that you are required to break open and expose the work for inspection later.

The stages for notification usually include:

◆ Commencement   2 day's notice
◆ Foundation excavation   1 day's notice
◆ Foundation concrete   1 day's notice
◆ Oversite preparation   1 day's notice
◆ DPC   1 day's notice
◆ Drains before covering   1 day's notice
◆ Drains testing   1 day's notice
◆ Occupation   1 day's notice
◆ Completion   2 day's notice

Additional inspection notices may be required by some authorities, such as exposure of existing foundations, so check with them before starting.

Notice should be in writing, and most authorities provide cards which can be used for this purpose. If you have one, a fax machine is an excellent way of giving notice, since it endorses the request with the time and date it is transmitted. Some authorities may operate a telephoned notice system. If you don't receive an inspection within the time limit, it is extremely unwise to carry on without first contacting the Building Control office to check why they haven't come out and give them an eleventh-hour opportunity to do so.

Building control officers do not supervise the work on your behalf. They carry out spot checks to ensure that the minimum standards of the Building Regulations have been met in the interests of health, safety and energy efficiency.

If you are in any doubt as to the quality of workmanship your builder will apply, you should appoint your own surveyor to oversee the project. A private surveyor can ensure quality control of the work, authorizing stage payments as the job proceeds.

Completion certificates

Once the work is finished, a Completion Certificate should be sought from your building control office. This is a valuable piece of paper which will be required should you sell the property or re-mortgage. It is a statement that the home complies with the Building Regulations. Until now, you may only have a Plans Approval Notice that says that your plans comply. On completion, you will have to submit a certificate of safety for the electrical installation from a competent person before you can receive a Completion Certificate. The Completion Certificate will also be needed to claim back your VAT, which is an excellent reason for trying to secure it as soon as you can.

Air tightness and Energy Efficiency

There are five key parts to showing compliance with the energy efficiency requirements of the Building Regulations.

1 The annual carbon emission rate must not exceed the target set for the home by calculations.
2 The fabric of the building and the services within it must have performance specifications within reasonable limits.
3 The glazed elements must be shaded to limit solar overheating in summer.
4 The completed home is air-pressure tested to prove that the air tightness achieved is equal to or better than that proposed in the design calculations.
5 Information is provided to you on the heating and hot water system and how to maximize energy efficiency in its use.

Insulation and air tightness are interlinked. These are two elements that will have a profound effect on the annual rate of carbon emissions from your home when it is finished. To comply with the Building Regulations, calculations have to be submitted at the design stage which illustrate how the proposed home will comply holistically with the energy performance requirements. A minimum level is set known as the TER (Target Energy Rating) that you must meet or exceed. The actual rate calculated is known as the DER (Dwelling Energy Rating).

Although the DER will have been established at the design stage, changing or modifying the specification in the build process can reduce the rating, causing it to fail compliance with the regulations. We aren't use to building to such rigid specifications in the UK and it is proving to be a bit of a bugbear. Everything

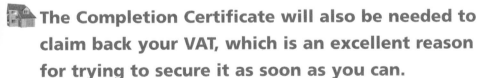

The Completion Certificate will also be needed to claim back your VAT, which is an excellent reason for trying to secure it as soon as you can.

from the light fittings (at least 30% have to be energy efficient) to the boiler type and hot water cylinder insulation is included in the calculations and much of it is assumed by the designer. You do need to ask for the details of those calculations in specification form to ensure you follow them, or are at least aware of it when you don't.

Your designer will have prescribed a rate of air leakage for your home within the DER calculations, between 3 and 15 cu.m/h/sq.m at 50 Pa. The rate illustrates how airtight and well sealed the building will be and, having set your stall out on this figure, you have to prove it. On completing works an air pressure test will be needed to check that the value has been achieved. If it the leakage rate is higher (worse), then remedial works will be needed. A benefit of designing and building an airtight home is that you can use a lower standard of insulation to achieve the same energy efficiency. A figure of 7 or 8 cu.m/h/sq.m at 50 Pa is a good standard to aim for and attainable with some care. Having your designer choose an achievable air leakage rate is however essential, and many adopt a safer leakage rate of 10 cu.m/hr/sq.m which really shouldn't be hard to achieve.

Air Testing involves employing a specialist registered (e.g. member of 'ATTMA' – Air Tightness Testing and Measurement Association') contractor to carry out the tests on your behalf. Essentially a small hovercraft size fan will appear on the back of a trailer and via a short air tunnel, air will be blown in through a doorway to pressurise the home to 50 Pascal's. The reducing air pressure through leakage is then timed, to calculate the rate.

At the design stage, you can always trade air tightness for insulation. The more your home leaks, the more insulation you need to counteract it. It is possible to design for the highest leakage (15) and avoid having to air test on completion, but to do that, you must have exceptional insulation levels and quite likely some renewable fuels, such as solar water heating. When the home is finished it won't be so easy to upgrade insulation and so it is better to avoid air leaks.

Avoiding leaks

For most new homes, air can leak out around door and window openings, around loft hatches and service holes for pipes and cables. These are the places where you must be vigilant and look for gaps to be sealed effectively.

Services are commonly brought in via ductwork, and so the gaps left around them will need to be filled too. Expanding polyurethane foam filler is ideal but leave the task until the services are connected up if you can. Any hole in the insulated envelope of your home can cause a failed air test. Careful workmanship by your tradesmen will avoid creating these holes to begin with, but failing that, careful reparations to seal them up afterwards is essential.

You can also help to improve your chances by using membranes to line ceilings and external walls in timber- and steel-framed homes, before plasterboard is fixed. Polythene sheeting can be pinned over the studwork but a better vapour barrier, and indeed a better air seal, can be found in the laminated aluminium foil sheeting products. Some encase bubble wrap polythene, whilst others comprise many sheets laminated together for added insulation. Aluminium tape is used at the joints to finalise the sealing process before the plasterboard is fixed.

Backing up dry lining like this, along with good quality draught-sealing openings should ensure that you pass the air pressure test later, and ensure that you get the energy-efficiency you need from your new home.

Sound insulation

Sound testing for detached homes is not required. Although the floors and walls separating bedrooms and bathrooms should be designed to resist a modest amount of airborne sound (about 40 decibels) this can be met easily by normal specifications. A doubled-up layer of plasterboard or acoustic mineral fibre insulation between timbers will achieve this. Only when you are semi-detached or terraced home building do you need to have to prove compliance. Sound tests have to meet prescribed levels set out in the Building Regulations as minimum standards of sound resistance between homes. You do, however, have a method of avoiding sound testing in new build situations. You can subscribe to the 'Robust Standard Details Ltd.' Scheme and select a standard detail to follow. It works a bit like a club, in that you have to pay to join the scheme and have your site registered. Upon which you will be sent a catalogue of the standard details from which you can choose one that suits you.

This chosen detail is registered for your site and to the building control office inspecting the work by you. All that remains is to follow the specification of the detail diligently and religiously when you are building. No variation, no matter how small, is permitted.

The system is only available for new builds and not for renovation projects where existing structures are part of the development.

With the exception of it being very prescriptive, I would advise that you choose this method as an alternative to sound testing. It is cheaper in the long run and much less stressful.

Test option

Airborne sound might be voices, music or televisions playing loudly next door. These days, entertainment systems come equipped with thumping bass tones and the test has to simulate those low frequencies too. A multi-faceted speaker blasts out pink noise at ear piercing volume. Unlike walls, floors are able to transmit noise through impact with the structure as well as air. Impact sound can therefore also pass through them. Impact sound is the sound of footfall or the moving of furniture for example. It is created during the sound test by a machine with mechanical dancing feet that frantically pummel the floor. Like the airborne sound test, it is unrealistically loud – but the point of these tests is not to see what can be heard, but how much sound is being cut out. The Building Regulations require sound reduction, not sound elimination.

Failed tests
Because the results of sound tests are independently certified, acoustic engineers have to be qualified and registered to carry them out. There are engineers trading who aren't and the results of their tests are unlikely to be accepted by Building Control. They should either be UKAS (United Kingdom Accreditation Service) accredited or a member of the ANC (Association of Noise Consultants)

As with air tightness, the fear amongst home-builders is of failing the tests. Having set out to install a system of acoustic insulation in the first instance, and not being able to test its success until the place is finished, is a bit nerve-jangling. Most tests that I've witnessed have succeeded, but not all of them. Following a recognised system of insulation is always going to help but it still isn't guaranteed to pass, because it is dependent on both the quality of workmanship employed in installing it, and also the fabric and design of the existing building – and both of these factors can be extremely variable.

One firm of acoustic engineers has reported about five percent of tests failing, and the reasons for these failures have included: using the wrong blocks in either separating walls or external flanking walls and in the bridging of cavities in cavity walls; walls with joists running through and mortar droppings; holes where they shouldn't be; and poor sealing of gaps in the construction of both floors and walls.

Other building laws

Private streets

Most of our roads are owned and maintained publicly by the Highways Authority, and it is they who employ and control safety standards and specifications for work on or near them. But not all roads have been adopted, some are maintained privately. They tend to be unsurfaced roads or at least unpaved ones, where collectively the residents living along them pay a sum of money every year for their upkeep.

Your local parish council should be able to point you in the direction of the residents group if yours falls into this category. I imagine that every year their elected committee would decide on how much is to be paid, but it would be worth knowing at the outset what the current and previous charges have been.

 The Highways Authority do not like private streets and try at every opportunity to avoid any more being created.

They also would like to see the future conversion of private streets into adopted public ones, and to this aim there is a statutory tool they can use. The Highways Act 1980 allows them to charge a set payment from the owners of new homes being built fronting them before they start work. Yes, even before you dig those foundations you may receive a bill along with a notice under Section 220 of the Highways Act 1980. Indeed, if their system is working correctly, it should arrive shortly after the Building Regulations Approval has been issued, and not more than six weeks later.

If the notice is served, it is an offence to start work on your new home until the payment has been made, and you risk prosecution if you do. The major housebuilders of estates tend to overcome this procedure by agreement (made under Section 38 of the Highways Act), but self-builders of one-off homes don't have that luxury unless they are building one in a consortium of many.

If you do really have to start work before you pay the full sum, a deposit agreed is normally acceptable. If you can't pay cash, some other form of security may be suitable, such as a mortgage or second mortgage on the plot, or a temporary bond written in a standard format.

Party Wall, Etc. Act 1996

You might think it is a bit premature at the design stage to be thinking of digging foundations, but there is a reason why you need to consider this early on. A private piece of legislation introduced in July 1997, entitled the Party Wall, Etc. Act 1996, surprisingly covers the digging of foundations in some situations as well as work on party walls. The act tries to prevent disputes between neighbours from getting out of hand and reaching the courts, as they are often prone to do.

In respect of foundations, you may be 6m away from the boundary, but if your excavations compromise the stability of the neighbours' property by virtue of their depth, then the Act requires you to consult with them and seek their agreement. Generally, a 45-degree spread of support is projected out from the bottom corners of foundations as the area within which the load or weight of the building is borne by the ground. This does really rely on knowing what the depth of their foundations is, and assumptions may have to be made until they can be exposed by a trial hole. Dig into this area anywhere up to 6m away (measured horizontally on plan), and you are at risk of affecting them.

If you are 3m away or closer, then the Act applies regardless, since it assumes that you are potentially close enough at that point to cause harm if you dig deeper than their foundations. This could mean you have to bear the cost of underpinning the neighbouring property to maintain its stability, but it could equally mean that both parties' surveyors agree there is no risk and nothing is needed. The Act is basically a procedural document that sets out your rights and your neighbours' rights and invites you (the self-builder) to notify them two months in advance of digging.

Each party can be represented by a party wall surveyor who is qualified in this respect, and if they can't reach agreement, a third party wall surveyor should be appointed to adjudicate between the two. You can find a surveyor in your locality by checking with the Pyramus & Thisbe Club. Named after characters in Shakespeare's *A Midsummer's Night Dream* who fell out over a boundary dispute, the society's motto is: 'The wall is down that parted their fathers.' You, like me, may look upon chartered surveyors differently now that you know of this fact.

If you forget or overlook the notification procedure, your neighbours are able to seek a court injunction or other legal redress requiring you to stop work.

Health and safety on your site

Even building designers have a responsibility under the Construction (Design and Management) Regulations 1994, commonly referred to as the CDM Regs, to minimize the risks associated with building work. They can do this by specifying safe working practice procedures when risks are involved, such as when digging deep foundations, by detailing the sequence of work and ensuring the trench sides will be supported.

As the self-builder carrying out the building work, you have some responsibilities under these regulations. Appointing your designer or another professional to act as planning supervisor is perhaps the best way through this tangle. The role of planning supervisor is an onerous one and carries most of the responsibility for health and safety. The Health and Safety Executive will be able to give you more information.

◄ Scaffolding should be maintained and checked regularly to ensure safety.

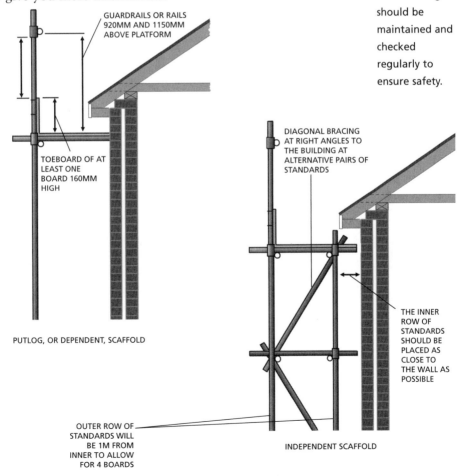

GUARDRAILS OR RAILS 920MM AND 1150MM ABOVE PLATFORM

TOEBOARD OF AT LEAST ONE BOARD 160MM HIGH

PUTLOG, OR DEPENDENT, SCAFFOLD

DIAGONAL BRACING AT RIGHT ANGLES TO THE BUILDING AT ALTERNATIVE PAIRS OF STANDARDS

THE INNER ROW OF STANDARDS SHOULD BE PLACED AS CLOSE TO THE WALL AS POSSIBLE

OUTER ROW OF STANDARDS WILL BE 1M FROM INNER TO ALLOW FOR 4 BOARDS

INDEPENDENT SCAFFOLD

CHAPTER 5

Contractors and Contracts

THE UK construction industry has a problem, and it's only got itself to blame. It has a massive skills shortage, and it's getting worse. Our skilled tradesmen who endured apprenticeships and learned their trade 'on the tools' are getting older and retiring now, and they haven't been replaced. Generally, young people have taken a dislike to building work in favour of IT and other more glamorous jobs, and for the ones who do want to, the industry has a habit of running around in a boom-and-bust circle.

Finding contractors

General contractors get by with a regular stable of sub-contract tradesmen who they use time and again, but as a self-contractor you won't have a reliable list of subbies to turn to and you will have to spend time finding suitable people well in advance. Once you've developed your programme of works and found contractors, book them in – only by doing this months ahead will you ensure their availability.

If the programme falters affecting their start date – and this often happens – keep them abreast of the changes. They are used to this; the building industry runs this way permanently, and working flexibly with time is part and parcel of it.

The knock-on effect of the skills shortage for the self-contractor wanting to employ skilled workers is that they are fewer and farther between than ever before, and filling the gaps are labourers if not actual 'cowboys'. It means you need to be extra careful who you employ, and to keep a close eye on the work. You should in any case avoid leaving contractors alone to make their own mistakes and decisions.

When trying to find contractors, look for recommendations and avoid looking at adverts. The local press can be full of 'cowboy tradesmen' advertizing their unique services. Instead, see if the local authority or large companies in the area are employing contractors on a regular basis, or whether any housing sites in the area have sub-contractors in attendance. You can always visit show houses on them. When you have a few names, run through this checklist. An invitation to tender and quote on a standard form, but with the scope for a separate schedule of work to be attached, is a good way forward and an example of one you can use yourself is shown on page 89, as both an invitation to tender (provide a quote) and a simple contract.

Health and safety

Building sites are dangerous places. Accidents that occur are often serious and all too frequently fatal. Under the Construction (Health, Safety and Welfare) Regulations 1996, some responsibilities lie with general contractors as employers of sub-contractors, or with self-employed tradesmen themselves – but also with you.

 It is essential that you are aware of safety on the site, not only for your own protection but also for those working on and visiting it.

If, for example, somebody should slip into an open manhole cracking a few ribs in the process, action could be taken against you under civil law for not ensuring it was covered over. This is a pertinent example, because over half of all injurious accidents on building sites are from people falling. As well as covering up holes and guarding edges, you should aim to keep the site as tidy as possible and keep an eye open for hazards such as discarded broken bricks, untied ladders and faulty scaffolding. Specific health and safety advice can be sought from the Health and Safety Executive, who have published a veritable library of brochures and booklets.

Cost control

The greatest challenge any self-builder faces when work begins is keeping hold of the costs and sticking to budget. Cost control is time-consuming but necessary if you are going to complete the project and be able to move in. It starts at the beginning, in inviting tenders for the work.

As a self-builder you may be engaging many different trade contractors in the project, and each should be invited to tender for the work. You can do this on a form that doubles as a simple contract. The one shown here has the advantage of requiring both parties to revert to the more complex conditions of the JCT standard form of contract if they become in dispute. Where individual contractors or sub-contractors are used for the various trades, as opposed to one general contractor for everything, it is important that you manage separate accounts for each if you are to keep control of the cost. Be aware of the status in law of a quotation and an estimate. They are very different.

Quotations

A quotation is a firm price that represents a legally binding contract between the parties. Having agreed a quotation, your contractor must stick to it. It is not acceptable for them to just incur additional expense on the basis that it 'had to be done' without you agreeing to it. If they do present you with a larger, unagreed final bill, in law you are not obliged to pay the extra amount, only the original quotation price. Inevitably, some variations will arise when the work is in progress, but it is important to document them, and the cost effect they have on a quote, with your contractor. Do not be tempted to let them ride and sort out the cost implications when the job is finished.

Variation orders

Agreeing the extras or variations should be done in writing whenever there is a cost variation.

The changes to quotations and contract sums that need documenting are labelled as variation orders or VOs. If you are engaging a project manager, then one of their key functions will be to keep account of them. They are written instructions to the contractor, authorizing him to carry out additional work or omit work that was previously agreed. Some contractor trade associations provide standard forms for variation orders to be written on, but you can create your own. A book of variation orders can be kept and jointly signed by both parties against the description of the work and its effect on the contract sum or quote. A copy should be kept by both parties, so a duplicate-type notebook with numbered pages is ideal for this purpose. If this system is diligently followed, you should be able to avoid differences of opinion later on.

Estimates

An estimate, on the other hand, is exactly that – a best guess. It allows the contractor to present a higher or lower final bill without warning and unagreed. An estimate is not legally binding unless it was supplemented with a written agreement stating that the price shown was a firm price.

EXAMPLE INVITATION TO TENDER/SIMPLE CONTRACT
For employing trade contractors
<name and address of contractor>

Dear............

Ref: ....<title description of job>

You are invited to submit a firm quotation for the above.

The work comprises the..

....and shall include for incidental works necessary to complete the work to my reasonable satisfaction.

Although a formal contract will not be entered into, the JCT Agreement for Minor Building Works 1980 Edition (revised 1991 and inclusive of all amendments to date) will be deemed to apply in the event of any dispute.

Damages for non-completion; liquidated damages will be at the rate of £........ per day/per week during which the works remain uncompleted.

An amount equal to 2.5% of the total value of the work will be retained for a period of.........weeks/months after the date of practical completion.

Where applicable, all work is to comply with the relevant requirements of the Building Regulations, NHBC or Zurich Home Warranty Insurers, BS: 8000, current Codes of Practice and other British and European Standards, material manufacturers recommendations and instructions appropriate to achieve a satisfactory performance.

The Contractor is to inspect the site of the work prior to submission of the quotation. No subsequent claim arising from failure to do so will be entertained. All costs incurred in preparing the tender shall be borne by the contractor.

Include in your quotation the contingency sum of .... For contingent or unforeseen works as identified in the schedule of works.

This sum to be deducted in whole or part as agreed by both parties if not required.

The works are to commence on ....and be completed by....................................

The specification shall be fully priced and a pricing summary sheet duly completed, signed and dated with the company address. The completed quotation should be sent to: -

<your name and address>

and must be received not later than..................<date required>

Yours faithfully,

....

Enclosed: Schedule of Work

If your contractor will only provide you with an estimate, and some will, it is important that you at least agree on a 'maximum price', not to be exceeded.

Whether quote or estimate, it should draw reference to the numbered and dated plans for the project (naming them as the 'contract documents'). If nothing else, it is a statement that the contractor has familiarized himself with the details of the scheme and priced in accordance with them.

Contingency sums

It is normally best to establish with each contractor an agreed contingency sum and have it included within the estimate or quote.

It may be represented by a percentage of the contract sum, but should be expressed as a round sum of money. Typically, a figure somewhere between 5 and 10 per cent of the quote would make a contingency sum for the average self-build, but clearly some trades will have a greater need for it than others, and there is no reason why you have to distribute it proportionally.

The sum is retained by you and is only used to pay for the unexpected extras (shown on the variation orders) should they occur. In this way, nasty surprises like 'bad ground' can be catered for, but care should be taken to ensure that the sum is only used for necessary work that was unforeseen when the job was priced. If the contingency sum isn't all used, then it can be deducted from the contractor's final bill when the job is complete. Do not be tempted to keep it out of quotes as a secret stash for emergencies. Contingency sums are meant to be obvious as a reasonable sum aimed at providing some security for both you and your contractor, and will in any case prevent them from bumping up quotes to cover any unexpected problems – the difference is, you won't get it back in these cases if it isn't used.

Provisional sums

When it is known that work on one particular element will be needed, but it is impossible to say how much or what work until it is carried out, a provisional sum is included. Again, this should be agreed as a round figure which should be capable of covering the actual cost. Once the work is complete and the actual cost is known, the adjustments can be made to the contract sum. A contract may include several provisional sums for various elements of the work that are unquantifiable. This usually happens when you haven't decided exactly what you want yet, and because of this, provisional sums are more prevalent at the end of the project with finishings. As an example, you might allow the provisional sum of £2,500.00 for landscaping works.

Prime cost sums

Prime cost sums, or PC sums as they are usually labelled, are similar to provisional sums but relate only to the material element of the cost and not the labour. So if you're supplying the materials you will not need to use them in contracts. However, you must have them recorded as cost-control measures in your bill of quantities or budget.

PC sums work the same way as provisional sums in that a round figure is set aside sufficient to cover the amount needed and then any necessary adjustments are made to correct the final bill. Often, they relate to materials needed in the final stages that you have yet to choose. Typical examples of PC sums might be:

Allow the PC sum of £2,500.00 for the supply only of bathroom appliances
or *Allow the PC sum of £30 per square metre for the supply only of glazed wall tiles to kitchen.*

Contracts

It has always been the case that anyone who wants to operate as a contractor can do so, without qualification or indeed previous experience. After all, we live in a country where DIY is so popular and materials are so readily available that general building is seen by some as requiring no particular skills, apart from the ability to labour hard – in other words, the perfect conditions for 'cowboys' to flourish in.

In a climate like this, it makes sense to enter into a formal agreement, whether you are engaging one general contractor or a dozen or more trade contractors. If you need a more detailed contract than the dual purpose one previously illustrated, the JCT (Joint Contracts Tribunal) publish the industry standard. There are others in plainer English, and the illustration given on pages 94–96 as an example shows the minimum detail needed for a contract to be worthwhile between a general contractor and self-builder.

If you are employing an architect or surveyor as the project manager, they will be able to advise you on the most suitable form of contract, indeed they may recommend using a standard form issued by their own professional institute.

The contract for the whole works shown can be used for cases where the entire construction of the home is awarded to a general contractor and specific conditions need to be addressed. It covers most of the clauses contained in approved standard forms, but more concisely. Sometimes particular issues that cause friction during building works could have been avoided by adding specific conditions to the contract like:

♦ Hours of working.
♦ Provision of site facilities, such as WC, water and electricity.
♦ Protection of trees or plants on the site.
♦ Whether radios/music players etc. are permitted.
♦ Lighting of fires to burn waste materials, removal of waste materials from site on a regular basis, etc.

Remember that specific conditions such as these may help to relieve the disruption arising from the work and reduce neighbourhood complaints, but conditions must be reasonable and practicable.

Workmanship standards

Perhaps the most difficult of all contract conditions is the standard of workmanship that you will need on your self-build.

It might surprise you to know that the Building Regulations are extremely ineffectual in this area – workmanship only has to be good enough for the building to perform its basic functional abilities as set out in the requirements. In a sense they are an irreducible minimum. A wall has to be horribly out of plumb before it becomes structurally unstable, and nobody in their right mind would want to pay for workmanship of that standard.

Your home warranty insurer has greater control in that they extend their requirements to issues of quality aimed at reducing the risk of claims. To extend this further, to fill in the gaps as it were, the best you can do is quote the British Standard BS:8000 series for Workmanship on Building Sites in the contract. In this way they become, in the various parts of the standard conditions, contractual and enforceable. If the workmanship at any stage becomes unsatisfactory and cannot be said to comply with these controls, your contractor will be in breach of contract and you will ultimately be able to terminate your agreement.

For your reference the 15 parts of BS:8000 are listed below, together with some of the bodies that self-certify other trades now if you use their registered members.

BS:8000

Part 1	1989 – Code of practice for excavation and filling
Part 2	1990 – Code of practice for concrete work
Part 3	1989 – Code of practice for masonry
Part 4	1989 – Code of practice for waterproofing
Part 5	1990 – Code of practice for carpentry, joinery and general fixings
Part 6	1990 – Code of practice for slating and tiling of roofs and claddings
Part 7	1990 – Code of practice for glazing
Part 8	1989 – Code of practice for plasterboard partitions and dry-lining
Part 9	1989 – Code of practice for cement sand floor screeds and concrete floor toppings
Part 10	1989 – Code of practice for plastering and rendering
Part 11	1989/90 – Code of practice for wall and floor tiling
Part 12	1989 – Code of practice for decorative wall coverings and painting
Part 13	1989 – Code of practice for above-ground drainage and sanitary appliances
Part 14	1989 – Code of practice for below-ground drainage
Part 15	1990 – Code of practice for hot and cold water services (domestic scale)

◆ ELECTRICAL INSTALLATIONS should be conditioned as 'installed in accordance with the IEE (Institute of Electrical Engineers) Wiring Regulations'.
◆ OIL APPLIANCES AND TANKS should comply with OFTEC requirements and be installed, commissioned and certified by OFTEC-registered operatives.
◆ SOLID-FUEL APPLIANCES should comply with HETAS requirements and be installed, commissioned and certified by the installers.
◆ GAS APPLIANCES AND SUPPLY PIPEWORK should be installed, commissioned and certified by CORGI-registered operatives.
◆ HEATING AND HOT WATER INSTALLATIONS should be provided with a Benchmark certificate of installation by the installer to you, the self-contractor, on completion of the work.

EXAMPLE FORM OF CONTRACT FOR THE WHOLE WORKS OF BUILDING A NEW HOME

This agreement between

<your name> . . . .

of <your address> . . . .

. . . .

(hereinafter referred to as 'the employer')

And

<Contractor's name> . . . .

of <Contractor's address> . . . .

(hereinafter referred to as 'the contractor')

is made on the   . . . . .day of . . . . . .20 . . . .

Whereas

1.The Employer requires the following building work to be carried out to construct the new home at

<Site address> . . . .

. . . .

For the registered owner of the title to the land

<your name)> . . . .

And has caused

Drawings numbered . . . .

and/or specification dated . . . .

and/or schedules dated . . . .

and/or structural design calculations and details dated . . . .

(hereinafter referred to with the conditions annexed as 'the contract documents') showing and describing the work to be done and which are attached to this agreement.

2.The Contractor has stated in his quotation the sum required for carrying out the work (the sum as stated in article two of this agreement.

3.The contract documents have been signed by both parties.

4.CONDITIONS (hereinbefore referred to)
(I) Standards
The Contractor shall diligently and professionally carry out the complete works as detailed within the contract documents in compliance with the applied Building Regulations, NHBC/Zurich Home Warranty Insurers requirements, British and European Standards, using approved materials and workmanship standards to BS: 8000, and with electrical installations installed in accordance with the IEE (Institute of Electrical Engineers) Wiring Regulations.

(II) Duration
The works may start on . . . .
And shall be completed by . . . .
Or may be extended to a later specified date by agreement of both parties, or a reasonable extended date for reasons beyond the control of the contractor such as adverse weather.
If the works are not completed by the completion date then the Contractor shall pay or allow for, in liquidated damages to the Employer at the rate of

£ . . . . . . .per week

between the contracted date of completion and the actual date of practical completion. The Employer may deduct such liquidated damages from any monies due under this contract.

(III) Defects
Any defects or faults including excessive shrinkage which appear within three months of practical completion due to materials or

workmanship shall be rectified and made good by the contractor at his own expense.

(IV) Variations

If any amendments or variations are required by the Employer, written instructions shall be given by him within two days of the oral instruction and the price agreed for it before works are carried out. Any inconsistencies or errors in the contract documents shall be corrected and treated as a variation.

(V) Payments

Interim payments shall be made for works carried out and materials brought on to the site at intervals of not less than four weeks. The Employer will pay to the Contractor any fair amount so specified in this respect, within 14 days of the date of invoice. Retention of.......% (not exceeding 5%) may be deducted from the final payment at practical completion to be released in two halves. The first half at 14 days after practical completion and the second half at 3 months after practical completion.

(VI) Quotation

The quotation shall be a fixed price that shall not take any account of changes to the cost of labour, materials, plant or other resources needed by the Contractor to carry out the work.

(VII) Legal Requirements and Notices

The contractor shall comply with all notices and requirements required by statute, statutory instruments, rules, regulations and bylaws. Including all necessary Notices for inspection to the Building Control Officer. If in complying with these matters of law additional works are necessary that are not shown on the contract documents he shall notify the employer immediately.

(VIII) VAT

VAT (value added tax) shall not be added to the cost of materials used in and around the new home build and the sum shown shall be taken as zero-rated for VAT purposes in respect of its material content. VAT at the standard rate of ....% is included within the sum for labour and plant hire.

(IX) Insurance

The Contractor shall indemnify the Employer against any liability, loss, expense, claim or proceedings in respect of personal injury or death of any person, arising from the work. He shall maintain an appropriate level of insurance under the Employers Liability (Compulsory Insurance) Act 1969 as amended. The Contractor shall produce evidence as required in respect of his insurance for the Employer.

(X) Determination

by the Employer

Should the Contractor without reasonable cause default by failing to proceed diligently or suspending the works substantially, the Employer may give notice of..... days to him allowing for the default to end. A notice of determination may then be served by the Employer on the Contractor. If the Contractor becomes bankrupt has a professional liquidator appointed or winding-up order made the Employer may by notice determine the employment of the contractor immediately.

by the Contractor

If the Employer fails to pay any interim payments or final payment within the specified time periods or pay any VAT due on the amount, or if the Employer unreasonably interrupts or disrupts the execution of the work or suspends the work for at least one month then the Contractor may give notice of..........days to the Employer, allowing for the default to end. A notice of determination may then be served on the Employer by the Contractor.

(XI) Settling Disputes
When either party requires a dispute to be settled, they shall give written notice to the other, of the appointment of an arbitrator. The arbitration shall be conducted in accordance with the Joint Contracts Tribunal Arbitration Rules as amended.

NOW IT IS HEREBY AGREED

Article 1
For the consideration herein after stated the Contractor will in accordance with the contract documents attached carry out and complete the work referred to, together with any changes or variations made in accordance with this contract.

Article 2
The Employer will pay the Contractor the sum of ....
For the works, exclusive of VAT (as zero-rated)

AS WITNESS

The signatures of the parties

the Employer ....

the Contractor ....

in the presence of (witness) ....

name in print ....

address ....

These certificates will need to be copied to the Building Control Officer, but they are statements of self-certification from the person directly carrying out the work which say that he or she is taking responsibility for its proper installation.

Contract time

Building contracts are drawn as programmes of work on bar charts. These charts are ideal because they show how stages (trades) overlap as they do in practice, and how some can only start when others are finished. For example, the electrical contractor cannot carry out his second fix before the plasterer has plastered the walls, but the windows can be glazed at the same time or at least in synchronicity with the plasterer.

If you can produce one on a computer or use a wall chart with stickers or marker pen, the charts can also be amended to keep abreast of the changes.

Plan carefully when each trade will start and how long it will last. Obviously there are no standards here, but you will need to ensure that your contractors have free access to the site at all times if they are to complete the work to schedule. Suddenly locking up the gates and going off on holiday in the middle of the job is likely to lead to them finding alternative work which may not fit in with your return.

You can agree 'delay penalties' in the contract of so much per week, but remember that they can work both ways. If the contractor delays the work, you can claim that it has taken longer than the agreed time and disrupted other trades. But likewise, if the delay lies outside of their control, you, the self-builder, may be held liable. With his follow-up work adversely affected, a contractor could claim the delay penalty himself.

Be wary of using your liquidated damages clause. If you give dates and periods that are unreasonable or unrealistic be prepared to change them. Some delays may be inevitable, and you may have to advise contractors of amended start dates right up to the eleventh hour.

Delays and liquidated damages

If you do experience delays of one sort or another along the way, as irritating as they will be, for much of the time it will be a case of riding them through.

Some delays with contractors not showing up on site or progressing slower than they should, can be and usually are covered by the conditions of contract. If one trade, for example, doesn't achieve its work in a given time, it may prevent the following trades from even starting, which may lead to them moving on to other jobs.

These delays can be addressed with liquidated damages that compensate you for the loss of time and production and the effect this has had on your cash flow. Usually liquidated damages are charged at a rate of so much per week. They can only be invoked when unreasonable delays have occurred that the contractor should have been able to prevent. Those that he couldn't have prevented are usually described as *force majeure* – meaning act of god – those uninsurable plagues of locusts, floods, outbreaks of war and terrorism, the sorts of things that come along from time to time and make life really inconvenient.

One of the items which often gets disputed under this heading is the weather, which gets blamed for everything that people themselves don't want to take responsibility for. Of course the weather is unpredictable but predictably so. In other words, it will

WEEK NUMBER/WEEK COMMENCE DATE

STAGE	1	2	3	4	5	6	7	8	9	10	11	12	13	14	15
SITE PREPARATION	▦	▦													
FOUNDATION			▦												
FOUNDATION CONCRETE				▦											
DRAINAGE				▦											
BRICKWORK UP TO DPC					▦	▦									
GROUND FLOOR						▦									
SCAFFOLD LIFT							▦								
WALLS TO FIRST FLOOR								▦							
1ST FLOOR STRUCTURE									▦						
SCAFFOLD										▦					
WALLS TO ROOFPLATE											▦				
SCAFFOLD												▦			
ROOF STRUCTURE													▦		
FASCIAS, ETC														▦	
ROOF COVERING															▦
GUTTERING															
WINDOWS AND DOORS															
ELECTRICAL 1ST FIX															
PLUMBING 1ST FIX															
JOINERY 1ST FIX															
PLASTERING															
JOINERY 2ND FIX															
ELECTRICAL 2ND FIX															
PLUMBING 2ND FIX															
SERVICE CONNECTIONS															
DRAINS TESTING															
INTERNAL FINISHING															
DECORATING															
LANDSCAPING															
COMPLETION															

▲ Example of a programme of works.

always be there, and in this country you can always assume it will be changeable. Some days it will rain, some days it will be hot, and some days the wind will try breaking you in half. The point is, you should expect to allow for some adverse weather in drawing up the programme. To assume that perfect weather conditions will prevail throughout the length of the contract is a little optimistic. So when does the weather become a good excuse? Traditionally when it becomes extreme. – hurricane, rain for 40 days and 40 nights, snow in the middle of summer, etc – in other words, exceptionally adverse conditions that couldn't reasonably have been predicted. Given this, you can see quite easily why appeals for delay due to weather are not often entertained in the building industry.

Other legitimate reasons for delays include strikes that directly or indirectly affect the supply of materials or labour, and general

16	17	18	19	20	21	22	23	24	25	26	27	28	29	30	STAGE
															SITE PREPARATION
															FOUNDATION
															FOUNDATION CONCRETE
															DRAINAGE
															BRICKWORK UP TO DPC
															GROUND FLOOR
															SCAFFOLD LIFT
															WALLS TO FIRST FLOOR
															1ST FLOOR STRUCTURE
															SCAFFOLD
															WALLS TO ROOFPLATE
															SCAFFOLD
															ROOF STRUCTURE
▓															FASCIAS, ETC
▓															ROOF COVERING
▓															GUTTERING
▓															WINDOWS AND DOORS
	▓	▓													ELECTRICAL 1ST FIX
		▓													PLUMBING 1ST FIX
			▓												JOINERY 1ST FIX
				▓	▓										PLASTERING
						▓									JOINERY 2ND FIX
							▓								ELECTRICAL 2ND FIX
							▓	▓							PLUMBING 2ND FIX
								▓							SERVICE CONNECTIONS
									▓						DRAINS TESTING
										▓	▓				INTERNAL FINISHING
											▓	▓			DECORATING
												▓	▓		LANDSCAPING
													▓		COMPLETION

civil commotion. I'm not sure to be honest what constitutes civil commotion; has anybody ever seen it? I imagine it involves gangs of people taking to the streets, rioting, pillaging and raping, but I'm not sure, because on this basis, and excluding some national sporting events, we haven't experienced much civil commotion since the Vikings left.

It has to be said that the most common reason for delays on self-build contracts is a failure by the self-builder or his agent to supply the necessary materials at the right time for tradesmen to use them. A contractor could claim for loss of productive time when you have failed to provide them with the materials they need. They will need to prove that they have suffered some kind of a financial loss resulting from this, but that shouldn't prove to be too difficult.

It is usually best to write it down as part of life's rich tapestry and work together to make up the time than pursue compensation. This can be done formally by agreeing on an extension of time to the contract.

If things do all go pear-shaped and you have to sue a contractor for damages, then the date at which delay started would need to be defined. Do not leave it to the court to decide on what is reasonable, in the absence of any evidence.

Snagging on completion

A snagging list is the term given to all those niggly bits that need sorting out at the end of the job. Ideally, you should inspect the work on completion with the contractor and point out anything that you consider needs attention – a crack that needs filling, paintwork that needs touching up, a door that needs easing, etc. A copy of the list is then kept by both parties, and should not be added to. The work is then carried out, and final payment can be made once you are completely satisfied and once you are sure that the building control officer is also completely satisfied.

If the contractor is providing you with a guarantee through his trade association, then make sure you have it signed and have it in your hands before releasing the final payment.

Disputes

The golden rule is to deal with contractor disputes quickly. Left unresolved, they have a tendency to grow. In instances where the work carried out is not up to standard and your contractor is unwilling or unable to rectify it, you should advise him that you intend to have it independently inspected by both the building control officer and warranty surveyor. This having been done, request a list of defective items from both parties. While the building control officer will only be able to comment with regard to contraventions of the Building Regulations, and the warranty surveyor with regard to the insurer's standards, their authority in these instances may help to at least get these points resolved.

If you do find yourself locked into a disagreement that cannot be resolved informally, or if either you or your contractor default on the contract, then a third party should be agreed upon to act as an arbitrator. This arbitration body or person (it could be a surveyor or a trade association) should be agreed at the start of the job, before communications have broken down.

The arbitrator, if needed, should be one who is suitably qualified and has no prior involvement in the project - in other words, not the designer or project manager. This is important, because some of the problems with the work may have derived from poor design or misunderstood instructions in the first place. The surveyor's list is likely to be more comprehensive, since it may include areas of poor-quality workmanship and aspects of the work not covered by regulations or insurance warranties.

 Once a list of defects is produced and everybody has a copy, a site meeting between all involved parties should be arranged to discuss how the problems are to be resolved.

If your contractor is unwilling or unable to co-operate in this respect, you may be forced to take a more formal action, ultimately through the courts. If this does become necessary, it will have helped your case considerably if the problems are well documented and you have given your contractor every reasonable opportunity to rectify them. Photographs of the defects should be signed on the back and dated at the time of exposure. Courts dislike photos taken with digital cameras since they are capable of being altered or enhanced. If you are using a camera with an automatic date stamp, check that the time and date are correct when you take the pictures, otherwise they are likely to be more of a hindrance than a help.

Self-building effectively depends on good communications and if you have reached the stage where they are gone, then you have already lost. You may have to change contractors to keep things going but if you do this before heeding to the warning procedures, you may end up financially sunk.

CHAPTER 6

Groundwork

THE extent of site preparation depends mainly upon the levels and degree of vegetation on the plot. Stripping the whole plot of all vegetation is seldom necessary, unless you want to build your garden as well as your home from scratch. With the groundworkers on site it can be just as easy to use the 'green' method of site clearance – ripping everything out from the roots up – with the digger.

GROUNDWORK

If you don't want to lose everything, selective cutting and digging out is the answer. Herbicidal treatment may be possible, but not if your plot adjoins a watercourse that you may contaminate. Some persistent weeds really do need removing; blackberry bushes are among the fastest growing and most invasive of all wild plants, and pruning them is a little pointless. Japanese knotweed has the same vigour, with the added threat that it can damage buildings if left untreated. Its control has to be undertaken by specialist contractors.

If the site is stripped with the knotweed stands in it, the spoil has to be relocated at least 10m below ground to prevent it reinfesting the new area.

Setting out

If you feel a little anxious about starting the work and getting your home built in the right place, then that's a good thing. You can't afford to be complacent about the setting out of the foundations, because getting it wrong is all too easy. It does happen from time to time, and extra trenches filled with concrete mean extra cost right from the start. Not only does it matter to you that your setting out is correct, it may be critical to the planning authority, or even building control, that your home is built to the dimensions and levels shown on the approved plans.

Setting out your home on the plot is the time when you find out how accurately your designer has measured the site, and whether the building is going to fit on it as comfortably as it does on the plans.

Boundary dimensions are not only important from a planning aspect, given the issues of overlooking and overshading and so on, but they can also have an effect under the Building Regulations on fire spread. With any non-combustible (unprotected from fire) elements on your boundary elevation, such as windows or timber boarding, being limited in area depending on the distance to the boundary, some errors in setting out can be disastrous. Up to 1m away from the boundary, a wall may be allowed only a small window, over 1m and the allowance in these non-combustible areas can be increased by five times or more. This can mean the difference between having your side entrance door or not. So double-check your boundary dimensions and make sure they are acceptable.

In reality not all of the dimensions may be critical, but if you have some discrepancies between the plot and the plan, now would be the time to get them resolved and the actual dimensions accepted – before you excavate the foundations. One other measurement that is often important is the distance the home is set back from the highway, often referred to as the building line. This is best described as a notional line that buildings along a street have been set to or behind but not in front of, for interests of visual amenity and highway safety.

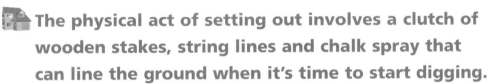 **The physical act of setting out involves a clutch of wooden stakes, string lines and chalk spray that can line the ground when it's time to start digging.**

But mostly it involves measuring and setting corners at exactly 90 degrees. You can do all of this with a 30m tape and some basic trigonometry – the square root of the hypotenuse (the diagonal) should be equal to the sum of the two opposing sides squared – or you can hire in some professional setting-out equipment. Theodolites can pinpoint the corners of a building with more accuracy than you could possibly want, while EDMs (electronic distance measurers) can measure across space with lasers to more accuracy than you could even begin to understand. In the end you are going to be digging a trench in the ground with the results, not building a telescope, so all the precision will fade a bit.

Along with dimensions for the centre line of the trenches and later for the outside of the walls, you will soon need some levels. Once the trenches have been dug, you will need to mark their sides with the level of the concrete proposed. Ordinary concrete is not self-levelling, but has the consistency of porridge and needs to be raked into level, so you need some pins on the trench walls or bottom to mark that level and rake the concrete to it. It is entirely possible and quite easy to let the concrete go off without levelling it properly, but your bricklayers will not thank you. With their trade following and the substructure masonry needing perhaps only a few courses of blocks to reach DPC level, it may be impossible for them to level it out over such a short lift.

A product worth considering is a ready-mix concrete with a plasticizer additive that does make it much more fluid and self-levelling, but it isn't widely used yet and I'm uncertain as to how effective it really is.

In addition to the dimensions on plan, you may also need to establish the levels on the site at the setting-out stage. Sometimes Planning Permissions are issued with conditions relating to the ridge height of the building or the finished floor levels. If you are to maintain your designed storey heights as the construction occurs, you need to start from the correct level at the ground. Since you only get the one chance to do this, a level survey may be needed to establish whether any reduced dig is needed across the plot before the foundations are set out and excavated.

The most effective is the laser level, set on a tripod head and left spinning laser beams. A levelling staff with a receiver attached at the critical position can be moved about the site where the level needs to be the same (oversite floor preparations for example), and beeps when it finds it. If you or your groundworker don't have access to such technology, more traditional tools like Cowley and Dumpy levels are just as effective.

With any site level survey, you need a datum point to reference all other levels from, and it isn't always easy to find.

A benchmark is the title given to a known datum. Benchmarks may occur on significant buildings or bridges, but more often you may have to use a public sewer nearby as a datum point.

Maps of public sewers are public records held by the water authority, who own them, and local authorities. Stored on computers as overlaid digital maps, they can be viewed and copies purchased on a site-specific basis. Included along with the pipe routes and the manhole positions are invert and cover level depths for the manholes, and these levels can be used as known ordnance datum points for your survey. Using a site level and measuring staff, the cover level of the manhole can be transferred, either directly or by a series of spot levels along the way, on to your plot. A temporary benchmark can then be established from which your building levels can be referenced. This temporary benchmark needs to be as solid a fixed point as you can muster, such as setting a stout peg in concrete, where you can read it but it's out of the way to avoid being accidentally whacked.

If you are totally and utterly lost for an ordnance benchmark, because you have no public sewer and nothing marked on the local Ordnance Survey maps, then you can only measure the building's height physically as work proceeds. You can guess that this adds more of a random excitement to the task, and poses the question 'where are you meant to be measuring from?' if the ground level varies. These are excellent questions and deserve a good answer, but not from me. It may be that your home is to replace another building on the site and conditions were imposed that it shouldn't be higher, in which case you need to record the height of the existing building.

Measuring the height of buildings can be done with a sextant, which uses trigonometry by recording the angle from the horizontal along a sight tube aimed at the building's ridge line or wherever and knowing the distance that the sextant is horizontally from it. Failing that, plumb lines that can be marked and measured are used where a straight drop can be found during the construction. This is an excellent way of checking the ridge height of a building by measuring straight down to the ground floor slab through the structure.

If I've given you the impression that all levels and dimensions are always critical, then I apologise; occasionally none of them are – but more often one or perhaps two of them are, and I recommend that you take some time in checking for yourself or checking with your builder or designer which these are, and ensuring they are correct.

Foundations

Foundations are dependant on two things: the load placed on them, and the nature of the ground they bear on.

The natural ground conditions across the British Isles vary tremendously. Silts, sands, rocks, chalks, gravels and clays – we have it all. Some materials like chalk are excellent for building on, and relatively shallow foundations, around 700mm deep, prevail in these situations, deep enough only to avoid frost damage. Others, like sand and clay, may have good load-bearing

Foundations near trees in shrinkable clay soil

Tree species	Distance from tree to foundation							
	5m	8m	11m	14m	17m	20m	25m	30m
	Minimum depth of foundations							
Oaks, willows, elms, poplars	3m	2.8m	2.6m	2.4m	2.2m	2.0m	1.5m	1m
Eucalyptus, cypress Ash, chestnut, fir, lime, sycamore, walnut, maple, cedar, yew, spruce, alder, whitebeam, plane	2m	1.8m	1.5m	1.1m	1m	1m	1m	1m
Beech, birch, hawthorn, holly, magnolia, pine, fruit trees (apple, cherry, pear, plum, etc)	1.4m	1.2m	1m	1m	1m	1m	1m	1m

characteristics but have a tendency to move and cause subsidence.

Clay, prevalent in the south and south-east regions, can vary in colour from blue to grey to brown and on to orange, and with the colour variations there are variations in plasticity. Clay is a shrinkable material that can change in volume dramatically. In the summer it can dry out and shrink, and in the winter it can become waterlogged and heave – either way, it can damage your home structurally. It is even more susceptible to change when trees and vegetation are present. A minimum depth of 1m is usually considered safe in clay soil without trees present (and where they haven't been removed in the last few years).

The effects are worse at the surface, and with depth they decrease, but with differing plasticity and with the water demand changes of various trees, extremely deep foundations can become necessary. Your home warranty surveyor and building control surveyor will be able to advise you on the minimum depth they are looking for in your foundation trenches after inspecting the site. As a means of warning the table above will give you a rough idea of what to expect, but it is far from comprehensive.

I haven't shown situations where foundations over 3m deep would be needed, because at this depth they are often uneconomic. You may wish to explore a pad and beam or raft system in these cases as a special foundation.

Measure the distance to the tree from the foundations and read off the minimum depth of excavation in shrinkable clay soils.

In the case of hedgerows, it would be appropriate to base the depth on the worst-case species to be found in the hedgerow. Even if the tree is young at present, the foundation depths must be based on its mature height when it is fully grown. For bigger trees that have to be retained, care should be taken not to damage the roots or branches, which may destabilize the tree.

Tree roots

Even with the advice given over depth it is important to extend your foundation depth below any visible root hairs to a depth of about 300mm to indicate that the soil will not suffer from desiccation. This is important with fully mature trees that may have developed a root system beyond the predicted length.

Cutting through a live root of 50mm diameter or bigger is not considered to be a good idea. Instead, your foundation should be designed to bridge over roots, allowing enough space for future growth without the structure exerting pressure on them. Tree roots in turn can exert considerable pressure on lightweight structures like a house, and during growth they may cause structural damage. If you are building close to a tree, seek the advice of a registered arboriculturist.

Removing trees

If you are able to remove a tree on the plot that will have an effect on the foundations it may not help, because the ground is likely to become waterlogged and swell to an extent which can cause damage to foundations. This effect is known as heave, and

▼ Building close to trees or removed trees can cause subsidence if precautions aren't taken.

SUBSIDENCE FROM SOIL DESSICATION BY TREE ROOTS

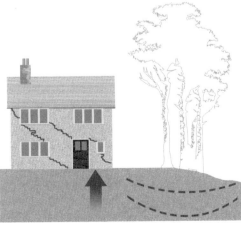

CLAY HEAVE AFTER TREES REMOVED

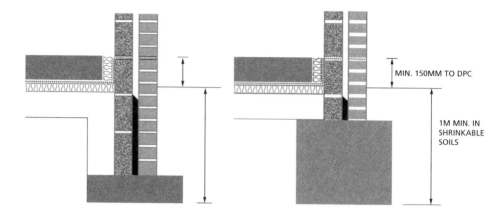

MIN. 150MM TO DPC

1M MIN. IN
SHRINKABLE
SOILS

▲ Conventional foundations formed by shallow or deep strip method.

while it is the reverse of shrinkage, the resultant damage can be just as bad. It is, however, possible to build in heave precautions at relatively low cost. Lining the walls of the trenches with heavy-gauge polythene will create a slip plane that will help to prevent heaving clay from exerting pressure on the sides of the foundations. Using anti-heave boards made from polystyrene to encase the walls of foundations is another solution. The boarding is castellated and weak enough to absorb the pressure of heave, but you will need to seek advice on what thickness to adopt. It can be anything from 50 to 300mm thick. You may have to use anti-heave precautions in some clay soils, even when trees remain.

Your surveyors should take the actual height of the tree – not its mature height when it was removed – into the equation for determining foundation depths. If you leave this out before removing the tree, you will face unnecessary expense from the depth of excavation and concrete. Removing a 5m tree will not require anywhere near the same depth as removing a 20m one.

Safety around excavations

Your self-build project should be classified as 'notifiable' as far as the Construction (Design and Management) Regulations 1994 – known as the CDM Regs – are concerned. You, as the self-builder, are required when digging over 2m deep, to provide protection to prevent people from falling in, i.e. a fence or barrier placed around them. Shoring of the sides of the trench only becomes necessary when your groundworkers need to get into the trench to bottom it up or level the bases by hand.

The risk of earth collapsing in is particularly high in made-up ground situations or where the soil has become desiccated by the sun or saturated by rain. Accidents like this are common on building sites, where risks are taken all too frequently. Even if your site is ring-fenced, if you have to leave excavations open overnight, make sure they are covered over with thick boarding.

Special foundations

RAFT FOUNDATIONS are reinforced concrete slabs cast with reinforced thickened edges around the perimeter, known as edge beams. Usually the slab reinforcement is preformed steel fabric mesh laid in sheets that are overlapped and tied to each other and to the straight bars in the edge beams. The concrete is a higher-strength grade than normal foundation concrete. Raft foundations have the advantage of needing only a minimal depth of excavation, and are hence ideal where groundwater or backfill material is on site. They might also be the choice for other reasons:

◆ To spread the load over a bigger area in soft ground, or in made-up ground, where they can be designed to bridge across weak areas in the soil.
◆ Where differential settlement is likely to be extreme.
◆ Where mining subsidence is likely to occur.
◆ Where the soil is susceptible to excessive shrinking and swelling. In this case the raft should be formed on top of selected non-cohesive fill material (such as clean stone) after the natural ground level has been reduced to a given depth.

There are some drawbacks, however: you need a level site for them to be worth considering, and your design needs to present a

▲ Typical raft foundation plan.

▼ Typical cross-section details of raft foundation.

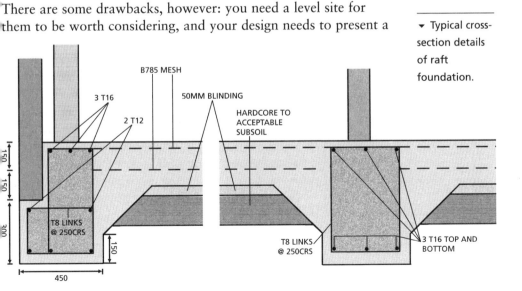

SECTION THROUGH EDGE OF RAFT

SECTION THROUGH BEAMS AT MIDDLE OF SLABS

fairly uniform loading along the edge beams and avoid concentrated point loads from piers. Raft foundations also tend to make pipework a bit more exacting in that you need to cast in ducts for pipes through the centre of the edge beams and slab at the formation stage. Coming along afterwards to connect up services to these ducts means you have no scope for altering or adapting them if they aren't perfectly in place.

PAD AND BEAM FOUNDATIONS consist of a series of mass-filled pads of concrete formed at whatever necessary depth and designed to carry reinforced ground beam foundations, which span between them much as lintels do above ground. The pads are usually located at corners and at intervals on lengthy walls. Designed as conventional foundations on an area basis, they are calculated by dividing ground-bearing pressure by the load applied from each pad. Consequently, the pads will often vary in size.

This type of construction may be used where deep foundations are required due to nearby trees, since the beams offer protection against ground movement. If this method is to prove economically worthwhile, you do need to have good load-bearing ground for the pads, which will otherwise become oversized. If heave is a problem, the same measures can be taken as described for conventional foundations.

PILE FOUNDATIONS have become more common in house-building since the advent of mini-pile systems. The piles act to support reinforced ground beams in the same way as pads do for the pad and beam system, but are more economical where excessive depths are required. Specialist contractors can design and install mini-steel-cased or precast concrete piles, which are driven down in sections to a given depth measured by the resistance from the ground. The system can be quicker than digging and filling large pads. It is suitable in clay soils, where trees exist or have been removed, or where nearby slopes or geological faults occur, but their main use could soon be on brownfield sites, because slip collars can be placed over the top sections of piles.

Piles are either subjected to a load test or over-designed in terms of load capacity by a factor of three to prove their adequacy. Sonic tests can be carried out to check if they have been damaged (cracked) during installation, and

▾ Typical pile layout.

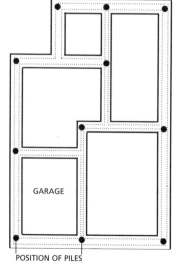

GARAGE

POSITION OF PILES

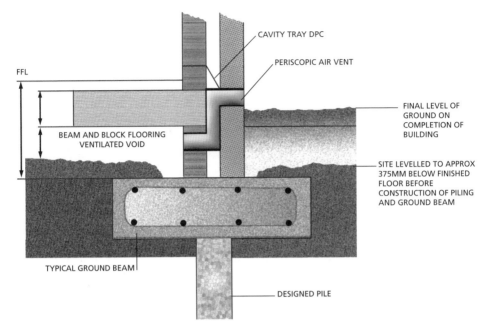

CAVITY TRAY DPC

PERISCOPIC AIR VENT

FFL

FINAL LEVEL OF GROUND ON COMPLETION OF BUILDING

BEAM AND BLOCK FLOORING VENTILATED VOID

SITE LEVELLED TO APPROX 375MM BELOW FINISHED FLOOR BEFORE CONSTRUCTION OF PILING AND GROUND BEAM

TYPICAL GROUND BEAM

DESIGNED PILE

▲ Typical ground beam/pile foundation detail in cross-section.

if this is the case extra piles will be implanted nearby the failed one to compensate. The foundation layout plan shown left, indicates where piles may be placed in a typical layout.

Systems are available which provide precast ground beams that fit to the pile caps and carry the walls and ground-floor beams in a modular floor. In these systems precast square piles are usually driven in, giving a suitable cap size for the beams to bear on.

Piles that are designed against heave have sleeves around their upper sections, but can also be designed extra-long to counter-balance the effects.

Inspections

Foundations are statutory inspections for building control purposes, and you must notify your building control surveyor before concreting them. Likewise, home warranty surveyors should also be notified, even if they choose not to inspect them.

Do not be tempted to press on with concreting until inspections have been made and they have been passed. Officers have sufficient powers to enable you to remove the concrete and lay open the trenches for inspection, or they may simply choose not to issue your certificates on completion. In some areas, planning conditions may be imposed which require all excavations over a certain depth to be inspected by archaeologists before concreting.

The Ancient Monuments and Archaeological Act 1979 creates

the conditions where you may have to give six weeks notice before any digging can be carried out on some sites, and where development may be delayed by a further 18 weeks to allow archaeologists to complete their investigations. Contact should therefore be made at an early stage if you have an archaeological condition imposed on your planning consent.

Fossils, antiquities and objects of value should remain under your ownership, although in declaring historically important finds, you can expect to be compensated if they are of national importance. I have never heard of anybody being able to fund their self-build in this way – but wouldn't it make a great story if you did?

Concrete

Readymix concrete has the advantage of quality control in the mix, guaranteeing its strength and workability. It also takes a lot of the hard work out of the job, particularly when it can be placed directly from the mixer truck into its position on site. You still have some levelling to do, however, because concrete has the consistency of thick porridge and shouldn't actually swim through the trenches to level itself like water.

Raking it to the level required is hard work in itself, but you can make the job easier by knocking in plenty of steel pins to mark the finished level you're after. With solid floors the hard work is tamping it to the level by using a straight length of timber that will span across the bay of concrete and over the substructure walls on either side, from which your level is taken. Tamping the concrete in this way helps to consolidate it in the same way that vibrating it does, and a gentle sawing and tapping motion combined brings the surface to the level and finish needed.

Mixes for concrete need to be specified when you order, and depend on the situation it is being used for, as well as whether it is reinforced or not.

The ST code relates to a standard mix that can be used in most home-building situations where reinforcement isn't required and ground conditions aren't aggressive. Section 4 of BS:5328:Part 1 defines the materials and proportions for these. The GEN code stands for general application as one of several designated mixes, that include RC for reinforced concrete situations and FND for foundations in sulphate ground conditions.

Readymix lorries can deliver concrete by pump if the chute on the truck can't be extended far enough or the drop into the trench is too much. Pumps need to be booked at an early stage, for one reason because there may not be that many of them available in

Situation	Standard mix	Design mix	Strength	Slump	Compaction
FOUNDATIONS					
Strip or mass	ST2	GEN 1	10	75	Tamping
Trenchfill	ST2	GEN 1	10	125	Self-compacting
Rafts, ground beams, etc.	–	RC35	35	75	Poker
Sulphate conditions	–	FND 1-4	35	75	Poker
FLOOR SLABS					
Finishings needed	ST2	GEN 1	10	75	Tamping
No finishings	ST3	GEN 2	15	75	Beam vibration
Garages	ST4	GEN 3	20	75	Tamping
DRIVEWAYS	–	PAV 1	35	75	Tamping

your area, and they are often preoccupied with civil engineering works. Barrowing readymix into position isn't really an option – the mix can't be left for that long on site, but transferring it by dumper truck could be an option if parts of the site are inaccessible to the lorry.

Relatively new on the market is self-levelling readymix concrete, premixed with plasticizer, that more or less does swim through the trench without raking and levels itself — at least that's what the suppliers say, and largely they say it to self-builders, at whom the product is targeted.

Floor structures

You wouldn't believe how much choice there is today for constructing floors. Some of the choice might be taken away from you if you are system-building. Timber-framed houses come with timber floors, for example, but you still have the option of using a webbed-joist floor for improving sound insulation and access for services. Given a traditional brick-and-block-built home, the options are much greater.

Ground-bearing floor slabs

The most common method of forming the ground floor is by concrete slab laid over a hardcore sub-base. This layer should be at least 150mm thick, before being compacted, blinded with sand

▸ In-situ
ground-bearing
floor slab.

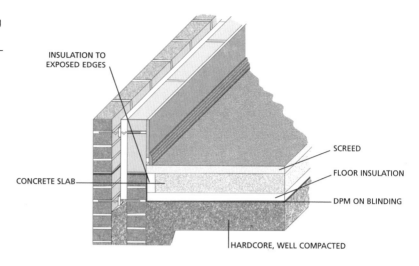

INSULATION TO
EXPOSED EDGES

SCREED

FLOOR INSULATION

CONCRETE SLAB

DPM ON BLINDING

HARDCORE, WELL COMPACTED

and overdressed with the damp-proof membrane (DPM), usually 1200-gauge polythene. Insulation can be used over the sub-base before the slab is cast, or it can go over the top of the concrete floor later on. The slab itself should also be at least 100mm thick.

Ground-floor slabs have in the past been a problem. When the wrong hardcore material is used or it isn't properly compacted, settlement is to be expected, causing the slab to crack. Because of this the oversite preparation, including the hardcore sub-base, has to be notified for inspection. Both the building control surveyor and your home warranty surveyor need to be notified at this stage.

Check out your options for materials with what is available locally. The material needs to be clean broken brick, concrete or stone that has been crushed or is naturally available in less than 100mm particle sizes.

Check that you have correctly calculated the depth of construction through to finished floor level and that your oversite level is correct. Make sure that the slab is at least 150mm in thickness but does not exceed 600mm in total thickness. On sloping sites where part of the make-up may exceed 600mm deep, it may be acceptable to use lean-mix concrete in layers with the hardcore to make up the difference, instead of switching to a suspended floor type.

Most hardcore materials need to be compacted in layers no more than 225mm thick, and you should use a mechanical plate compactor to do this. Take care not to push out the external walls where a stone-type fill is used. Stone just rattles around and doesn't exactly compact; like water, it finds its own level very quickly.

If you've got a sharp-edged material, it will need blinding to protect the polythene DPM from puncturing. A fine material such as sand is used, but don't overdo it: a maximum thickness of 20mm is enough.

Lap and tape down 1200-gauge polythene for the DPM and make sure it is dressed up over the outside walls (inner leaf) so it can be lapped with the damp-proof course (DPC) later. Polythene DPMs also help to protect the concrete slab from sulphate attack and sulphates may be found in some hardcore, such as brick rubble.

Use the correct depth and type of insulation graded for floors, not walls! Expanded polystyrene is rarely used now; instead, phenolic foam boards, often 70–80mm thick, are commonly required.

If you are insulating at this stage beneath the slab, the joints will need taping and strips must be stood up the sides of walls to the slab depth so it is fully encased.

The exact depth of insulation needed to meet the current standards will depend on the P/A ratio as well as the product type, where P is the perimeter of the outer walls and A is the area of the floor. The larger the area in relation to the perimeter of your home, the less insulation you need to meet the standards. This is because the heat loss from a ground floor is mostly around the edges.

Make sure you are not forming the hardcore on filled ground, or where subsoil heave will cause problems. Your foundations and the precautions taken for them will need to be reflected in the slab design. Even on good subsoil, the addition of a lightweight fabric reinforcement such as A142 is beneficial to avoiding settlement cracks, and it can also be used in garages, where 150mm thick concrete slabs are common. In very large slabs movement joints such as fibrous material strips should be used, to allow some expansion to occur without cracking the slab.

Reinforced suspended slabs

If you do have ground problems or if your floor level is just too high off the ground to permit a ground-bearing slab, you can adopt the same construction but with fabric reinforcing mesh or fibre-reinforced concrete to strengthen it. A truly suspended slab will bear on the walls and not the ground and your structural engineer will be able to design the most economical solution to the problem.

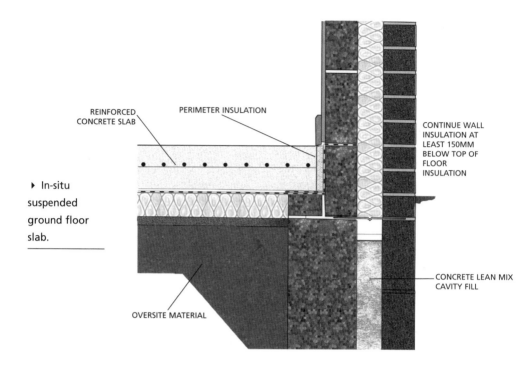

REINFORCED CONCRETE SLAB

PERIMETER INSULATION

CONTINUE WALL INSULATION AT LEAST 150MM BELOW TOP OF FLOOR INSULATION

▸ In-situ suspended ground floor slab.

CONCRETE LEAN MIX CAVITY FILL

OVERSITE MATERIAL

Generally speaking, all suspended floor methods work up to a span of about 5.5m. If you have dimensions greater than this between your external loadbearing walls, it is likely that you will need to provide extra loadbearing walls internally to provide support in between and break up the span.

As an indication of the specification you can expect to employ, here are some examples depending on the distance between the loadbearing walls, assuming:

◆ A maximum 63mm thick cement/sand floor screed finish with domestic floor loads.
◆ A 40mm depth of cover between the reinforcement and the underside of the concrete.

Span between foundation-bearing walls	Mesh size	Concrete grade	Slab thickness
up to 2.4m	B385	C35/	130mm
2.4–3.0m	B785	"	130mm
3.0–3.7m	B1131	"	150mm
3.7–4.3m	B1131	"	180mm
4.3–4.9m	B1131	"	200mm
4.9–5.5m	B1131	"	230mm

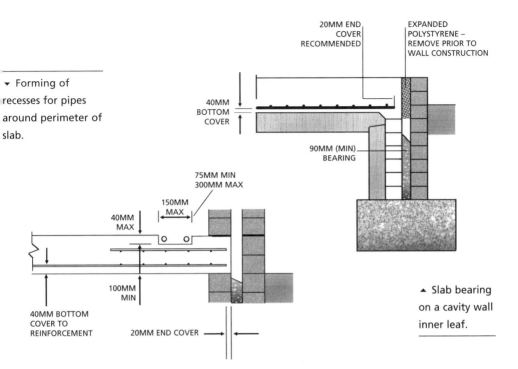

20MM END COVER RECOMMENDED

EXPANDED POLYSTYRENE – REMOVE PRIOR TO WALL CONSTRUCTION

◂ Forming of recesses for pipes around perimeter of slab.

40MM BOTTOM COVER

90MM (MIN) BEARING

75MM MIN 300MM MAX

150MM MAX

40MM MAX

100MM MIN

40MM BOTTOM COVER TO REINFORCEMENT

20MM END COVER

▴ Slab bearing on a cavity wall inner leaf.

◆ The table opposite is only a guide and allows for one standard height (2.4m) partition, cement sand floor screed and the weight of the concrete slab itself.

◆ Note that 'B' type mesh has main bars running one way and lesser secondary bars running the other, and is laid in rectangles. It is critically important to place it with the main bars running with the span shown in the table.

◆ Where more than one sheet of mesh is used, joints must be overlapped at least 400mm and tied together with tying wire.

◆ The mesh should be seated in position on preformed stools to achieve the correct cover on the bottom of the slab.

◆ Where internal walls occur, an extra strip of mesh should be placed in the top of the slab beneath the walls.

Fibre-reinforced concrete is often used in commercial buildings where a power-floated floor finish is needed. Instead of using reinforcing mesh in the concrete, plastic or steel fibres are mixed in at the plant to a given proportion, and these strengthen it to a similar degree.

Suspended timber floors

If you are using this method for your ground floor, some precautions are needed to avoid rot and decay. The ground will

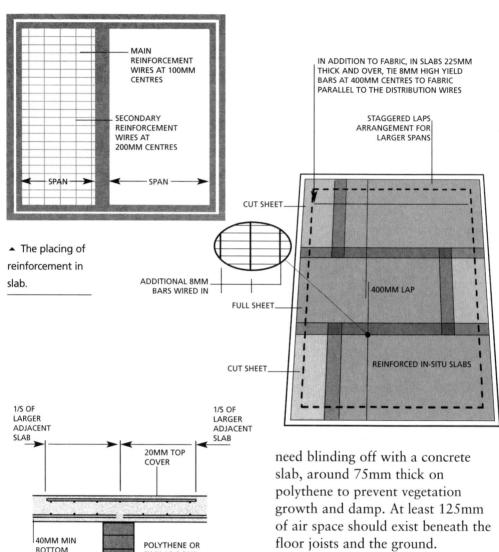

MAIN REINFORCEMENT WIRES AT 100MM CENTRES

SECONDARY REINFORCEMENT WIRES AT 200MM CENTRES

SPAN

SPAN

▲ The placing of reinforcement in slab.

IN ADDITION TO FABRIC, IN SLABS 225MM THICK AND OVER, TIE 8MM HIGH YIELD BARS AT 400MM CENTRES TO FABRIC PARALLEL TO THE DISTRIBUTION WIRES

STAGGERED LAPS ARRANGEMENT FOR LARGER SPANS

CUT SHEET

ADDITIONAL 8MM BARS WIRED IN

FULL SHEET

CUT SHEET

400MM LAP

REINFORCED IN-SITU SLABS

1/S OF LARGER ADJACENT SLAB

1/S OF LARGER ADJACENT SLAB

20MM TOP COVER

40MM MIN BOTTOM COVER

POLYTHENE OR SIMILAR BOND BREAKER UNDER SLAB

190MM MIN WIDTH

▲ Continuous slab over supporting wall.

need blinding off with a concrete slab, around 75mm thick on polythene to prevent vegetation growth and damp. At least 125mm of air space should exist beneath the floor joists and the ground.

A good cross-flow of air through this void is essential, an absolute minimum of vent area equal to at least 550sq mm of air per 1m run of wall – plastic periscopic air vents are best at achieving this. To protect the joists, DPCs need to be placed beneath the timber plates on which the joists will be sat and fixed.

◆ The table opposite is based on sawn softwood sizes.
◆ The maximum clear span between support is shown.

◆ No allowance has been made for partitions (common practice is to double-up joists beneath studwork partitions where they run parallel).
◆ Standard floor loadings for domestic use apply (i.e. 2.0kN/sq m).

Noggins
Timber floors need some cross-bracing, and you can do this either by using offcuts of the joists as solid noggin or herringbone strutting. Strutting can be bought in steel strap form or cut on site as 50 x 50mm softwood. It needs to be positioned in floor spans between 2.5m and 4.5m in the centre, and for joist spans over 4.5m as two rows of struts at one-third centres.

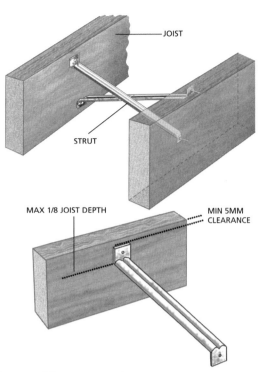

▲ Herringbone joist strut.

Ordering structural timber
There are specific requirements for timber used in construction, particularly in the case of structural members.

GRADING There are many strength grades for timber, ranging from the weakest softwood to the strongest hardwood, but only two are used for structural softwood: C16 and C24. It is a requirement of the Building Regulations that structural timber is dry-graded, meaning that its moisture content is limited to a maximum of 24 per cent. Every piece of structural timber must be stamp-marked to say what stress grade it is, and among other

Floor joists	C16		Grade	C24	
	400 mm	600mm	Centres	400 mm	600mm
50 x 150	3.10m	2.65m		3.30m	2.90m
75 x 150	3.60m	3.15m		3.75m	3.30m
50 x 175	3.60m	3.10m		3.85m	3.35m
75 x 175	4.20m	3.70m		4.35m	3.85m
50 x 200	4.15m	3.70m		4.30m	3.75m
75 x 200	4.75m	4.20m		4.75m	4.20m
50 x 225	4.70m	3.95m		4.75m	4.20m
75 x 225	5.20m	4.70m		5.30m	4.85m

information to say whether it is dry or kiln-dried (KN). You should insist that dry grading is required when ordering timber.

PRESERVATIVES These should be requested on ordering. Treatment is carried out under pressure/vacuum and affords protection against fungal and insect attack. This is essential in areas known to suffer with house longhorn beetle (*Hylotrupes bajulus L*), such as parts of Surrey, Berkshire and Hampshire. All timber preservatives contain harmful chemicals, and any on-site treatment of timber should be done with extreme care and protective clothing should be worn.

SELECTION Before accepting the delivery of any timber, check for splits, shakes, knots and any bent or warped lengths, and reject anything unsuitable before signing the delivery ticket or paying. The quality of timber varies, and it isn't unusual for some of it to be so low it isn't suitable.

ENVIRONMENTAL ISSUES These may be of importance to you, so you will want to see that any timber you buy has been marked with the FSC (Forest Stewardship Council) trademark. This means that the timber has been cut from sustainable managed forests that have been certified by the organization throughout the world.

▼ Timber
suspended
ground floor.

Insulating timber floors

This has never been easy, but it's usually cheap. Glass or mineral-fibre insulation can be suspended between the joists with chicken wire fixed between them as a net. A thickness of 150mm or more may be needed to attain a satisfactory standard using these products, but this is awkward to support and invariably means pinning chicken wire to the underside of the joists. Some higher-performing floor insulation products can be draped over floor joists before boarding or supported on battens between them.

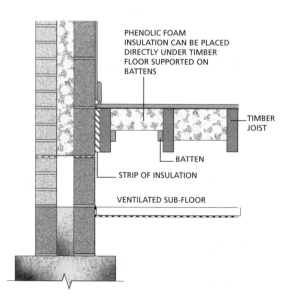

PHENOLIC FOAM INSULATION CAN BE PLACED DIRECTLY UNDER TIMBER FLOOR SUPPORTED ON BATTENS

TIMBER JOIST

BATTEN

STRIP OF INSULATION

VENTILATED SUB-FLOOR

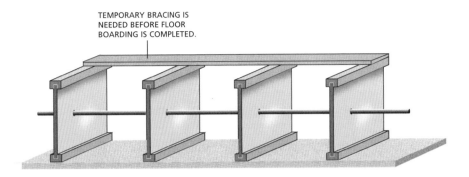

TEMPORARY BRACING IS
NEEDED BEFORE FLOOR
BOARDING IS COMPLETED.

TJI® floors (truss joist)

Relatively new to the industry, these come in two forms, the first as I-beams made of boarding in the web and softwood on the top and bottom flanges, the other as steel diagonal bracing in the web. The advantages of both are span, which is better than ordinary joists and noise reduction from the absence of creaking boards.

▲ TJI® floors with easier services penetration.

Wooden joists creak because they shrink, and the boarding fixings are loosened when this happens, but webbed-joist floors don't have the mass of timber to shrink. They are also lightweight, making them easier to install, and the steel-web type can have services running through them without any notching or drilling needed – even 100mm soil pipes can be run through them, an impossibility with any other floor system.

Beam and block

Precast concrete T-beams have the advantage of being able to span greater distances than solid timber, and don't suffer from insect attack. The infill between beams can be done cheaply with standard wall blocks laid flat and grouted over, or with expanded polystyrene insulation blocks specially made for the purpose. Manufacturers will normally provide a layout plan to work to, showing where the beams are to be positioned. It has become standard practice to sit them on the DPC direct, and also to provide a second DPC on top before proceeding with the wall structure. This seems to have come about because the placing of the beams has occasionally displaced the first DPC, but if you're careful this shouldn't occur.

Since 2002 insulation upgrades under the Building Regulations, floors on the ground level have had to meet higher standards for thermal resistance, and this has meant that laying blocks flat in between concrete T-beams benefits you less than it used to. Even when your system allows you to use aerated concrete blocks with

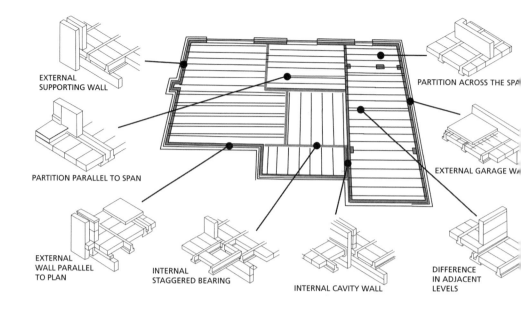

EXTERNAL
SUPPORTING WALL

PARTITION ACROSS THE SPA

PARTITION PARALLEL TO SPAN

EXTERNAL GARAGE WA

EXTERNAL
WALL PARALLEL
TO PLAN

INTERNAL
STAGGERED BEARING

INTERNAL CAVITY WALL

DIFFERENCE
IN ADJACENT
LEVELS

▲ Beam and
block floor
system.

some degree of insulation about them, they remain only 100mm thick and in need of plenty of extra insulation over the top before they can be finished by screed or boarding – which can be more of a problem than you might think. Once the roof is on and your home is weathered and ready to receive its insulation and floor finish, the surface of those beams and blocks can look a right state, with mortar splashes and built-in unevenness of the two products.

All insulation sheets need a level surface to be laid on, and inevitably this means grouting over the floor or laying down a bed of dry mortar to get a reasonable face. If you've been using a concrete-filled insulation block system for your walls, then you are probably wishing at this point that you'd covered the floor with some protection, as pumped concrete can be messy.

To overcome the insulation problem, some T-beam manufacturers have diversified into making insulation panels to fit in between the joists instead of blocks. These expanded polystyrene blocks can eliminate the need for further insulation and give 'U' values as low as 0.20 W/m sq k to the overall floor. They can do this by virtue of being shaped to cut around and over the T-beam for support and reduction in cold bridging.

There are benefits in using ordinary beam-and-block floor systems for the upper floors, where you don't have to worry about thermal insulation. The system is quite effective for sound deadening given the mass of the beams and dense blocks together, compared with timber floor joists.

Manufacturers will provide from your plans their own layout

diagram, indicating where the beams are to be positioned and their spacings, which will ensure that you get them correctly positioned on site. Getting them in position can vary from easy to difficult, depending on the site's accessibility and the length of the beams. Usually most new home spans aren't that great and they can be lifted manually, but for upper floors and larger spans a crane may be needed to bring them in.

Hollow pot concrete floor slabs

Not often used in new home construction but still worth considering, especially where you have wide spans between loadbearing walls (over 5.5m). These precast concrete slabs tend to be made in sections 1 or 2m wide, and to reduce their weight they are pocketed with circular holes (tubes, if you prefer) running through their core, making them partially hollow. Even so, they still require crane lifting into position. You have the advantage of an instant floor deck from the moment they are placed onto the walls, which is extremely handy for the next lift of walls. Again, though, they do need an insulated finish when used for ground-floor construction.

The drawbacks, apart from the cost of the product itself, really come from the essential crane hire that goes with placing them and from the health and safety risk of placing them recklessly. You really don't want to see a chain break or a beam dropped; it can flatten walls and anything else in the way quite suddenly.

For sound insulation, all they need is a phenolic insulation sheet (a thin, rolled-out layer) to give them some isolation from the screed, and you have exceptional sound resistance.

In garages, the beams are set at 225mm centres rather than 450mm for the blocks to be fitted the other way. Since you have to finish these floors with something, a reinforced screed at least 65mm thick is essential in a garage.

Ventilation

What is needed in the way of damp-proofing and ventilation in these areas differs tremendously from one designer and control authority to another. The site conditions have a marked effect. If you are taking gas pipes through the void, or if radon gas or methane (or marsh gas) is likely to occur, then you must ventilate the void with air bricks in the walls. If there is a high water table or sloping site, it will need to be drained by weepholes and damp-proofed. On a dry and level site with no gas threats, nothing in particular may be needed.

Having said that, the cost of treating the site with weedkiller or laying down polythene with a sand or weak concrete blinding to weight it is negligible.

Drainage

Whether you choose to install the drainage system at the moment is up to you. Some people prefer to get all the groundwork done at one time, and others prefer to leave the drains to the end. Doing them in the middle of the project usually isn't an option because the scaffold or the stored materials are in the way. There is a risk of backfilled shallow drainage becoming damaged with plant moving about the site, and so there is some advantage in leaving them to the end.

100mm diameter PVCu shallow access drainage has been the preferred system since the beginning of the 1980s, although clay is still available. A clay pipe system means site-built manholes, whether they be brick or concrete chambers. Plastic preformed inspection chambers are available in all sizes for shallow or deep access – shallow is defined as anything down to 1m deep.

You should aim to lay pipework in straight lines and avoid bends whenever you can. If bends have to be employed, try to locate them in gradual radii and place them as close to inspection chambers and rodding points as you can. Ventilate your drainage system at the head of the run – this means a soil vent pipe with an open-air termination – not an air admittance valve.

As with foundations, drains are listed as a stage requiring inspection notice to the building control service. They are usually bedded in pea shingle and laid to fall with all chambers in place and joints correctly made before the inspection. A test can be placed on them at this stage to check that they are watertight.

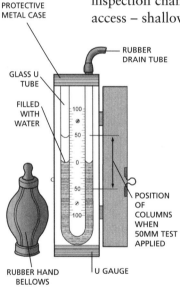

▾ Air test equipment.

PROTECTIVE METAL CASE

RUBBER DRAIN TUBE

GLASS U TUBE

FILLED WITH WATER

100

50

0

50

100

POSITION OF COLUMNS WHEN 50MM TEST APPLIED

RUBBER HAND BELLOWS

U GAUGE

Sewer connections

Connecting your new drainage system to the public sewer may be a final task before occupying the home, but leave plenty of time to organize it.

Written consent is needed from the water authority who own the sewer, and if it's in the highway, from the Highways Authority. The road may have to be excavated and traffic controls may need to be introduced.

The water authority will require one of three options for the

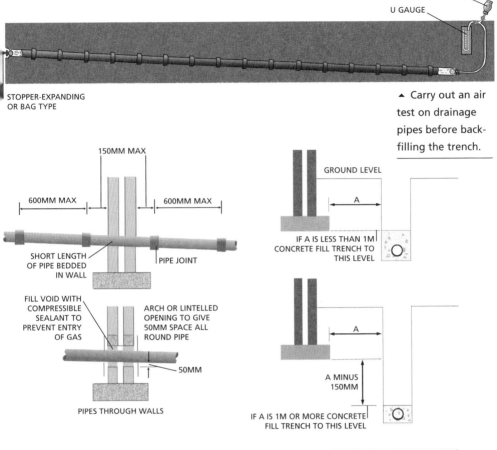

HAND BELLOWS

U GAUGE

STOPPER-EXPANDING
OR BAG TYPE

▲ Carry out an air test on drainage pipes before back-filling the trench.

150MM MAX

600MM MAX   600MM MAX

SHORT LENGTH
OF PIPE BEDDED
IN WALL

PIPE JOINT

FILL VOID WITH
COMPRESSIBLE
SEALANT TO
PREVENT ENTRY
OF GAS

ARCH OR LINTELLED
OPENING TO GIVE
50MM SPACE ALL
ROUND PIPE

50MM

PIPES THROUGH WALLS

GROUND LEVEL

A

IF A IS LESS THAN 1M
CONCRETE FILL TRENCH TO
THIS LEVEL

A

A MINUS
150MM

IF A IS 1M OR MORE CONCRETE
FILL TRENCH TO THIS LEVEL

PIPE RUNNING CLOSE TO BUILDING

▲ Protecting drains.

connection – either a new manhole, a connection to an existing manhole or a saddle connection. A new manhole will need to comply with their specification right down to the benching height, grade and type of cover, and everything else. When working on adoptable drainage, there is no situation where you can choose the specification yourself. The work is usually inspected by the authority as well as the building control surveyor.

Saddle connections are when the new drain is joined to the existing sewer obliquely by cutting a hole in the pipe topside and grafting on the new pipe. They are possible because sewers are usually formed in thick vitrified clay material 150–300mm in diameter. Sometimes when new sewers are laid, saddle connections as spurs are provided (blanked off) for future homes to be connected to.

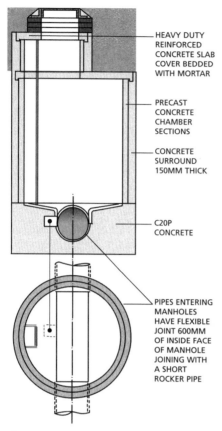

HEAVY DUTY REINFORCED CONCRETE SLAB COVER BEDDED WITH MORTAR

PRECAST CONCRETE CHAMBER SECTIONS

CONCRETE SURROUND 150MM THICK

C20P CONCRETE

PIPES ENTERING MANHOLES HAVE FLEXIBLE JOINT 600MM OF INSIDE FACE OF MANHOLE JOINING WITH A SHORT ROCKER PIPE

▲ ▼ Cross-section details of manholes.

Cesspools

These are probably the oldest method of drainage; no rocket science involved here. In the past they were built of brickwork and then concrete blocks, but today they are prefabricated in fibreglass.

Whatever the material, they remain simply as storage tanks that from time to time require emptying. Site-built ones usually consist of a rectangular tank with a double chamber, while fibreglass models are more capsule-shaped like a giant pessary (there is an irony there somewhere, but I'm not going to look for it), and can be installed in a single day. They are produced in a variety of volumes for different-sized families, and if you are in any doubt as to the one you require, most manufacturers will calculate it for you based on the occupancy of your home and the storage time required.

The minimum storage time, controlled under the Building Regulations, is 28 days, but if you so desire you can increase this. The minimum size cesspool for a single dwelling is 18,000L, requiring an excavated hole of some 6m length by 4m width. This capacity of tank will be sufficient for only two people, however, and a family home will need considerably

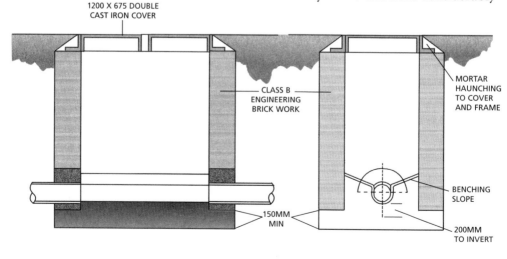

1200 X 675 DOUBLE CAST IRON COVER

CLASS B ENGINEERING BRICK WORK

MORTAR HAUNCHING TO COVER AND FRAME

BENCHING SLOPE

150MM MIN

200MM TO INVERT

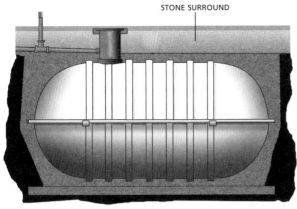

STONE SURROUND

DRY WELL DRAINED SITE

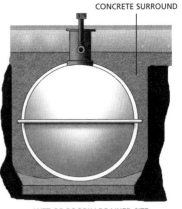

CONCRETE SURROUND

WET OR POORLY DRAINED SITE

more. You should add 6,800L of extra capacity for every person over the first two. Most of you will thus need something larger, and the standard capacities available are predominantly the 27,000L, 36,000L and even 45,000L versions. The bigger you get, the more the installation hole begins to look like the pit from *Quatermass*.

▲ Cesspool installations depend on site conditions.

Rarely have I seen the 45,000L tanks installed, but when I have, I have approached the edge of the 12 x 4m pit in awe. Of course the depth required is partly determined by ground levels and the depth at which your drainage arrives. Normally you are looking at excavating to almost 3m from the incoming drain depth or invert level, but your cesspool manufacturer will provide you with the exact dimensions. The hole is bottomed out with a 150mm thick concrete base on which to sit the tank, so that it doesn't sink when it's full and remains level.

The most exciting thing about these huge tanks is that when empty they are extremely buoyant and will happily float in saturated ground. This means that you must backfill them carefully and with the right material to hold them in place. In wet subsoil or at least clay subsoil with the potential of becoming wet and heaving, the tanks may easily pop out of the ground after emptying; to prevent this from happening, a backfill of concrete around and over the tank is needed, plus a layer of pea shingle over the concrete base to provide a bedding.

▼ Glass fibre cesspool.

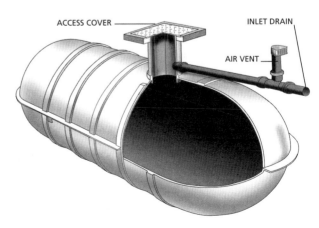

ACCESS COVER

INLET DRAIN

AIR VENT

Of course, backfilling the pit around a giant pessary with concrete comes with its own problems. If the tank isn't filled with water and held in position the concrete can itself displace it, and once it has shifted out of position, your chances of getting it back are not good. Many cesspool installations have had to be abandoned before they could be used because careless installation has pushed them over or raised them higher than the incoming drainage, rendering them unusable. I have watched people struggling with them chained to the back of Land-Rovers in an attempt to pull them upright, having just dumped several tonnes of gradually setting concrete all on one side – to no avail.

If the cost of cesspools and their installation has put you off a bit, it is possible – subject to getting the design approved – to build your own using a concrete reinforced cover slab and base. Engineering bricks suitably rendered on the inside can be used for walls, but should be laid one brick thick at least, and the same goes for concrete blocks, which could be used laid flat.

Be aware that as the owner of the cesspool, you are responsible for ensuring it doesn't leak, pollute the ground or cause a nuisance with smell. If the ground around your tank is susceptible to seasonal movement, you'd be better off buying a fibreglass one and surrounding it in concrete.

A water test to check it doesn't leak is a minimum spelling on a site-made tank. Check the water level over a day and see if it drops beyond any reasonable evaporation.

Septic tanks

The alternative to a sealed cesspool is a septic tank. These bulb-shaped tanks allow a separation of the solid and liquid matter, the latter of which is then dispersed out into land drainage, where it percolates into the ground. Obviously this water is not entirely pure, and for this reason septic tanks are prohibited in sensitive areas like aquifer zones where water is collected for supply.

Although the tanks are smaller and with less capacity, their process allows them to require emptying less compared to cesspools, and they are much cheaper to buy. A 2,700L tank is suitable for a family of four, but you should add 180L of capacity for every additional person – as 1,000L equates to 1cu m in volume, you can see how the size and the cost relate to a standard cesspool. They are much smaller and cheaper, but of course they only work effectively if the secondary treatment of the drainage is working correctly.

As with rainwater soakaways, the nature of the subsoil is critical to the design of the drainage irrigation system. In clay or

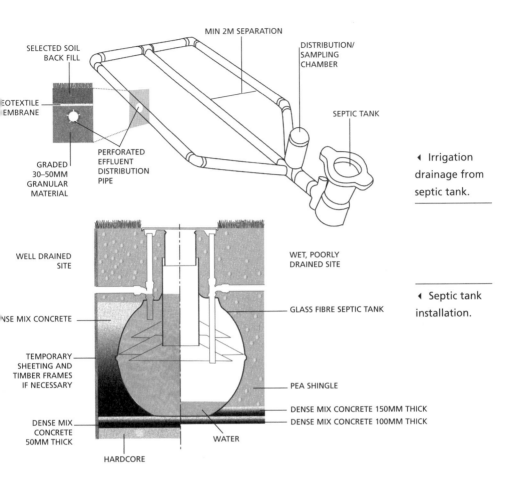

SELECTED SOIL
BACK FILL

MIN 2M SEPARATION

DISTRIBUTION/
SAMPLING
CHAMBER

GEOTEXTILE
MEMBRANE

SEPTIC TANK

GRADED
30–50MM
GRANULAR
MATERIAL

PERFORATED
EFFLUENT
DISTRIBUTION
PIPE

◄ Irrigation
drainage from
septic tank.

WELL DRAINED
SITE

WET, POORLY
DRAINED SITE

◄ Septic tank
installation.

DENSE MIX CONCRETE

GLASS FIBRE SEPTIC TANK

TEMPORARY
SHEETING AND
TIMBER FRAMES
IF NECESSARY

PEA SHINGLE

DENSE MIX CONCRETE 150MM THICK
DENSE MIX CONCRETE 100MM THICK

DENSE MIX
CONCRETE
50MM THICK

WATER

HARDCORE

other heavy soils the percolation rate can be poor, and a large
system of perforated pipes may be needed laid out across a big
area to compensate. The only true way to establish the porosity is
to test it by digging a small hole and conducting a porosity test as
for soakaways.

In the case of septic tank drainage, however, you don't actually
want the drainage to work too quickly. A Vp figure of between 12
and 100 is essential for effective treatment (see box on page 130).
Outside these figures, and you may need to look at another stage
for the drainage treatment, perhaps a final soakaway pit.

Irrigation pipework is perforated; often flexile corrugated and
slotted piping is used and laid out to a very shallow, practically
level, gradient of 1:200. Granular bedding and surround of the
pipes is essential, with at least 50mm of cover over the crown of
the pipe. It helps enormously to cover the pipes with a geotextile
membrane before backfilling over, keeping the soil from washing
through and clogging them up. 10mm pea-shingle is not ideal as

Percolation testing

At the end of the day excavate a pit of safe working size in the location of your soakaway drainage. In the bottom of the pit, hand dig a smaller hole 300 x 300 x 300mm in size and fill it with water. Let the water drain away overnight and refill the hole in the morning. This time record the time it takes (in seconds) for the water level to drop from being 75 per cent full to 25 per cent full, since this will equate to a drop of 150mm in the water level (it's easier if you can mark the side of your hole in advance of filling it). By dividing the time by 150 you have the porosity value of the soil, known as the Vp. For this figure to be reasonably accurate and reliable, you should carry out a few tests in different trial holes around the site.

drainage bedding for percolation drains, as it's a bit on the fine side; crushed or rounded stone up to 50 mm diameter with larger voids between is far better.

Chapter 12 includes advice on other forms of treating and disposing of foul water from septic tanks, such as reed beds and drainage mounds.

▾ Exploded view of septic tank showing the settlement process.

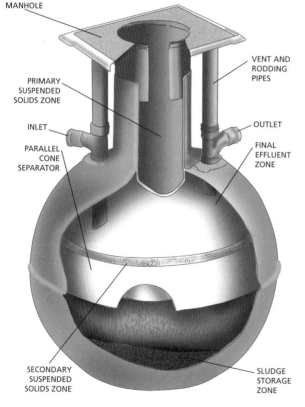

LOCABLE MANHOLE

PRIMARY SUSPENDED SOLIDS ZONE

INLET

PARALLEL CONE SEPARATOR

VENT AND RODDING PIPES

OUTLET

FINAL EFFLUENT ZONE

SECONDARY SUSPENDED SOLIDS ZONE

SLUDGE STORAGE ZONE

Location of drainage tanks

Both types of tank need emptying up to once a month, periodically in any case, and so siting the tank in a position where the emptying vehicle can get at it is important. The vehicles may be able to link hoses together to exceed these distances and overcome other obstacles, but they are pumping out effluent here and you really don't want them to experience any difficulties. About 30m from the driveway or the highway is as far away as you can locate a tank, at the same time a corner of your plot that fits in with the fall of the land and is at least 15m away from your home is ideal.

Of course, with percolation

drainage from a septic tank you may need a large area away from the house. These pipes are installed relatively shallow and cannot be located beneath a driveway or near to services like the mains water supply. It is not acceptable to discharge these drains anywhere near a water catchment area, or even within 10m of a stream or river.

 If you find you can meet all the conditions but are on a viciously sloping site, it is important that the incoming drainage doesn't arrive at high speed from the steep gradient. There is a biological process taking place inside the tank that relies on the contents not being disturbed too much. A steeper-than-normal gradient for the first section of drains or a back-drop manhole system is needed, so you level out the last 12m before the tank to a gentle 1:50 to 1:70 fall in PVCu pipework.

GROUND LEVEL
BACKFILL
GEOTEXTILE SHEET
150MM CLEAN GRAVEL SURROUND
150MM
150MM

▲ Section through irrigation pipe trench.

Mini-treatment plants

What can you buy for the self-builder who has everything? Their very own miniature sewerage treatment works. These products take the aerobic processes of a septic tank one step further, treating the liquid by-products to the point where they are discharged as clean water. The manufacturers claim that the water is entirely pure and could be drunk, but I've yet to meet anyone who was keen to prove this point. Certainly, the Environment Agency have permitted their use in water catchment zones where septic tanks would not be allowed, and the water may be discharged direct into watercourses from them.

▼ Septic systems can require a lot of space.

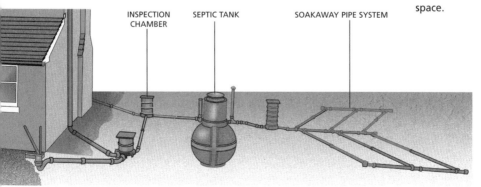

INSPECTION CHAMBER   SEPTIC TANK   SOAKAWAY PIPE SYSTEM

CHAPTER 7

Traditional Build

Brickwork

Facing brickwork is the showpiece of the house, and if it's up to standard nobody will notice it. It's a fact – we are all so used to seeing brick walls that we only actually see the really bad ones. Brickwork, to be good, above all needs to be uniform – the mortar joints need to be of equal thickness in each course and of equal width in the perp joints (the vertical ones.) Not only that, but the mortar mix needs to be consistent for each lift of the wall.

When you write these requirements down they seem so matter of fact and obvious, but the really sad truth is that they are commonly ignored. A good bricklayer will cut bricks to ensure his perp ends are equal, a lazy one on a price will simply increase the mortar joint width to make up the difference. I have seen the latter done frequently to the extent where the wall appears practically rendered with mortar. Years ago, brickies had to whack quite a few bricks with their trowels until they got one the right size to use, now they have brick cutters that do the job accurately, so there are no excuses; it really comes down to whether or not they take pride in their work. The same goes for gauging the mortar to make sure it always looks the same colour and is equal in strength.

The next time you find yourself on Primrose Path or Bluebell Boulevard or some other incongruously named new housing estate road, take a look at the walls as you stroll by and judge for yourself. It doesn't even seem to matter how much the properties are on sale for – the quality of brickwork can be good or bad on any given house.

To keep a close eye on your own brickwork as it proceeds on your new home, there are some things that you should pay particular attention to:

◆ Is the mortar being used within an hour of its mixing, and not being recycled with extra water once it starts to harden?

◆ The bricks should be rising 300mm in four courses, with the perp ends lining up in alternate courses.

◆ Check that gauge rods are being used to ensure the work is vertically and equally coursed.

◆ The brick wall isn't being built more than 1200mm above any adjacent work at any time and is therefore unsupported. This includes the inner leaf of blockwork (unless it is a thin-joint system).

◆ New brickwork is being protected against bad weather (rain, frost, snow) by hessian sheeting.

◆ The sand is kept clean (which means covering it on site or having it delivered in 1-tonne bags).

◆ The wall ties are being correctly spaced and are embedded by at least 50mm into the joints.

◆ The lintels are the right sort (as specified) and bear at least 150mm on the walls either side of the opening.

◆ Expansion or movement joints are being installed where they are specified by the designer (some facing bricks will only need them at 12m centres) or brick manufacturer.

What does plumb mean? Because we are dealing with building here, not micro-engineering, some tolerances are acceptable. The brickwork must be equal in:

◆ LENGTH   up to 5m: 10mm either way
5–10m: 15mm either way
over 10m: 20mm either way

◆ HEIGHT   up to 3m: 5mm either way
3–6m: 15 mm either way
over 6m: 20 mm either way

And it must be vertical and true in:

◆ LEVEL   up to 10mm over any 5m is considered level

◆ PLUMBNESS   in 8 courses: 5mm either way
in 3m: 10mm either way

Bricks and blocks

With energy-efficiency standards being what they are and bricks being what they are – poorly insulating – it is important that they aren't used in place of cut blocks on the inner skin. Thermal blocks could not be more easily cut to size: manufacturers have even gone to the trouble of making some smaller to avoid the saw on site. Alas, some bricklayers are still using bricks to make up their blockwork at window openings and beneath the wall plate. This rather destroys the thermal insulation qualities of your wall unless you are relying on a insulated thermal plasterboard or drylining system. Using bricks will produce a cold bridge for heat to transfer through even if your cavity is insulated, so it is essential to cut blocks, even if this takes a little more time.

The best way of closing the cavity at openings is the insulated cavity closure, a really good invention that takes the workmanship question away.

These plastic, foam-filled closers are vertical DPCs and sometimes even frame fixers all in one. The traditional alternative of cutting the blockwork and building in a vertical strip of DPC is thus made redundant, which is not a bad thing.

When ordering cement, the following figures may prove useful:

40 bags of cement (at 25 kg each) equal 1 tonne (metric)
60 bags of cement (at 25 kg each) equal 1cu m (approx)

Walls can be put into one of two categories – loadbearing and non-loadbearing. The loadbearing ones can be defined as those that hold up something other than themselves, and the non-loadbearing ones as partitions that serve only to divide up space and don't contribute at all to the stability of the home.

So loadbearing could mean that the floor joists sit on the wall or the roof structure, a beam or the ceiling, for example, or indeed another wall. In the last instance, an upper-floor partition springs to mind, but it could just as easily be helping to support another wall perpendicular to it by providing buttressing support against wind pressure.

This doesn't leave a lot to fit into the category of non-loadbearing, but you could design a small house where all the internal walls were non-loadbearing and the roof was supported only on the outside of the walls. However, once the outer walls exceed 5m in length, some internal support for floor joists becomes necessary and beams or walls with foundations become more critical.

Loadbearing walls themselves need to be supported from a foundation or a beam or some other structural element that can carry the load imposed on it. In most cases a floor slab isn't going to be sufficient, and a foundation will be needed. The width of the foundation is directly related to the nature of the subsoil, its bearing capacity and the load on it. Mathematically, the load in kiloNewtons per 1m of wall divided by the bearing capacity in kiloNewtons per 1sq m of ground equals the width required in metres from the foundation.

Vertical loads through your structure can be designed right down to the ground by your design engineer if necessary, but that level of design isn't required unless your home is built on questionable ground, or has high loads focused into piers or columns perhaps.

Lateral stability

Horizontal loads aren't so easy to visualize. They come from one of two sources – the wind, or the ground in the case of basement and retaining walls. Wind loading can vary tremendously, and some method of calculating the maximum wind pressure on a wall has had to be derived by British Standards over the years. BS:6399 does this and allows the design engineer to pick basic wind speeds off the map appropriate for your region and then tweak them with a series of factors based on your site's altitude and level of exposure or shelter. The basic wind speed itself can vary from 36–48m per second regionally, so the resulting pressure can be very different from one site to another. From this the pressure (the load) on a square metre of wall can be derived and its stability assessed. Whether it will stand up depends on the strength of the masonry used, the size of the panel between buttressing walls, and the thickness of the wall.

Again, this depth of structural analysis isn't needed 95 per cent of the time, and it may be avoided by simply making sure your external walls don't get too long. A good rule of thumb is to keep them within 50 times of their effective thickness between buttressing walls. Your buttressing walls are basically the ones running at 90 degrees to it internally or externally that have a foundation. Cavity walls have an effective thickness that is two-thirds the sum of both leaves, so for example if you have a wall of 100mm blocks outside and 150mm blocks inside, you need to calculate the thickness as two-thirds of 250mm – 167 mm – and multiply that by 50 to see that your wall shouldn't run for more than 8.35m before being supported at the ends.

Buttressing walls only work as props if they have some integrity themselves – if they are riddled with holes for door or window openings, their supporting ability is removed. The rule of thumb here is to make sure the total width of those openings doesn't exceed two-thirds of the length of the wall itself. This can be a problem if you adopt a sun lounge or conservatory element to part of your home, because you may have more window opening here than wall.

Internal walls or chimneys are good for support so long as they have some basic minimum sizes.

With internal walls, they need to be sat on a foundation to qualify, and you need at least 550mm of wall before you locate a door opening in it. Door openings can represent almost the entire storey height and have a nasty habit of occurring in the corners of rooms to free up space, but if you want the wall for support you have to shove them in a bit. You could build in a pair of architectural piers, perhaps, to form a cupboard or shelf display unit, in which case they need to be solid one-brick-wide piers that project out at least three times the thickness of the wall. In a cavity wall situation that is going to give you more depth than your average bookshelf, but about the right amount for a TV or hi-fi system.

Chimneys are not such a problem, so long as they are at least twice the thickness of the wall and you make sure that the mass of the brickwork is at least that equal to a buttressing pier in the cross-sectional area. Obviously you can't include the flue or fireplace itself in working that out. Buttressing elements need to be storey height, by which I mean at least the height of the supported wall and where the measurement of length runs from centre line to centre line of the supported wall structure, not internally.

If the need for buttressing support is present and for one reason or another your walls can't provide it, you might have the chance to build in a wind-post to the closing cavity of a door opening for instance. Wind-posts are steel hollow-sectioned posts that can be built in to a wall and tied top and bottom to transfer the load into other structural elements – the foundation at the bottom and a lintel beam at the top.

You can buy proprietary ones made of stainless steel, or you may have a steel fabricator form you one to suit your needs. They are often the choice for strengthening the outer walls in large open-plan homes, devoid of inner walls.

Lateral restraint

If I refer to your prized new home in the next sentence as a box, let me apologise now. New homes, and indeed most new buildings, are essentially boxes. Boxes are strong when small, but the bigger they get the thicker the sides have to be, as we've already discussed, or the more subdivided they have to be inside for strength. Your roof and floors can add to that strength from their lateral support the same way that buttressing walls can, if you tie them in properly.

The tying in of floors is easily done with straps of galvanized or stainless steel. At 30mm wide and 5mm thick they run across three joists and bend 90 degrees, enough to hook over the wall they are built into. The important bit here is to recognize that they are meant to be built in as the wall is raised, and not nailed or screwed onto the face of the wall later. Perforated with holes, the long ends can be screwed down to the joists and the noggins between them. You won't get enough fixing points from the joist alone, and to stiffen the whole connection up lumps of wood called noggins (usually joist offcuts) are packed between the joists in a line beneath the straps to help. Noggins can be less than the joist depth, if need be by up to 50 per cent, but the deeper the better.

The straps are inserted at maximum 2m centres and either side of openings for doors and windows, and run perpendicular to the floor joists whenever you have a wall longer than 3m.

All internal walls should also be tied in at the floor level and to restrain them. We tend to use 100mm thick blocks now as standard, but in the past 75mm ones were common with space-hungry house builders. With the floor joists shrinking away as they dry out, the block partitions can be left freestanding with no support at the top and quite capable of being shoved to the point where they would move an unsettling and crack-inducing amount. For the sake of a few lateral restraint straps, they can be tied in.

If you have gable end walls, the next level, even on a trussed roof home, is the ceiling at which you should copy the lateral restraint strapping detail used for the floor. Up from that is the rafter level and the top of the wall as it runs along the verge. Here is the most vulnerable place in the whole wall for movement from wind. In the hurricane of

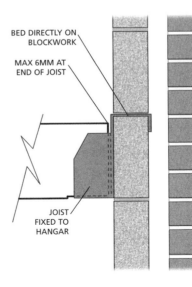

▼ Lateral restraint type joist hangar.

BED DIRECTLY ON BLOCKWORK

MAX 6MM AT END OF JOIST

JOIST FIXED TO HANGAR

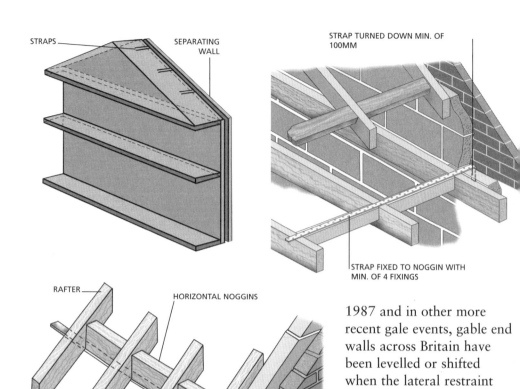

STRAPS

SEPARATING WALL

STRAP TURNED DOWN MIN. OF 100MM

STRAP FIXED TO NOGGIN WITH MIN. OF 4 FIXINGS

RAFTER

HORIZONTAL NOGGINS

STRAP BEDDED UNDER A CUT BLOCK TO BEAR ON A FULL BLOCK

▲ Lateral restraint straps.

1987 and in other more recent gale events, gable end walls across Britain have been levelled or shifted when the lateral restraint strapping wasn't present as it should be. In the years preceding, builders had complained that it was pointless using such thin bits of metal so poorly connected up here, but they proved their worth then and have done ever since.

Vertical stability

Roofs

The wall plates on which your roof will sit are anchored down with vertical restraint straps, which are basically the same as lateral ones but half as thin. Because they often have to be fixed to the masonry of the inner leaf of cavity walling, the fixing isn't always easy. Lightweight aerated blocks can't be nailed into, and plugging and screwing these straps on is essential if they are to work. Given the substantial weight of some concrete roof tiles, the truth is they aren't so important as lateral straps. The dead weight of the roof is sometimes enough to hold itself down against wind uplift, but for the cost it is worth putting them in anyway, particularly if you have a wide overhanging soffit that the wind can push up on.

Walls

When bricks and blocks are made they are awarded a compressive strength; the denser and heavier they are, the higher their strength. The problem here is that they can all look the same and often the weight difference is too small to tell, so you have to rely on the manufacturer's information to tell you the strength of the product you have bought. Blocks are marked in different styles to identify them and bricks aren't, but the markings can be very subtle. It can be critical to build walls to a minimum strength if they are loaded by excessive amounts, perhaps from concrete slab floors or multiple storeys and sometimes point loads if they are to remain stable and crack-free.

Cavity wall ties

For a very long time we built our cavity walls with 50mm cavities, but in April 2002 when the England and Wales Building Regulations requirements for external wall insulation were increased to a maximum 'U' value of 0.35W/m sq k, wider cavities began to prevail – albeit cavities that were filled with insulation. Up to 75mm wide you can use the standard ties at 900mm horizontally and 450mm vertically, but if your design calls for an even wider cavity than 75mm, you have to use a suitable tie, such as the vertical twist type, to achieve the structural bond. The maximum horizontal centres have also been reduced to 750mm from the standard 900mm. Now the U-value maximum of 0.30 W/m sq k means 100mm cavities are common and 450mm spacings in both directions are needed. In any case, 150mm is the absolute maximum cavity width.

Calculating the number of wall ties needed

Cavity width	Maximum spacings		Number of ties per sq m of wall
	vertical	horizontal	
50–75mm	900mm	450mm	2.5
75–100mm	750mm	450mm	3.0
100–150mm	450mm	450mm	4.9

Cavity wall insulation

Whether you retain a clear cavity or use a total-fill insulation is a matter worth considering in depth. In helping you to make the decision you have a few factors to ponder on, not least of all the

▼ Different types of cavity wall tie are available.

VERTICAL TWIST TIE

DOUBLE TRIANGLE TIE

BUTTERFLY TIE

DOUBLE TRIANGLE WITH RETAINING DISC

DOUBLE TRIANGLE WITH RETAINING ROD

VERTICAL TWIST TIE WITH RETAINING DISC

degree of exposure to wind-driven rain. As we've already revealed, brick skins of cavity walls at only half a brick thick (112mm) can leak dramatically when the rain is pushed in to them by wind pressure.

As anyone who has lived in Britain for at least one winter will know, the combination of wind and rain is a popular one, and it's a rare plot that has all four sides sheltered from the elements. Usually the worst direction to be exposed to is the south-west – great for the sun in summer, but prone to bringing in the wet stuff with gales in winter. Cavity-wall insulation products are treated for water repellency, and shouldn't absorb the water if it arrives on their outer face. Instead, it should drain down the surface of the material and out through the foundations or weepholes in the perp ends at DPC level.

Like all water-resistant or water-repellent products, they come with a definition of the wording, which is very different to the one defining 'waterproof'. The conditions of use for these products are quite onerous, perhaps too onerous for bricklayers in a country with a massive skills shortage – and only they can be sure of keeping your inner leaves dry.

The insulation batts have to be neatly inserted and fitted together, without any mortar splashings or droppings occurring between them. They have to be kept clean and dry, and not wedged or forced into gaps and protected at the exposed tops by cavity tray DPCs. If water gets a chance it will track across the gaps between the batts and soak down into them until they are saturated, and from there on it is inevitable that damp will find its way through the inner leaf and into your home.

Because of the risk and the high standard of workmanship needed to avoid problems, many builders have steered clear of total-fill insulation in brick-faced walls. Where clad block walls are specified, the problem shouldn't exist. Render, tile hanging or boarding will resist rain totally if properly carried out.

The clear cavity was always there to keep the inner wall dry, and it wasn't until the 1980s that we started to change that and bring insulation into it. Even so, with standards for energy efficiency being less then, it was still possible to keep a clear cavity and use partial fill

▼ Partial fill insulation should be installed with a clear cavity retained.

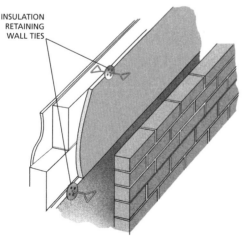

INSULATION
RETAINING
WALL TIES

nsulation or an insulating inner block. Today's standards are much higher, and using a partial-fill insulation board will inevitably mean using a wider cavity. Ideally a 50mm cavity is needed for bricklayers to ensure keeping it clear and clean. They may have to use a gauge rod to knock off mortar droppings as they proceed, or better still a cavity board to stop them dropping in the first place, but that 50mm gap will ensure a dry cavity.

Finding an insulation board that suits the standards and your needs will take a bit of research and designer advice, but be aware that the higher performing the insulant, the higher the cost. You can use multi-layer reflective sheets or phenolic foam boards in relatively thin thicknesses compared to mineral fibre or polystyrene, but you pay for their performance in the initial outlay.

If you want to take the problem of workmanship away from the brickie, then you

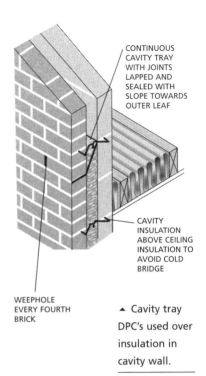

CONTINUOUS CAVITY TRAY WITH JOINTS LAPPED AND SEALED WITH SLOPE TOWARDS OUTER LEAF

CAVITY INSULATION ABOVE CEILING INSULATION TO AVOID COLD BRIDGE

WEEPHOLE EVERY FOURTH BRICK

▲ Cavity tray DPC's used over insulation in cavity wall.

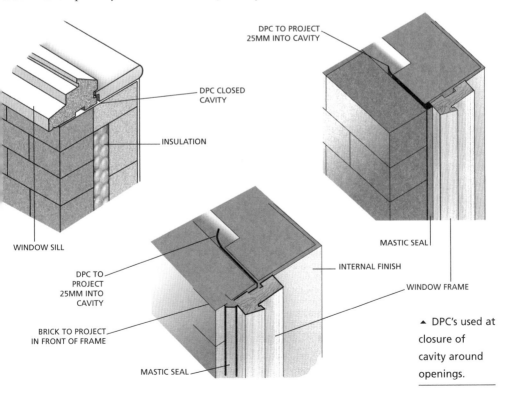

DPC TO PROJECT 25MM INTO CAVITY

DPC CLOSED CAVITY

INSULATION

WINDOW SILL

DPC TO PROJECT 25MM INTO CAVITY

BRICK TO PROJECT IN FRONT OF FRAME

MASTIC SEAL

MASTIC SEAL

INTERNAL FINISH

WINDOW FRAME

▲ DPC's used at closure of cavity around openings.

might decide on pumping in the insulation once the walls are up and the roof is on. Unlike the existing homeowner having this done, you have the luxury of working from the inside, drilling and filling before the walls are plastered, leaving no tell-tale signs of the job when all is complete. You still need to ensure your cavities are kept clean, but at least this system can be guaranteed by the installers or under separate insurance.

Movement joints and masonry reinforcement

Mortar strength is as variable as brick strength. Your bricklayer should use a mix of cement and sand that reflects the strength of the brick, often 1:6 (cement:sand), or 1:1:6 (cement:lime:sand) if lime is added for flexibility. Mortar that is stronger to keep abreast of loadings and stronger bricks can have a knock-on effect when it comes to how the walls move.

You might want to read that again – many of us prefer not to think that our homes move. Alas they do; brick walls have to have some flexibility to cope with shrinkage and expansion, and if they are too rigid and brittle they will crack. Most facing bricks will expand and shrink around 0.5mm per metre with heat or water. It's a good idea to add a mortar plasticizer, if not lime, to the mix. Even so, in very long walls you would be wise to consider movement joints. These are straight vertical breaks in the bond of the wall that divide it into smaller panels and are ideally placed at window or door openings where the side of the opening reduces the height of the joint. A compressible filler material is used to separate the panels of masonry and is recessed into the joint, later to be covered by mastic sealant or a PVC gasket of an appropriate colour. If you do have to install a joint from roof to ground, it might be worth coinciding it with a rainwater or soil vent pipe because they don't look pretty. Another solution is to incorporate it within a recess in the wall or a return.

Because bricks expand with saturation mostly in the first two weeks of their life, it is best to avoid using those that are fresh from the kiln. If they arrive still steaming and warm on the lorry, send them back. The same goes with blocks: I've seen lorryloads of them steaming as they arrive on site in winter, kiln-dry, and then spend the first few weeks of their lives in torrential rain. Not surprisingly, they crack before the home is finished.

Frogged bricks

Some manufacturers indent their bricks to make them lighter. These indents are called frogs. BS:3921:1985 allows manufacturers to frog bricks by up to 20 per cent of the overall volume of the brick.

Some companies don't put any frogs in, some put frogs on both faces, and some put frogs on just one face. Some manufacturers of sand-faced stock bricks have always used the full frog size allowable on one face of their bricks only. With this type of brick it is better to lay them frogged face up, improving the odds of the frog becoming filled with mortar by the bed joint; this method is considered best since it overcomes poor workmanship. In reality the vast range of superior facing bricks available now have little in the way of frogs, and the quality of their appearance and competitive price has meant that few new homes are being built with the old-style sand-faced stock bricks that were so common in the 1970s and 1980s.

Lintels

For some reason lintels aren't always given the design treatment. They are left as brickwork accessories that can easily be obtained when they are needed – except that invariably they can't. And without lintels your work will stop at first lift for as long as it takes for the order to be supplied. More than any other element, lintels are often misused because the type that was designated for the task was not instantly available and another sort that was is used instead.

Take the case of the closed eaves lintel, for example, which is short enough to sit up there above a window beneath the roof. It has been designed to take a small amount of masonry between it and the wall plate to spread the load evenly, but often an ordinary cavity lintel will be incorrectly used and the plate will be bedded directly to it, potentially invalidating the guarantee and compromising structural stability.

Not only are lintels shaped to fit particular constructions and

▾ All cavity wall lintels require cavity tray DPCs to protect them from rain penetration.

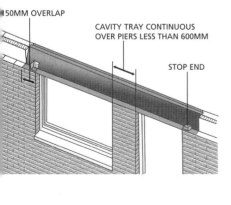

50MM OVERLAP

CAVITY TRAY CONTINUOUS OVER PIERS LESS THAN 600MM

STOP END

OVER LINTELS

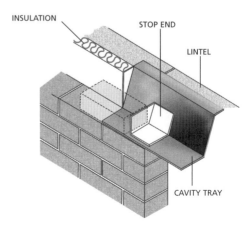

INSULATION

STOP END

LINTEL

CAVITY TRAY

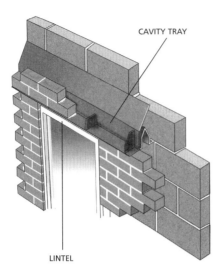

CAVITY TRAY

LINTEL

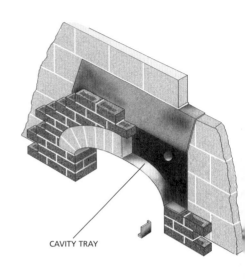

CAVITY TRAY

▲ Lintels and cavity trays are purpose-made for specific situations.

▼ Circular windows may have straight lintels above but cavity trays should be purpose-made.

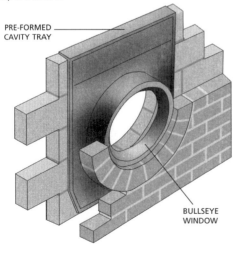

PRE-FORMED CAVITY TRAY

BULLSEYE WINDOW

positions, but they are gauged in steel thickness to carry varying loads. The thicker the gauge, the greater the loadbearing capacity. A manufacturer may therefore have a hundred different lintels in a catalogue to select from at the design stage.

◆ Prepare a lintel schedule before you dig the foundations, and obtain some quotes by hawking it around the merchants. Most manufacturers will prepare a schedule for you if you send them your plans.
◆ Lintels should not be cut down in length to adapt them. Apart from negating the manufacturer's guarantee, you will cut through their galvanizing protection, leaving the end exposed to corrosion.

◆ The prestressed concrete lintel is perhaps the most misused of them all. Commonly available in 63 x 100mm section to suit a cavity wall leaf, it is widely used to carry loads it was never designed to carry. It is in fact only suitable for small openings, such as internal doorways up to around 1.3m in width. There are deeper PCC lintels for higher loads and greater spans, but these usually prove harder to obtain. It is also worth remembering hat lintels are designed to carry uniformly distributed loads. Where point loads are placed on them, from the bearing ends of other beams for example, they should be checked out by a structural engineer, who can assess the maximum bending moment placed on the lintel and compare it to the allowable moment quoted by the manufacturer. Some lintel companies provide a structural design and checking service for their customers free of charge.

Security

Our home is our sanctuary from the pressures and threats of life. To be so it must be secure from unwelcome intruders. You can design in security right from the very beginning by positioning your home thoughtfully on the plot, by locating doors and windows in viewable positions, by avoiding recesses in outside walls and flat roofs beneath upper windows, and so on.

The UK police authorities started a scheme of advice called 'secured by design', aimed at encouraging building designers to think of 'security' early on, rather than leave it to the last-minute specifying of bolts and latches. The scheme allowed for the registration of new homes by developers when liaison had taken place with the local architectural liaison officer and the security features of the new home had been adopted and implemented.

It's a little unrealistic to think you can ever guarantee against suffering a burglary, but you can adopt measures that reduce the risk. Burglars are looking for homes with easy access, an unlocked door or window or a means of entry that needs only the minimum of force, so by introducing robust design for fittings and fixings as well as vigilance, your home can be made safer from the start.

Windows and doors that are located at the rear away from the street and its users are at most risk. Ground-floor windows and those above flat roofs or with balconies are at the top of the league for entry points, and these need special consideration.

Start from the plot layout

With your refuse collection points and meters located at the front of your home, there should be no need for officials to gain entry to the back, and so side entry gates within walls can be erected to enclose the rear garden at the boundaries and keep it secure.

In itself this will only draw attention to anyone trying to access the rear of your home who shouldn't be there; it does, however, mean that if they can get in from common land or a neighbouring garden they are less likely to be seen, so this is only the starting point for keeping them out.

Entrance doors

There is little point in hanging a robust door to a poorly fixed door frame that can be thumped out of its opening.

Door frames need secure fixings deep into the reveals of openings, spaced at no more than 600mm apart. Frame-fixing screws are commonly used for this purpose, but it helps if you locate two screws at the corners, no further than 150mm from the corners.

The door itself ought to be hung on at least three solid hinges of no less than 100mm, with the hinge pin internal, and for added strength hinge bolts can be added to supplement them. These bolts are essential if the hinge pins are external.

The door itself needs to be as solid as you can afford. The British front door was always solid timber, but since the plastic door and window explosion of the 1980s and onwards, PVCu front doors are often used instead. They have good locking facilities, with five-lever mortice locks as standard for most now, but the door material itself is relatively soft – great for thermal insulation, but not solid like wood for security.

Timber front doors are often better, and you should choose one with stiles at least 119mm wide and 44mm thick. Invariably panel doors are sought for their appearance and the panels themselves are thinner, but if they are restricted in width the risk of forced entry through them can be reduced.

Glazed parts of the door are best restricted to head height panels that are out of arm's reach from the lock; 1m is considered the minimum. As with any glazing, laminated safety glass is considered to be the best since it may fracture when hit but won't shatter or craze like toughened glass will. It achieves this by being made of two panes bonded together to form a resilient sheet.

A circular spyhole door viewer that is around 1.5m above the floor or a bit less to suit the outside ground level is invaluable when combined with a security chain or arm that restricts the opening of the door.

As far as locks go, the most favoured are mortice locks that are key operated on the outside only and lever- or latch-openable internally without needing a key. This has as much to do with fire safety as convenience because you may need to leave the house in an emergency, when playing hunt the key seems less fun than normal. The bolt it throws should be of hardened steel that resists sawing through, and its fixings into the door and frame need to be sound enough to ensure that the lock can't be removed without damaging the surrounding material. Deadlocks are fine, but as always, they rely on you taking the key with you. Even with mortice locks, the key needs to be used to throw the bolts rather than relying on the latch to avoid intruders.

Letterboxes are normally set centrally in the door for a reason beyond making life easy for postmen – within 400mm of a lock, they could be used to manipulate it.

You can buy limited opening flaps, but make sure these comply with BS:2911 – the fitting of letter plates is solely internal, preventing them from being removed from the outside.

Porches

The main reason for having a porch is for protection. Porches offer you some protection from the elements as you stand by the front door, or they offer your home some protection from you as you take off your wet coat and shoes before entering. Porches are thus one of two things – secure or unsecure. An unsecure porch can be designed with varying levels of weather resistance, from a canopy roof and open sides right on to enclosing walls and entrance door. To my way of thinking, if you're going to go to the trouble of fitting a door you might as well make it a secure door – I'm always a little confused by the porch door that swings open when you knock on it and never quite sure whether I'm meant to go in and knock on the next door or not.

If it is your intention to take the porch as the secure point and leave the inner door as a standard internal one, then the security obviously needs to be extended around from the door to any side windows or glazed sidelights and walls, for example. Speaking of which, glazed sidelights should also be laminated glazing, as this will serve in security as well as accidental impact from stumbling and children, or possibly stumbling children. Those hinges we spoke of just now for your entrance door need to be located on the glazed side panel side, just in case somebody wants to use the glass as a point from which to reach your doorlock.

Rear and side entrance doors

Invariably these are the most at risk, and the locks for these are best specified as five-lever deadlocks to BS:3621. You should add to them though with sliding bolts at the top and bottom if you can – 100mm barrel bolts with security screws are ideal, since burglars may feel they have the time and seclusion in these locations to force through the door of the empty home. No. 8 screws at least 30mm long will grip efficiently into timber, but plastic doors and their frames are not so easy to fix to, and self-tapping screws that bite into the steel reinforcing of the PVCu frame may be needed. Plastic, I'm afraid, just isn't so easy to get a good fixing to. If the doors are French or patio ones, with the risk of glazing, the key-operated lockable bolts are the type you need, which also prevent sliding doors from being lifted off their runners. To lock this type of bolt you normally have only to push the barrel in and release it with a key to open.

Remember that if you have a door serving an internal garage, this is also a potential risk and should be lockable.

Although it is a fire door, self-closing and so on, it is not ordinarily considered as an escape door so there is no problem with key locking from the inside. The fire resistance is to separate the garage from the home should a fire break out from a parked car or stored materials like oil.

An up-and-over garage door can also be provided with a pair of deadlocks that should be morticed into the frame as an add-on extra to whatever lock came with the door. These standard locks are never sufficient in themselves and seem to become less convincing with use.

Windows

I have known of burglaries where the windows have been taken out to gain access. The burglars obviously felt this was easier than opening them or breaking the glass. Admittedly, some windows on older properties do seem to just rot there waiting to be pulled out, and your new home shouldn't suffer the same consequences. Even so, the fixing of window frames is important. As with doors, the frame-fix screws that normally get used for the task should be closer than 600mm apart and in the corners at least to within 150mm of each corner.

I still believe that windows should be glazed internally, i.e. with the glazing bead fixed on the inside, but not all windows are manufactured this way. It may not be easy to prise out the glazing beads of some plastic windows, but it will be impossible if they aren't on the outside of the glass. If they are on the outside, then make sure that they are fully bonded or mechanically fixed in before the installers leave the job. With timber windows that are glazed traditionally, look to pin the beads at 150mm centres at least, as well as bedding them in mastic sealant or putty.

Background vents have to be included in new habitable rooms, and this is best achieved by trickle vents to the window frames. These are high enough to be draughtproof and controllable by sliding covers on the inside, as well as being entirely secure. Basically what lies beneath the covers is nothing more than a chased-out slot or series of holes 10mm wide. Alas, the plastic window industry has steered its customers towards the crack vent, a catch that has a double position, one in which the frame is totally shut and locked and the next in which the frame is left marginally ajar and locked. In spite of controlling bodies' best efforts to advise people of the security risk of the latter, they are being used in lieu of trickle vents all over the country for the sake of economy.

I'm almost certain you won't be considering this on a new self-build home, but I have seen a few people lately building their own rooflight windows onto new flat-roof extensions. I can barely bring myself to talk about it, but by using polycarbonate sheeting of the triple-walled stuff we see adorning conservatory roofs, they have formed upstands, dressed them with felt and mastic sealant and screwed down the polycarbonate into an openable rooflight.

 This has to be the weakest element of the home from a security aspect, to say nothing of the long-term weather resistance.

Security alarms

I speak from personal experience when I say that trying to wire up an existing home with a burglar alarm system is less than fun if you loathe surface wiring of any description. To install one in the construction along with all the other first-fix wiring must be blissful. In choosing a security alarm system, a BSI-kitemarked product is highly recommendable, and many installers of these systems price their work economically for new-build installations.

Control panels can be located where you like, but of course to arm the system and vacate the premises is a timed exercise and you really need to give yourself a chance of achieving it. Panels are ideally located in the hallways, or even the cloakrooms or understair cupboards fairly close to the front door.

Some systems, such as the wireless ones that emit a signal to the alarm box, can be supplemented with external building alarms and smoke alarms.

Roof structures

Cut and pitched roofs

Once upon a time all roofs were made this way. Trusses hadn't even been thought of, and if they had, carpenters the world over would have laughed themselves silly. A school of thought remains that this is the only proper way to build a roof, with graded straight timbers of stout size and thumping great nails. As points of views go it is one that's hard to beat, but the truth is that cut and pitched roofs can be difficult, if not virtually impossible, to form over large spans if internal loadbearing walls or beams aren't available. Individually, rafters, joists and purlins will only span so far, and not so far as you might think. The tables in this section look at the maximum distances for various sections both of standard C16 grade timber and the better C24 grade.

Rafters

When you consider that anything steeper than 10 degrees is classed as a pitched roof and anything steeper than 70 degrees is a wall, anywhere between the two and you have rafters with some variation in the weight they might be carrying as a load per square metre. The spans in the table are measured along the pitch – whatever it is – but if you're off the tables and into structural engineered solutions, then it is more than likely that your engineer will take account of the exact pitch of the rafters in calculating the load imposed on them from the tiles and equating it to a load on plan. The span of the rafters will then be measured on plan accordingly, as will the snow-load figure. The snow load is the only imposed loading we stick on to roofs – wind or leaves or anything else are ignored, only snow counts – and how much we

▸ Traditionally framed roof.

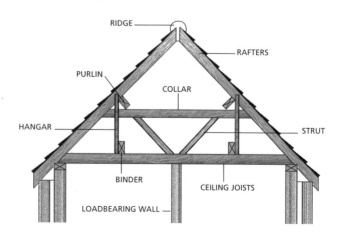

have to allow for depends on where you are, and particularly where you are above sea level.

Commonly the figure is 0.6Kn/sq m, which equates to something like 600mm depth of snow, and this is what the tables are based on. If your building is more than 100m above sea level or if you just want to allow for the next Ice Age, then the figure is upped to 1.0Kn/sq m and you should read the spans for one depth of section size less, i.e. for 50 x 150mm read 50 x 125mm.

Rafter size	Max. span (measured along rafter between supports)			
(C16 or SC3 grade)	Roof pitches from		Roof pitches from	
angle	22.5–30 degrees		31–45 degrees	
spacings	400mm	600mm	400mm	600mm
50 x 100mm	2.45m	2.14m	2.53m	2.21m
50 x 125mm	3.05m	2.67m	3.15m	2.76m
50 x 150mm	3.65m	3.20m	3.76m	3.30m

Ceiling joists		
Size of joist	Max. span (measured between supports)	
(C16 or SC3 grade)	at 400mm spacings	at 600mm spacings
50 x 100mm	1.84m	1.73m
50 x 125mm	2.47m	2.31m
50 x 150mm	3.11m	2.90m
50 x 175mm	3.72m	3.44m
50 x 200mm	4.37m	4.04m

Flat roof joists		
(C16 or SC3 grade)	Max. spans (measured between supports)	
	at 400mm spacings	at 600mm spacings
50 x 125mm	2.53m	2.37m
50 x 150mm	3.19m	2.97m
50 x 175mm	3.81m	3.47m
50 x 200mm	4.48m	3.97m
50 x 225mm	5.09m	4.47m

Purlins

Purlins were ever so popular in the 1930s, when the cut and pitched roof was made solely of 4 x 2in timbers. Rafters had to be supported, even on fully hipped roofs, and purlins were run

Purlin spans for various sizes, grades and spacings

Purlin size	C16				Grade	C24			
Strut Spacings	1500	2100	2400	2700		1500	2100	2400	2700
75 x 150mm	2.00m	1.80m				2.10m	1.90m	1.80m	
50 x 175mm	2.10m	1.95m	1.80m			2.15m	1.90m	1.85m	
50 x 200mm	2.40m	2.10m	2.00m	1.85m		2.50m	2.20m	2.10m	2.00m
50 x 225mm	2.70m	2.35m	2.20m	2.00m		2.80m	2.45m	2.35m	1.90m

around the middle of them, often in a complete ring, propped up by struts. Which is more or less where the design input stopped, because the struts often just landed on the 4 x 2in ceiling joists, placing them under even more stress than they had to start with.

These days we can't accept purlins so casually supported. They have to have a very definite span, the same as any other simply supported beam, a beginning and an end with some proper support at each. If you absolutely have to do some cantilevering of the purlin, you will definitely need the services of a structural engineer to design it for you. The table above is for use only in simplistic situations where the purlin beam is loaded uniformly by the roof and simply supported like any other conventional beam would be.

The spans, you will note, aren't great – they aren't great at all. Indeed, a purlin spanning between gables without any intermediate support is likely to be a steel beam purlin or a ply box beam purlin, and not a sawn timber purlin. These creatures need support at more frequent intervals, and struts are still the member of choice for the discerning carpenter. Struts should be pretty much perpendicular to the purlin, that is to say at 90 degrees to it, to transfer the load down to the next line of support, be it wall or beam.

This does have a nasty habit of putting the purlin higher up the roof than is ideal for reducing the rafter span to something sensible, which is often the reason for providing the purlin in the first place, so it needs some careful thinking on the designer's part beforehand. In shallow-pitched roofs, a purlin and strut roof can be difficult to arrange if there aren't any convenient loadbearing walls from which to prop up the struts.

It is possible for an engineer to design struts at reduced angles to the perpendicular. Essentially they have to adjust the 50/50 split between vertical and horizontal forces accordingly and assess the difference as bending, and adjust the horizontal forces on the strut. With the strut placed under bending instead of just compression, the depth of the member may be increased from the usual 50 x 100mm to something bigger. There is also the question of how the connections will transfer the load at the strut ends, and some detailing will be necessary with the answer.

Raised collar roofs

Raising the ceiling from the usual 2.4m level in some parts of your home will change the aspect and potential for those rooms considerably – they feel so much more spacious and airy once that level deck above rooms is raised beyond our immediate perception. Yes, you do pay a price in that if you attempt this on a ground floor of your house, forming a gallery in the floor above will lose you valuable space. Beneath the roof, where all you may encroach into is the attic, the price is easier to bear and you can add some welcome dimension to a small room like a bathroom or box bedroom by introducing a raised collar roof. There are some structural limits to the design, aimed at preventing the roof (rafters) from spreading.

As a rule of thumb, the ties shouldn't be raised higher than one third of the distance from plate level to ridge; beyond this and the rafters will need to be larger sections to deal with the point loads from connections and the bending that this will induce. You should always bolt the connections and include double-sided toothed plate connectors to avoid their rotation.

▾ A standard fink truss is designed to these elements.

Trussed rafter roofs

Roof trusses have been with us since the 1960s and remain the most popular method of forming a pitched roof on new homes. Their beauty lies solely in the speed of their erection, since the whole roof can be created and weathered with felt in a single day.

Critics of trusses dislike them because the timber sections used are remarkably slim compared to those required in a cut and pitched roof, and the punched metal nail plates which hold them together seem even more fragile. They also have the disadvantage of creating a largely inaccessible roof space due to the web of diagonal members that are present in conventional trusses.

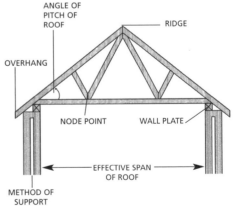

ANGLE OF PITCH OF ROOF

RIDGE

OVERHANG

NODE POINT

WALL PLATE

EFFECTIVE SPAN OF ROOF

METHOD OF SUPPORT

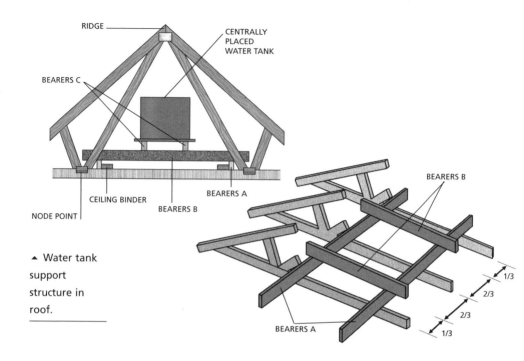

▲ Water tank support structure in roof.

Truss fixings

The truss clips are metal plates used to secure trusses to the wall plate in favour of bashing in 100mm nails, because the truss timbers are easily damaged by skew-nailing. Square twisted sherardized nails are used in the holes provided in the clips

 A checklist to tick off before ordering a quote or confirming an order for trusses

- ◆ Carefully measure the span over wall plates (not the clear span between walls).
- ◆ Check the roof pitch required.
- ◆ Check the type and size of any overhangs required.
- ◆ Check the type and weight of all roof coverings.
- ◆ State the size and desired position of any water tanks to be housed in the roof space.
- ◆ Details and positions of the supports for the roof (although they will not design these supports).
- ◆ Positions and sizes of any openings for chimneys, loft hatches, skylights or dormer windows, etc.
- ◆ You will also have to confirm if you will need their straps and clips, or gable ladders and wind-bracing timber.
- ◆ You will need to request whether you wish the timber to be pressure-treated with preservative or not.

because they have improved withdrawal strength, making them ideal for this application.

The stability of the trussed rafter roof relies upon elements other than just the individual trusses themselves. To form a roof that is stable under wind loading, the trusses must be braced with additional timbers running across them both longitudinally and diagonally. Even the tiling battens across trusses also help to brace them against the wind. If wind bracing is omitted or improperly installed, the stability of the roof will be compromised. Your trussed rafter manufacturers will be able to provide you with information regarding the position of wind braces in addition to supplying the structural design calculations for the trusses themselves – but they are unlikely to do either until a firm order has been made. When the building industry is buoyant you need to place orders a couple of months in advance of delivery; it is far better to get in early and store them on site for a couple of weeks than have to stop work and wait.

▾ Trusses need careful handling and protection on site.

Delivery and site storage

The location of the building and access for delivery – overhead cables, narrow roads – can be problematical for the long HGVs delivering them.

Give some thought to how they are going to be lifted into position. If they are not too large at least three men will be able to manhandle them, but the larger trusses will need mechanical handling by crane or teleporter. To give you some idea of weights, a single fink truss of 30 degrees pitch and a span of 7.7m will weigh 35kg. An attic truss for providing an accessible space in the roof of the same span will weigh 110kg. There may be fewer members in the latter, but the design demands much larger sections of timber, particularly in the ceiling ties.

It is important when storing trusses on site that they are stacked clear of the ground on

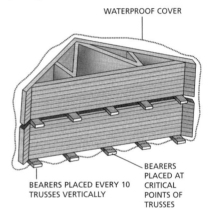

WATERPROOF COVER

BEARERS PLACED EVERY 10 TRUSSES VERTICALLY

BEARERS PLACED AT CRITICAL POINTS OF TRUSSES

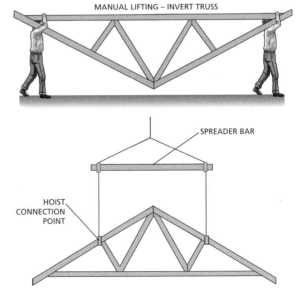

MANUAL LIFTING – INVERT TRUSS

SPREADER BAR

HOIST CONNECTION POINT

bearers and protected from the sun and rain by tarpaulins.

If your roof shape involves smaller intersecting roofs, these may be supported by girder trusses of two or three ply, depending on the span and the loads, from which other mono-trusses can be supported. Complex roof shapes with numbers of smaller intersecting roofs, hip ends or dormer structures get a bit too fiddly for the truss system, and areas of your roof plan can get hived off as 'infill by GC' meaning general contractor – although they might just as easily label them as 'somebody else's problem'. Some truss companies will supply you with the sticks to do this, but if it requires some design work it is better that you get that done first and shop around for the timber. It kind of defeats the object of using trusses if you have so much loose infill to build. Trusses have limitations, and although simple roof shapes are easy and efficient, complex ones aren't.

Wind bracing

Without wind bracing, trusses cannot share the loads exerted on them by the wind and the roof structure as a whole could rack over. Truss manufacturers will always supply the bracing material (25 x 100mm boards), but not always the information on where to put them. British Standards and warranty insurers seem to review their requirements for wind bracing periodically, and they

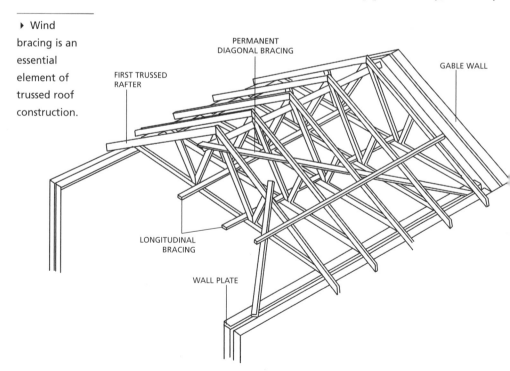

▸ Wind bracing is an essential element of trussed roof construction.

PERMANENT DIAGONAL BRACING

GABLE WALL

FIRST TRUSSED RAFTER

LONGITUDINAL BRACING

WALL PLATE

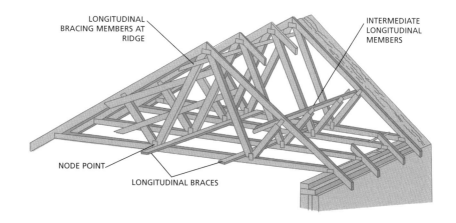

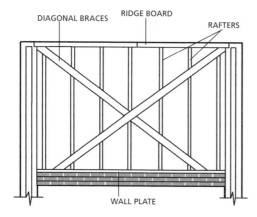

▲ Longitudinal bracing secured as trusses are erected.

never seem to align with each other anyway. Your warranty surveyor should be able to advise you as to what bracing is needed for his certification, and your building control surveyor on what is advised by British Standards. The structural Approved Document A has yet – at the beginning of 2003 – to address the subject strangely enough, but hopefully the next edition of it will.

Four different methods of bracing exist, and you could require any, if not all, of them in your roof design. The shape and span of the roof, together with its degree of exposure, have a bearing on which apply. All bracing should be double-nailed to each truss member it crosses to ensure proper transmission of the wind load. Monopitch roofs should have different types of bracing. It is entirely possible to end up with a small forest of timber in a correctly braced roof.

◆ LONGITUDINAL BRACING
Straight timbers overlapping past each other are the basic

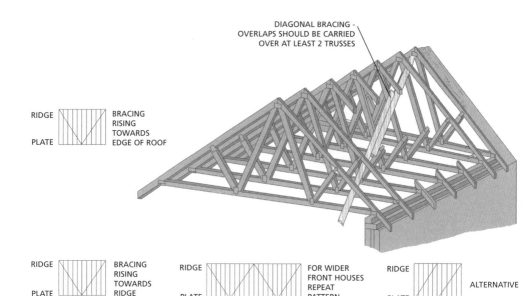

▲ Diagonal bracing shown here across rafters.

minimum wind braces. They should occur at the node points where struts meet rafters and ties. For a typical Fink truss you would have five positions. It sometimes proves useful in gable end roofs to run the lateral restraint straps to the gables across these braces, eliminating the need to nog out beneath them.

◆ DIAGONAL RAFTER BRACING

Again, standard bracing configured on plan view at 45 degrees to run beneath rafters from the corners to the ridge. In this way at least four braces are needed, but if the roof is longer, more.

◆ DIAGONAL CEILING BRACING

These braces are positioned across the top of the ceiling ties and run diagonally from the outside corners to the node points of the trusses. They would not normally occur in the centre of a roof truss, only on the two outer parts of the ceiling tie.

◆ CHEVRON WEB BRACING

These are diagonal braces that run in this case across the web struts where the span of the truss is over a certain limit.

Roof ventilation

Cold roof voids beyond the insulation layer are prone to condensation. The warm moist air from your home has permeated the plasterboard and the insulation and found itself in a much colder void, where possibly the air could be trapped and still. If it is, the vapour will condense on the cold face of the roofing felt

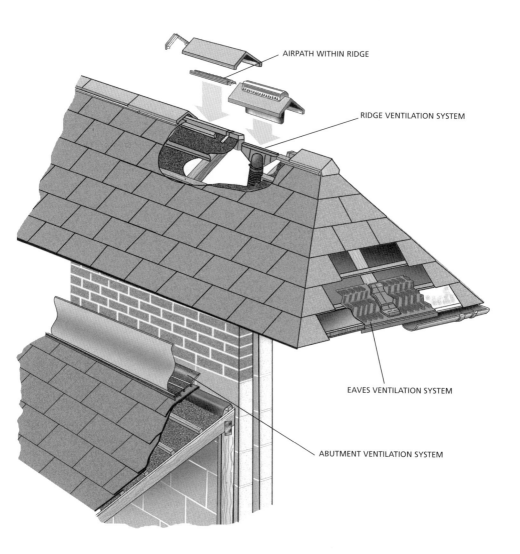

AIRPATH WITHIN RIDGE

RIDGE VENTILATION SYSTEM

EAVES VENTILATION SYSTEM

ABUTMENT VENTILATION SYSTEM

because its journey ends here. Condensation isn't a nice thing to have within your home anywhere but left unnoticed up here, the damp could corrode the roof plates and fixings, rot the timbers and generally damage anything you want to store in the loft.

The whole process can be made much worse with cold- and hot-water tanks for the heating system. If they aren't totally sealed up with covers and lagged with insulation, the vapour will be permanently present. When I changed my boiler for a combi and took out those tanks, creating a dry loft, the effect was instant. There was no more condensation, even though I had ventilation up here from eaves and gable vents as well.

Vents should be installed in all cold-air roofs to keep the air

▲ Roof void ventilation is critical in avoiding condensation.

and its vapour moving on and out. An inlet and an exhaust vent are needed for this to happen. Exhaust vents are best as ridge tile vents, but on roofs up to 9m span they could just be on the opposite eaves. The eaves vents are the neatest and most discreet; they can be bought as preformed soffit or fascia models, or even as under-tile combs that are more or less invisible from the ground.

Tile vents can be used for open-eaves situations where other vents can't be used, or against valley sides where no eaves are present. The wealth of ventilators on the market is extraordinary. Some are pretty obtrusive and downright ugly, others are slimline and discreet, and they all have a different quantity of air space.

Some arithmetic is needed here to work out how many tiles you need for your given situation, and I'm not sure that a chart will help you much.

A 10mm wide continuous gap along the eaves of a pitched roof is usually sufficient, but if you want to use tile or spot vents, look for this 10mm width per metre length of roof, i.e. 10,000sq mm per metre.

A 5mm wide continuous ridge vent is needed to exhaust air in room-in-the-roof situations or where roofs are wider than 9m. Ridge vents can thus be used that give the equivalent of 5,000sq mm per metre length of roof.

In these room-in-the-roof structures, ridge vents need to be combined with wider eaves vents of 25mm continuous, or 25,000sq mm per metre and a gap of at least 50mm over the insulation for the air to flow through.

What has helped tremendously in recent years is the manufacture of permeable roofing felt that allows the vapour to pass through it. In fact, if it is used correctly, in some situations you can avoid having to use any extra roof vents at all. Sounds good? Yes, of course it costs more and you might have to counter-batten the rafters with vertical battens over the felt, but it could free you of a time-consuming job and I'm sure it will speed up construction, avoid awkward fixings and keep other costs in timber sizing down.

Roof coverings

The great British climate presents a challenge to any roof. It isn't just the rain, it's the wind that sometimes accompanies it and the cold that sometimes frosts it over and the heat that sometimes bakes it. In other words, the full spectrum. Roofs in Britain have to cope with most of the elements at their worst at some time or another. With negative suction on the leeward face of the roof, rainwater can be forced beneath the tiles, and on the windward side positive pressure can do the same in wind-driven rain conditions.

 ## Keeping the weather out begins with the very shape and design of the roof.

Up to 30 degrees in pitch and the negative wind pressure or suction on it is far greater than with steeper pitches. Valleys channel water into streams on the roof covering, and that means increased risk of water penetrating if they aren't correctly formed, sized and durable. Hip ends give a better appearance and are less vulnerable to wind pressure than gables.

It's worth remembering that the actual angle of a slate or tile is always a bit less than that of the roof pitch and the rafter, simply because they overlap each other. If you don't follow the manufacturer's guidance on the recommended minimum pitch for tiles, the covering becomes aesthetic and can't be relied upon for weather resistance. In these situations the guarantee of the product is usually voided and the underlay becomes the sole means of defence. Having said that, roof underlay felt is particularly good at keeping out the weather. If it's well lapped and supported at the eaves by tilting fillets, and if vertical battens are used to run down the rafters before cross-battening is done, it will work as a drainage system to take water to the gutters. Felt should always be extended out at the eaves into the gutter in any case. However, in most tiling situations a vertical batten isn't necessary and the roof tiles should be thought of as the sole weathering element.

The weight of the tile also has a bearing on its weathering ability. Some slates only weigh in at about 20kg per square metre, while other concrete tiles may be three or four times that. With heavy coverings, vertical restraint straps might not be needed to anchor the wallplates down, as the dead weight of the finished roof is often enough to do that by itself. Not only that, but heavy tiles that interlock with each other are seldom going to be lifted by negative wind pressure, compared to lighter ones.

Where any tiles are vulnerable is at the overhangs of the eaves and along the verges of gable walls. In the latter, only a modest overhang of 20 or 30mm might exist, but wind pressure can force these off in severe gales. Verge tiles tend to be weathered at the edge with mortar filled to an undercloak material that is pinned to the gable ladder, but it is easily damaged. The same is true of

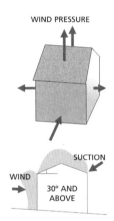

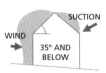

▲ Negative wind pressure or suction can occur on both roof faces of shallow roofs but typically only on the leeward face of steeper roofs.

eaves – if the wind can get under the overhanging tiles, in time they can be loosened and lifted off.

If you are building in a severe exposure zone you could choose a tiling system of dry fixings where the ridges and verges are screwed or clip-locked down rather than bedded in mortar.

The cost league of roof coverings tends to look something like the list below, starting with the cheapest concrete interlocking tiles and building up to natural Welsh slate at the top.

8 Interlocking concrete tiles
7 Plain concrete tiles
6 Chinese natural slates
5 Cement fibre slates
4 Spanish natural slates
3 Plain clay tiles
2 Brazilian natural slates
1 Welsh natural slates

Like all building materials, the price varies with the state of the housing market, property value and demand. They can rocket after severe gales, when half the neighbourhood are having to patch up their roofs or when house prices are soaring. As always, you need to shop around to get the best deal.

Tiles

Tiles can be split into two broad types, interlocking and plain. The interlocking type accounts for most of the modern tiles manufactured today. With grooved and lipped edges each tile along the course locks to those alongside it, providing greater resistance to wind uplift and thus better resistance to weather.

▶ Ventilated verge.

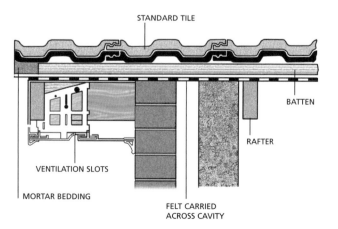

STANDARD TILE

BATTEN

RAFTER

VENTILATION SLOTS

MORTAR BEDDING

FELT CARRIED ACROSS CAVITY

Because of this feature and in combination with the size and weight of the tile, the need for nailing is reduced. In certain cases tiles may only need to be nailed every seventh or eighth course, and in others, only at the edges of the roof, increasing the speed of tiling. Whatever the manufacturer's minimum requirements, you may actually want to nail more frequently to add peace of mind the next time a hurricane comes along.

Plain tiles are small, cambered tiles that have a traditional cottage look. In parts of the country, clay peg tiles were once handmade and used as the main roof covering, and tile manufacturers have sought to produce tiles by machine that reflect their character. Clay has a much warmer and textural quality over concrete, and hence it is difficult to find anything that quite matches it, other than another handmade clay tile. As a material, clay ages very well, and some would say it improves with age, lasting for up to a hundred years.

▲ Concrete interlocking roof tile.

Traditional handmade tiles are still produced in some regions, but needless to say they are at the top of the list as far as cost goes. Since the size of a plain tile is standardized to 165 x 267mm or thereabouts, there are always 60 to the square metre, and labour costs for laying them remain constant, whatever the material may be.

You can always look for secondhand or reclaimed tiles from architectural salvage yards, but if you need a large quantity you may have a problem finding them. These businesses are really aimed at extensions and repairs where they can sell small quantities of them at a price per tile.

Even if you do strike lucky and secure enough plain tiles, can you also obtain the ridges or hip tiles you need? Clay hip tiles are usually produced bonnet-shaped and are wonderfully aesthetic, particularly when the mortar bedding is carried out neatly.

Some better plain tiles are cambered from top to bottom as well as from side to side, and this contributes to their rustic appearance when laid. As clay tiles vary in shade and colour, modern lookalikes are produced in colour bands for mixing on site. This is an absolutely essential task if you are to avoid patches of brown or orange tiles on the roof instead of a blended mixture.

With interlocking tiles the hips are usually covered with the same half-round or angles that run along the ridge, looking rather bulky and heavyweight in the process, particularly where the hips are small such as on dormer roofs or barn hip ends.

Slates

If your new home is sited in a Conservation Area or a Special Landscape Area, you may have to use the indigenous materials of the area rather than their modern counterparts.

Natural slate is available from new, so you needn't be faced with having to obtain secondhand slates in large numbers. Welsh slate is still quarried for this purpose and produced in a variety of traditional sizes, with different mines producing slates with distinctive colours – some mines will, for example, produce a purple-hued slate, while others may be nearer black than grey.

With slate, the laps vary with the size of each one and the degree of exposure. The shallower the pitch, the greater the lap needed to counteract it and maintain the weather resistance of the roof. Wind uplift increases with lowering the angle of a roof and rain can be driven beneath slates that are lifting. The more they overlap, the less chance there is of them uplifting.

Average Exposure
(figures are minimum overlap in mm)

	Roof pitch (degrees)					
Slate size	20	25	30	35	40	45
500 x 250mm	115	90	75	75	65	65
600 x 300mm	115	90	75	75	65	65
460 x 250mm	–	85	75	75	65	65
400 x 250mm	–	–	75	75	65	65
350 x 200mm	–	–	75	75	65	65

Severe Exposure
(figures are minimum overlap in mm)

Slate size	Roof pitch (degrees)					
	20	25	30	35	40	45
500 x 250mm	–	105	95	85	75	65
600 x 300mm	–	110	100	95	80	70
460 x 250mm	–	115	85	85	85	75
400 x 250mm	–	–	90	85	75	65
350 x 200mm	–	–	75	75	75	65

The only drawback with new slates is that they usually don't come holed for nailing. Holing them is a painfully laboursome business if you aren't skilled and don't have the traditional hammer for the purpose. They are whacked on the reverse side to allow a countersink to form on the fixing face for the nail head to sit in. Drilling them will not achieve this.

The gauge for holing is usually set as the batten gauge + the lap + 8–15mm (to allow for variations in size and batten gauge). This measurement is taken from the base of the slate. The hole should end up 20–25mm from the top of the slate.

Copper slate nails of sufficient length are used to embed at least 15mm into the battens. If you are laying your own natural slate roof, do not be tempted to fix them tight together – natural slate doesn't interlock and is traditionally fixed with a gap of 4–6mm between each to allow for drainage through to the sarking felt. The slates are obviously laid in a broken bond, and cutting them is best done with specialist tools that nibble the edges to form a shaped edging. You can't realistically cut slates too thin without them breaking soon after, and the minimum width for a slate is therefore around 150mm.

Start battening at the eaves with two battens so that the eaves course and the first real course can be laid. The eaves course of slates needs to overhang the fascia by about 50mm to drain into the gutter. Normally you'd have a tilting fillet to support the underlay at the eaves here, unless you actually want small birds to come and nest in the sagging material between the rafters.

CHAPTER 8

System Building

THE reason I have devoted an entire chapter to system-built homes should already be evident to you: they are perfect for self-builders. To start with, manufacturers often have a range of standard house models that you can visit on show sites, walk around and see exactly what the end result looks like, the kits are factory-produced to finer tolerances than you could expect to achieve from site construction, and the speed of their erection is nothing less than impressive. For most systems you can achieve a weather-resistant home in a couple of short weeks, with little mess to the site.

Combine these factors with the fact that higher thermal requirements are making them more attractive over traditional construction, and the choice of systems is expanding and you have a reason why every self-builder should seriously consider them.

Timber-frame kits have of course been with us for some time, although they did go a bit quiet in the final decade or two of the 20th century, not entirely undue to a certain *World in Action* TV documentary revealing the poor practices of a national house builder at the beginning of the 1980s. Because that builder was known for specializing in timber frames, the system got the rap rather unjustly.

Frankly, mass house construction of any kind can be seriously lacking in quality control, where speed of development takes precedence over quality and supervision is scant. If you were to carry out sample inspections of work on housing sites in your area, you could expect to find a plenitude of short cuts gone unnoticed, including plumbing waste pipes and fittings that should have been glued together left push-fitted only, and painted fascias where the topcoat arrived over the timber minus any undercoat, or where rubble was buried in the garden instead of removed, and the gauge of the mortar mix varies with each lift of the brick walls. Everything that can be overlooked without causing any immediate effect often is, and some things which do cause an effect sometimes are.

My point is the fact that this company was bodging timber-frame was almost irrelevant; they could just as easily have been bodging traditional or prefab construction.

Prefabricated panel build

Speak of prefabs and we all, including me, have a psychological hurdle to leap.

Post-war sheds spring to mind, as opposed to images that could grace the cover of a *My Beautiful Home* magazine. Clearly there is some major marketing to do if the new, and very different, prefabricated house kits are to take-off.

People who live in these new, super-insulated homes have been reported in the trade-press as saying, 'It is just like living in a normal home', which, frankly, isn't helpful and seems to underline even their preconceptions of prefabs along with everybody else's. Abnormal generally isn't what people want.

It's a shame really, because the new insulated panel kits, where your walls, roof and floors all arrive in factory-made slabs to be crane lifted into place and joined together, take so much of the hard work out of building and are very effective both structurally and thermally.

With prefabricated roof panels as well as floor cassettes, you can weather in your new home very quickly. The roof panels make it easy to form large galleried rooms with sloping ceilings – a side effect of forming a roof with an insulated and strong structural panel instead of the usual trusses or struts and ties. From an environmental view, many of these prefab panels are constructed from sourced timber and can claim to be free from nasty substances. They also display breathable construction qualities that allow moisture to disperse to the outside rather than condense within the structure, causing damp and ultimately damage.

You still get to employ the outer

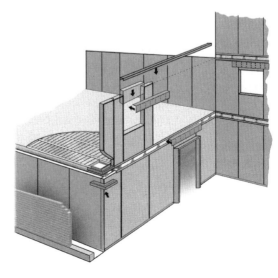

▼ Prefabricated wall and floor panels speed construction.

skin weathering of your choice, be it facing bricks, cedar shingles, clay tiles or whatever, and the roof can be tiles or slated traditionally too. In effect the end building can look very much the traditional home, the only possible hint of its modern nature coming from the overhanging roof plates at the eaves which can extend out considerably to offer sunshading to the windows immediately below.

Thin-joint masonry system

I'll be honest – I don't know if you can describe this method of building as a 'system', as it isn't so different to traditional construction with bricks and mortar. I'm really including it here because it has great potential for the DIY bricklayer. The hard thing about conventional bricklaying is the mortar, getting the gauge of the mix right, getting the depth of the joints right and the courses level and the perp ends consistent – in fact everything to do with actually bedding the bricks and blocks, all of which pretty much disappears in a puff of cement with the thin-joint system.

Instead of using cement and sand mortar, you use a prefabricated adhesive that sticks the blocks together. I say blocks because the system is available only for aerated lightweight block construction. Armed with a bit of practice, a spreading tool that looks a bit like a scoop, with teeth designed for the task (hired or, better still, bought), and a block saw to cut them when needed, anyone can be a bricklayer. Well, almost anyone – the harder bits are around the peripheries of openings where the cavity has to be closed and the vertical DPC built in – block lintels are available, and the first course on the foundation has to be laid conventionally in mortar to get you off on an even keel.

The benefits, apart from the reduced skill level, really only come from the fact that without 10mm mortar joints, the thermal insulation of the wall is better. When 'U' values are calculated for walls, the surface area of 1sq m of blockwork includes 10 per cent of low-insulation mortar that leaks some of your heat and reduces the value of the wall. Using the thin-joint system maximizes the thermal performance of the block, meaning that less insulation is needed in the cavity to meet the standard you and the regulations are after. The same is true of sound insulation although to a lesser extent.

Is it quicker? Probably not if you've never done it before, but with practice, yes. The glue is fast-setting so you can't lay too many blocks at once before spreading out the next section of the stuff. With some systems, the roofs and floors can be purchased as tongue-and-groove plank elements which will offer some sound insulation values that timber roofs and floors lack. Even staircases are available preformed.

The beauty really is in the flexibility of taking the system as far as you like – you can go the whole way with two skins of blocks and spray on a single coat elastomeric render, or just use it for the inner leaf and internal walls of a traditional brick-and-block home.

With the adhesive being much quicker to set than mortar, the walls can be built up higher each day without fear of finding them spread across the ground in the morning. It should also be possible to keep waste down to a minimum because the blocks have to be neatly cut before use to fit together, as opposed to just being whacked with a trowel and patched in with mortar. That neat cutting takes a bit of time, and you won't want to waste the offcut if you can use it elsewhere, thus making the site tidier and free of broken blocks as well as gone-off mortar.

Some manufacturers also produce a larger than average block (more than double the usual size) to speed up the progress. Because you get to build a high inner wall first, leaving the brick or outer skin to be constructed later, you can fix the insulation batts carefully without fear of getting them mucked up with mortar, one of the major problems with cavity wall insulation.

The preferred wall ties for this purpose are the helical type that you can drive into the wall anywhere, regardless of where the block courses occur, but to suit the brickwork leaf courses.

Timber-framed construction

Here in Britain, timber-framed construction normally means providing a timber-frame inner leaf as the structural element and a masonry outer leaf as a rain shield in a cavity-wall format.

The insulation within a timber-frame structure can be perfectly located between the timber studs of the framework, and because of this it can be considerably thick and yet still maintain a clear cavity for weather resistance. The greatest risks come from condensation forming within the structure, but modern materials can reduce these risks to acceptable levels. With the construction lending itself to system building, where manufacturers produce a design and supply package with the option to erect it as well, the timber-framed home can be built fast in a one-stop shop.

Many countries prefer to use a deeper timber section for the framework than we do in the UK. 50 x 150mm (2 x 6in) is more normal in Scandinavia, and 50 x 100mm in Britain. Either way the frame still needs to be braced, with diagonal timbers between

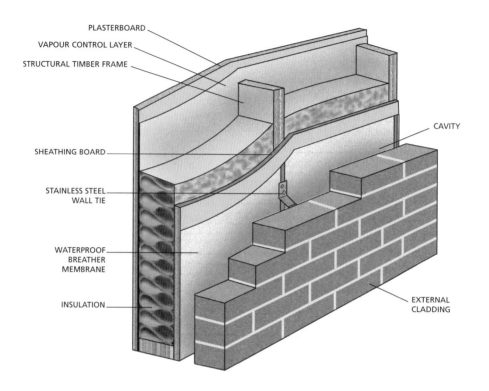

PLASTERBOARD

VAPOUR CONTROL LAYER

STRUCTURAL TIMBER FRAME

CAVITY

SHEATHING BOARD

STAINLESS STEEL WALL TIE

WATERPROOF BREATHER MEMBRANE

INSULATION

EXTERNAL CLADDING

▲ Traditional timber-frame wall structure.

the vertical studs or by lining with plywood sheathing. The latter is preferred since it provides a diaphragm-like structure which is highly resistant to racking movement under wind loads, and ply or OSB (orientated strand board) is used. Either way the walling is made up in manageable panels on the ground and erected into position on site by crane, and you can expect to hire one for a couple of days to get all the walls up and the roof trusses on. The sole plates of timber-framed walls need securing down without penetrating the DPC. To achieve this, special anchor plates are used which allow it to be fixed to the ground floor structure rather than the wall substructure.

Sheathing is normally covered with a breather membrane (building paper) which adds some weather resistance behind the cladding. It is usually stapled to the sheathing and needs to be well lapped at joints and repaired after it gets torn or damaged, as it usually will. You can't use traditional roofing felt for this task because it isn't that breathable, but other perforated sarking felts are available for a dual purpose of roof and walls.

Internally the plasterboard finishing is fixed over a vapour control layer (polythene) to restrict the path of condensation. 'Warm wall' construction, where the insulation goes on the outside of the sheathing, does not need a vapour control layer.

As with breather membranes the insulation is stapled to the stud frame, with joints well lapped and damage repaired immediately before plasterboarding.

 It is entirely possible to erect the timber frame of a four-bedroom home in a single day.

Two hours to unload, half a day to stand up the panels and nail-gun them together, and the trusses put on and braced in the afternoon. Some companies will send along a chippy with the kit on the first day to help you set it up. This is an invaluable aid because this person is going to be familiar with the product and all its quirks.

The least radical of all system-built homes, we've been building timber-framed houses the same way since the 1970s: brick outer skin, cavity, timber inner skin with insulation stuffed between the timber studs, dry-lined with plasterboard. They do make for energy efficient designs but the increase in U values now means that the insulation should be something better than the old glass-fibre quilt. Now, 150mm-deep studs which are filled with phenolic foam insulation boards can create a highly energy efficient home. I do like timber frame myself but there are undeniably still issues with it that need to be addressed.

Whichever sheathing you use, ply or OSB, both are wood-based products that are combustible, and you will be lining the inner face of your cavity on one side with them. Keeping the cavity free from electrical wiring and gas services is absolutely essential to reduce the fire risk, along with ensuring that there is correct fire stopping at the junctions of all floors and walls. This is done by mineral-fibre cavity barriers being fitted carefully, continuously and tightly to the cavity in these positions. The aim is to prevent a fire from spreading throughout the home via the cavity. Where fires have occurred, they have usually been started as a result of later work, where cutting through the wall has friction heated the sheathing, causing it to smoulder and ignite. If the cavity is incorrectly stopped, the fire can spread and the whole home can be lost.

For years, we have had controls under the Building Regulations in Britain to limit, as much as possible, the spread of a fire across interior room surfaces, such as walls and ceilings inside our homes, but these have unfortunately yet to be extended to the surfaces of cavities, where fires can spread

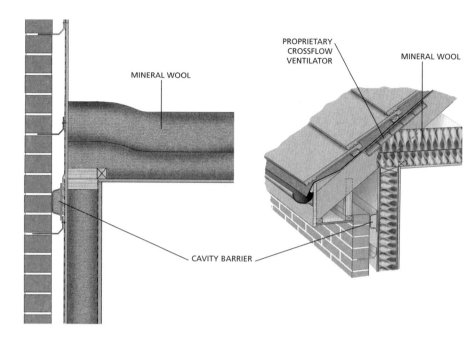

MINERAL WOOL

PROPRIETARY
CROSSFLOW
VENTILATOR

MINERAL WOOL

CAVITY BARRIER

▲ Timber-
frame construc-
tion needs
careful installa-
tion of cavity
barriers to
prevent fire
spread.

unnoticed. Regulations only go as far as cavity barriers to stop
fire from spreading from one house to another or too far, but you
may wish to reduce the risk of fire spread by lining the cavity face
with plasterboard on both sides or using ply sheathing that has
been treated to inhibit fire spread. Any timber can be treated to
retard fire, although usually the most effective methods are those
carried out under pressure in factory conditions and are thus
relatively expensive.

What will also make a difference is workmanship standards.
Check to make sure mineral-fibre cavity barriers are installed
correctly, and if you want to, install them more frequently than
you need to – perhaps at the intersections of internal walls
dividing rooms as well as floors. In the unlikely event that a cavity
fire does occur, the barriers could save the whole home from
damage – as well as you.

Some site checks for timber-framed construction:

◆ Check that foundations have been accurately set out within
plus or minus 10mm per 6m length of wall.
◆ Check floors and walls below base plates (sole plates) are level
to plus or minus 6mm in 6m, and take great care in levelling
beneath base plates on a mortar bed and DPC.
◆ Secure them using special base-plate angle fixings, **not** by
bolting through the plate and DPC.

◆ Do not allow the wall panels to be moved out of plumb to accept incorrectly made trusses or beams.

◆ Avoid gaps between wall panels and poor nailing between panels.

◆ Check that the upper floor wall panels are nailed securely to floor joists and are packed out beneath properly between the joists.

◆ Discard split timber caused by nailing too close to the edge of timbers.

◆ Make sure the outer breather membrane overlaps the sole plate and the DPC beneath it is lapped up the inside of the plate to protect it from wet floor finishes (i.e. screed).

◆ All timber should be regularized and bear a stress grade stamp, and be marked 'dry' or 'KD' to show low moisture-content. External walls timber should also be vacuum- or pressure-treated with preservative.

◆ Protect the chipboard floor decking from the elements. Some boarding comes prelaminated with removable protection.

◆ Ensure all the cavity barriers are tightly and continuously fitted at the floor levels and wall junction positions to divide up the cavity.

◆ Soon after completing the erection of the timber frame, the roof should be pitched and covered and the windows glazed. Do not allow the frame to stand exposed to the elements for too long.

A concrete home

Concrete panel construction was a popular way to build homes after World War Two, when a national shortage of housing demanded a quick and easy method of building. Most of the houses have now been condemned as structurally unsafe: the panels were thin, cover to the reinforcement was less than generous, and the disease of concrete cancer set in. Well, 50 years was probably longer than they were intended to last anyway.

Today it is still possible to use precast concrete in construction, but this is rare because of the poor thermal insulation values and appearance of the product, and the house needs total cladding inside and out. Precast concrete floor joists are popular, because you can achieve a solid-floor effect from a suspended system quickly. Appearing in the early 1980s, these prestressed floor joists are T-shaped, allowing concrete blocks to be loose laid to form a flush floor – well, flush to a level with a slurry grouting over the top to fill the gaps. They still need insulation added unless you use the specialized polystyrene infill blocks in lieu of concrete ones, and this can be overlaid on them before the final finishings are carried out.

In so far as walls go, the concrete system-build method at present is really a polystyrene block-build method. Hollow-pot interlocking blocks of expanded polystyrene (EPS) are stacked Lego-style on top of each other and then concrete is pumped into the hollow pots. The blocks themselves are little more than permanent shuttering and perform no structural role in this relationship; they just make up for the lack of thermal insulation that concrete walls offer. Retaining walls can be built this way too, with steel reinforcing bars inserted into the pots in exactly the same way as precast hollow-pot concrete block walls are built.

The same applies to lintels, with special blocks being used to accept reinforcement laterally rather than vertically. At first glance the system appears to be a very clean way to build, but only up to the point where the concrete has to be added. Pumping concrete can be a messy business at the best of times, but pumping into small hollow pots is especially so. Once the walls have cured the wall plate can be shot-fired or bolted to the top, the roof can be pitched, and the doors and window frames can be fixed to the openings. The system has been used in this county by self-builders looking for an alternative to timber frame, perhaps where the walls are more solid.

Internally, a dry lining of plasterboard on dabs will finish the walls, but for extra strength a paper-reinforced plasterboard will allow heavier fixtures and fittings to be hung from the walls. Externally a thin coat render system can be spray-applied in two coats to give a flexible and low-maintenance finish that is so clean when new that it doesn't need painting.

This system is widely used in Germany and other Northern European countries where insulation and robust construction are key values. One manufacturer did, I believe, have National Type Approval from the LABC (Local Authority Building Control) at one time but it wasn't maintained, perhaps because their market share wasn't large enough to make it worthwhile. Even so, every year homes are built throughout the country using this method, and more than one manufacturer supplies to the UK.

The design work, however, seems to be down to the self-builder's architect and structural engineer, who essentially must design to the standards for reinforced concrete. Methodology is important, though, particularly as in situ concrete does not reach its full (characteristic) strength until 28 days after it has been placed. This fact means that retaining and buttressing walls may need to be loaded with floor structures before work can proceed to another level if they are to remain stable.

The polystyrene may be treated with a flame-retarding additive to reduce fire spread, but that doesn't mean it won't melt in a fire. Blocks that have accidentally caught fire on site have been superficially damaged, making finishings awkward and compromising the thermal insulation qualities. I don't see that they can be too easily repaired once this has happened.

Steel-frame construction

A steel-framed home might seem a touch industrial and heavy-duty, but these systems do not involve RSJs and arc-welders – quite the opposite, in fact: they are made of lightweight galvanized sections cut from thin steel sheeting and formed to joist shape by rollers, with holes pre-punched in the factory. When I say thin, I mean only 1 or 2mm thick. Essentially, Meccano. When panels are assembled off-site, they might just as often be screwed or riveted together as welded or bolted.

Steel-framed housing is as rare in the UK as insulated-panel housing, but it is extremely popular in Japan, where around 150,000 homes are built every year by this method; and in the USA, where stick building is everything, it amounts to a fifth of the market.

 In Britain to date, we have only built steel-framed homes in small numbers, and only then with angle iron after a war had ended and fast construction was needed.

Because it is a 'specialist' product only a few companies manufacture the kits, but those that do can offer a house kit design similar to the major timber-frame specialists. The price is still higher than traditional brick-and-block construction but on a par with timber frame, although it is of course more of a specialist job to erect the frame, and this can push up the cost. So what are the advantages of building your structural frame in steel?

Being factory-galvanized, steel is never going to rust or rot, and to my knowledge the world has no metal-boring beetles to eat it. Steel framing is particularly good at resisting earthquakes (hence the popularity in Japan) and lightning strikes, which are harmlessly conducted to the ground through the structure. You should also have no worries about handing the home down to your grandchildren – or their grandchildren, come to that – because some studies have reported that steel framing like this can last in excess of a millennia, although presumably the results of

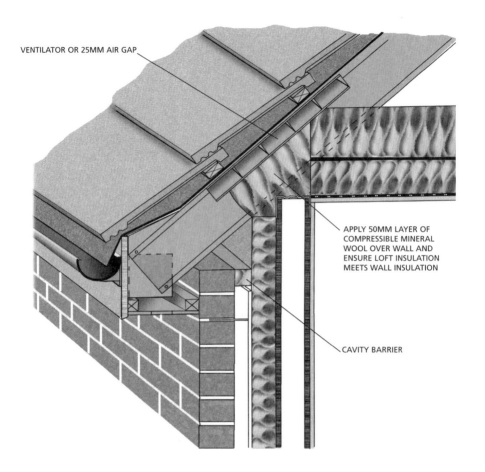

VENTILATOR OR 25MM AIR GAP

APPLY 50MM LAYER OF COMPRESSIBLE MINERAL WOOL OVER WALL AND ENSURE LOFT INSULATION MEETS WALL INSULATION

CAVITY BARRIER

▲ Continuous insulation is important with steel-framed homes.

site trials are still awaited. From an environmental point of view, I shy away from the idea that any product we manufacture will last that long. On the other hand, the material used to make these sections is up to 60 per cent recycled from drink cans and the like, so perhaps if in the future somebody wants to dismantle your home they can recycle them again to satisfy a crushing thirst.

Because the structure is lighter than timber-frame or masonry construction, the load to the foundations is reduced, which will be of some advantage if you are building on poor ground. If the ground is consolidated fill or simply has a low bearing pressure, this system could well reduce your foundation costs by allowing you to use mini-piles or less reinforcement to a raft or ground-beam foundation.

I've heard it said that from a fire-resistance point of view, steel buildings are the best since steel doesn't burn and the connections mean the building will never completely collapse. A British Steel design engineer once told me that he had never heard of a total collapse of a steel-framed building – but this was before 11 September 2001. It is true that steel doesn't burn – it melts, and before that, once the temperature of the fire is reached, it will warp and disfigure beyond recognition.

 I would ignore any suggestion that you and your steel home may be totally safe from fire, but clearly it will not have the structural combustibility of timber frame.

Steel, however, is too good a conductor of heat for the insulation to reside between the sections as it does with timber: cold-bridging would abound, and so this system lends itself to insulating over the outside of the frame – which, in the case of a masonry outer leaf, simply means cavity wall insulation. That way the frame is included within the insulated fabric of the building.

As with timber frame the downside is that you can only line the frame internally with boarding, leaving a hollow structure that is difficult to fix anything of any weight to and that gives the feeling of living in a drum because you simply lack the density of solid walls to keep out noise. You can go someway to overcoming these problems by using a heavyweight paper-reinforced plasterboard, but this of course will add to the cost.

Steel-framed buildings with pre-punched holes are accurately formed in factories. This means that your home will be perfectly square and your walls perfectly upright. No other form of construction will achieve this, but that also means that any other element of construction, such as the foundations, will have little margin for error. The setting out of the building on the footings becomes critical. If the permitted minor tolerances are not met there could be insufficient bearing at the sole plate or variations in the width of the cavity. To achieve these tolerances packing shims or grouting will be necessary, placed beneath every stud and above the DPC. I would advise you to use packing shims cut from thin pieces of galvanized steel, available from the manufacturers.

CHAPTER 9

Green Build

APOLOGIES **for the title of this chapter – but it could have been worse: it could have said 'The Green House'. There is something about the word 'green' that just sounds so – well, over-employed now. The fact that we still have to give it a label at all is rather sad. I had hoped that all homes would be more environmentally friendly by now, but the truth is they aren't.**

The principles of building construction didn't change much in the 20th century, which when you think about it is pretty odd, given the massive leaps that we made elsewhere with technology. When the sci-fi writers of the last century wrote of the millennium they predicted bubble houses and theme parks on the moon, but in reality the biggest leap we made was trussed rafters. Perhaps they have just had to move the dates back a bit – one company in Japan still has plans drawn up for a lunar theme park where the rides will take advantage of the low gravity, but it's now targeted for 2050. I hope that I will be too old (if not actually on the wrong side of the ground) to avoid the temptation of a long weekend in space then.

So we've colonized the planet with tiny portable phones, yet we still have to open our front doors with a soft metal key. Why haven't we pushed back the frontiers of science when it comes to building houses? Two reasons – one is conservatism, in that we tend to like a traditional approach when it comes to the home, and having found what we like, we tend to want to stick with it. The other is the cost of construction and land. The premium of construction land translates to so many pounds per square metre of floor space and linear foot of frontage, all of which spawns one question - how many homes can be crammed onto the site? This 'never build four when you can squeeze five on' approach is kind of restrictive when it comes to innovation.

So home building has deep roots, and traditional methods still rule. It's possible that the dramatic change in architecture required is putting a lot of people off – 'green' homes do tend to look like a cross between Teletubby Land and the London Aquarium, all grass and glass. And those seem to be the two main characteristics associated with the genre – a floor-to-roof glass house built over the south face of the home, and a grass roof sloping down the back.

Take the 'Dream House' built in 1998, known in the industry as the 'Integer House' (an acronym for Intelligent and Green, or at least Intelligent and Gern), the star of a BBC-TV series. An experimental home built with every conceivable eco-friendly, high-tech product available, that ignored most if not all of the home-build traditions but at a phenomenally high cost for the floor area achieved, it was destined to remain as an experiment. If nothing else, the 'Dream House' proves that change has to come gradually in little steps and not in leaps and bounds. Even so, its architecture became the prototype for green design. So what did it look like?

It was set into a bank, earth-sheltered from the elements and barely impacting on the visual amenities of the area. Like a lot of homes in this position, the upstairs becomes the downstairs and vice versa. But if you are going to have bedrooms below the main living rooms you will need good sound insulation (something the 'Dream House' didn't have). Floors that creak when people walk around upstairs and televisions that are nearer the floor than the ceiling all help to confirm that the best place for bedrooms is upstairs under the roof, where it's quiet. To add to the noise problem, the utility room was placed next to the bedrooms, and with the washing machine running on nighttime cheap electricity... I don't think so.

Glass

The main feature of the 'Dream House' was a full-frontal greenhouse that stretched down from the roof, covering the whole of the front elevation, and this feature remains prominent in green homes today – 10m high and steeply sloping, which is a tremendous help when it comes to cleaning the glass. Near-flat glass or plastic roofs soon green over, but with rainwater shooting down a steep roof it should be virtually self-cleansing. A steel frame with some pretty chunky sections, solar panels on the small roof

WATER CIRCULATES THE LOOP BY PUMPING EXCHANGING HEAT

HEAT EXTRACTED FROM THE EARTH PUMPED UP TO THE HOME

HEAT EXTRACTED FROM THE HOME TRANSFERRED TO THE GROUND AND COOLED

▲ Underground heating loop system.

near the ridge, and a rooflight thrown in for good measure made the prototype look more like the Mir space station than a house.

In the green house (I knew it would sneak in eventually) the glass is there more for solar gain than the view and because of the amount of it, it must normally be separable from the remainder of the house if it isn't to turn your home into a fridge during the winter. This means you need to design it in as a giant conservatory that can be used to harness the sun's warmth and light when it is needed, but can be shaded out to prevent overheating and separated off to prevent heat loss. Glass has many sides to it, but only one is acceptable.

Window technology has been forced on, with Building Regulations demanding higher insulation standards from glass. The use of low-e-coated 20mm cavity double-glazing became the industry standard in 2002, but glass like this comes at a price and you only need it to keep the heat from escaping. Single-glazing in toughened panels is much better at letting in the heat in the first place, and openable doors and warm air ducts that free heat can then be distributed into the living rooms of your home.

An overhanging roof will help to shade the glass from overheating, but to effectively control the solar gain you are going to need blinds. Electric-powered louvres are available, and many can be powered from a single plate switch, but how eco-friendly is that? In the true green house, low-tech is the way to go and blinds can be manually lowered by a long pole that has a hook on the end.

The green house is there to attract solar heat. But homes with south-facing conservatories can quickly overheat in the summer, and to help reduce the problem the 'Dream House' used single-glazing instead of double. Even so, the roof had to be equipped with blinds for shading and the glass tinted to reduce glare. Automatic louvres built in at low and high level and programmed to open at a preset temperature allow air to circulate through, cooling things down. A large conservatory façade can generate enough solar gain to maintain a temperature of 19–21°C.

Ventilation

For warm air to circulate and rise throughout the house, louvred vents should be incorporated; in the 'Dream House' they were over the doors. Passive stack technology has been available since the 1980s in the UK, and I've seen it used in a few homes instead of electric extractor fans. Basically you have pipes, air stacks if you like, rising vertically through the house, taking warm, moist air out of the wet rooms – kitchen and bathrooms – and drawing it up and out through the roof, chimney-style. Because warm air rises on cold or temperate days this works fine, but on hot summer days it may be colder inside than out, and a fan is then needed in the roof void to draw the air up.

A whole-house ventilation system that runs continuously at low speed will draw out moist, warm air and recover the heat from it for re-introduction to fresh air being drawn in. Air management systems like this need to recover the vast majority of heat from exhaust air and be capable of changing hundreds of cubic metres of air per hour.

Green roofs

I like a grass roof, particularly when the building is built into a bank or cliff, camouflaging the structure from behind and above. A home that takes full advantage of the natural cover is a true eco-home in this book.

Actually the roofs are invariably not covered with grass at all, but sedum, which is a kind of low-water-demand succulent that stays green much easier and requires no maintenance. Grass is a different kettle of fish; it requires much more water to keep it alive, and it needs mowing every so often. The few buildings where I have seen grass used have experienced some difficulties. I tend to think that if you are building on a sloping plot, a valley side or whatever, a grass roof that runs off from the natural level of the ground would be wonderful. Stood by itself two storeys

▾ A whole house ventilation system.

A – TEMPERED AIR

B – COLD INCOMING AIR

C – WARM CIRCULATED AIR

D – RECLAIMED HEAT

above the high street makes it a statement of individualism, rather than a building that blends in.

Getting onto the roof for maintenance is going to be difficult if it is separated by fresh air from the ground. The RSPCA are going to want a wire fence around it to stop a goat from falling off, and the HSE are going to want a tether wire to stop a gardener with a hover mower from falling off. Guinea pigs might be the answer, but you may attract every falcon for 20 miles towards what looks from the air like a picnic table. All things considered, if you can design in the grass roof as an escarpment of Mother Earth thrusting skywards, not only will it look better but also you'll be able to maintain it in safety.

How are green roofs kept alive?

The roof structure may not be that much different to start with, albeit perhaps a little stronger. The dead loads of the roof covering will, after all, be significantly higher than roof tiles. The rafters are boarded over with plywood before being felted by a specialist membrane that incorporates a copper core root barrier. A series of polystyrene trays of the sort you see at garden centres (eggbox-shaped) cover the felt and are partially stone-filled before being filled with about 125mm of topsoil. The stones are both the drainage layer and the ballast to hold them in place.

Before the turf or grass seed is laid, a system of irrigation pipes must be laid out over the roof so that in dry periods water can be pumped up to keep it alive. The porous rubber of recycled car tyres makes a good environmental choice for irrigation pipes that are laid within the surface of the topsoil.

Given the high evaporation rate of a grass roof, not much water is going to make it to the cobblestone-filled gutters, but what does should be directed via drainage pipes to a below ground storage cistern, where in times of drought it can be pumped back on to the roof for irrigation.

Finally, before the turfs are laid or the seeds spread, a sacrificial reinforcing of timber trellis is laid to give the grass a chance to get established and knit the whole thing together. The roots of the grass plant will of course bind the topsoil wonderfully when it is established. It is an amazing plant and a great colonist that can grow quite happily on a vicious angle without fear of being washed away in a downpour. Its biggest threat will come from dry periods, when turf will shrink back and resemble a badly made patchwork quilt, and if this is followed by gale winds you could find your roof covering lying face-down in a nearby field.

If you can keep it lengthy, this will protect it from the sun and

allow wildflowers to spring up. For a while you are going to have
to get used to the idea of looking up from ground level to see the
shoots of grass sprouting from the eaves, derelict house-style.
Maybe you'll even have to take the odd nosy visitor up there to
show them just how out of hand things have got.

You can mix into the topsoil some wildflower mix seeds from a
local supplier. Choose plants that are indigenous to the grasslands
of your locality if you are going to do this, but I suspect that
nature will soon introduce some herself anyway.

Wild grasslands are untidy, so don't manicure the roof into a striped masterpiece of Englishness.

Instead, let the rye grass in, and who knows, you may have spider
orchids popping up in years to come and your home will nestle
beneath the buzzing of bees and fluttering of butterflies.

Sedum is the preferred option over the grass roof because it
retains its greenness much easier and is on the whole less
troublesome. The procedure is the same, it is just the covering
species that has changed. If the roof could be kept damp enough,
you may be able to use such evergreen plants as camomile,
dichondra and cotula to form a soft green cushion of growth.
These species are often used in ornamental gardens but aren't
tough enough to be trampled underfoot continuously and could
hence do well up here, although cotula can die off in severe frosts.

The back of the 'Dream House' was by far its best bit, sporting
a green living roof, not grass but sedum; with a cedar-clad timber
frame above ground it looked a lot like Grandma's place from
Little Red Riding Hood.

There is always scope in experimental design to pass off a
mistake as innovation, but the rainwater drainage pipe from the
'Dream House's' greenhouse roof challenged this opportunity to
the limit. A large box-section gutter discreetly collected the
rainwater and carried it along to the edge of the roof, where I
guess it was hoping to find a downpipe connecting to the
underground drains. Instead, it connected to a piece of white
10cm circular pipe horizontally for 30cm or so in thin air, turned
down a 90-degree bend, coloured grey, into a brown piece of
underground pipe stood upright 60cm above the ground. If this
was innovation, it could only have formed a surreal doorway
down the side of the house, encouraging dwarfs to use the back
door. If you are not building to a TV show's schedule, you will be
able to give more thought to these details.

The bit cut into the bank, and thus underground, was formed from precast concrete. The bedrooms were located back here, the darkest part of the house which is fine when you're asleep, but when you wake up it is always nice to throw back the curtains and find the world still there. As I say, this was an experiment for television (it only had planning permission to stay up for two years), but the ideas, particularly the environmental ones, were sound and have lived on.

Insulation

Thick walls will need to be insulated along with the ground floor and roof to an extent where heat loss simply doesn't occur. No artificial heating should be needed in winter or summer. In the summer heat will need to be exhausted out through skylights. High-performing triple-glazing with argon-filled cavities between low-e-coated panes will bring levels of thermal resistance to the windows that are comparable to thick brick walls.

The 'Dream House' was wrapped up like a pig in a blanket, with the walls and roof having U values of thermal transmittance much lower than the accepted maximums required by the Building Regulations of its day. To achieve this a timber-frame structure was used for the walls above ground so that the insulation could be built in between the timber posts and hence to the whole thickness of the wall. Normally the posts, or studs as they're known, would be only 100mm or 150mm thick, but in this case they were 200mm thick and so a much greater thickness of insulation was used. The insulation itself could be anything available on the market, but the 'green' choice they made is still available, a product made from recycled newspaper mashed to a pulp and treated with a fire retardant which is sprayed into the gap and trowelled off.

The outside of the frame was lined with cedarwood clapboard, very American. I'm not sure just how eco-

▾ Energy efficiency depends on many things.

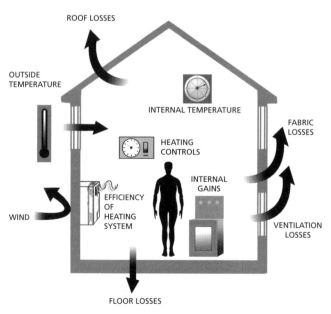

friendly this is, with the Canadian forests being overlogged annually, but I believe that the argument goes something like this – it's okay to cut down trees in a managed forest, when they are mature and have stopped growing, because they aren't doing much by then to suck CO_2 out of the air, providing you replace them with saplings, which will. I'm not sure if woodpeckers would agree with this idea, but that's the way we see 'sustainable' timber production. The cedar looks a wonderful orange-brown colour when new, but over time it fades to a silvery grey.

The green sedum or 'grass' roof was highly insulated. Apart from the turf itself, a warm-deck insulant was laid over plywood. The sedum itself grew in a vegetation blanket overlaying a mineral wool matting and root barrier. I was able to inspect a similar grassed roof system being constructed on the National Trust's new restaurant on the white cliffs of Dover. The root barrier here was copper-lined, and maintaining its integrity during installation was critical. Some drainage of rainwater was allowed for beneath the turf, but as you can appreciate, with sedum most of the water is taken up by the plant – as much as 95 per cent is claimed – and so gutters are almost redundant. Because of its high saturation it can go without watering or without rainfall for up to ten months before dying. It does, however, need treating with a slow-release fertilizer in the spring of each year, and presumably weeding if it isn't going to turn into a cornfield.

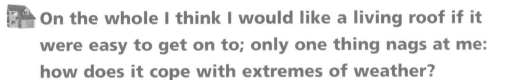 On the whole I think I would like a living roof if it were easy to get on to; only one thing nags at me: how does it cope with extremes of weather?

In heatwaves could dry grass ignite? (A grass fire can spread really quickly in a drought.) In a flash flood will it cope with total and continuous saturation or slide off the roof, or in a hurricane will it peel away from the vegetation matting and become airborne?

Water

It has been reported that the millions of new homes being built in the south-east have overstrained our water resources. A dry winter followed by a hot summer will be all that it takes to expose the crisis. So one idea that must soon become a feature of new homes is the 'Dream House's' ability to store rainwater from the conservatory roof in an underground tank. From here it can be recycled for use in the garden in summer, but it can also go

▲ This rainwater storage system uses the garage floor void beneath a beam and block floor.

one step further by recycling what is known as grey water.

Water from washing is collected from the sink, hand basins, bath and shower and directed away from the WC's foul drains to be filtered and reintroduced to the house. It can't, of course, be used for drinking or cooking, but it can be kept separate from potable water supply and used in the WC cisterns. Low-capacity (6L) flush toilets are now required as standard, but perhaps if you were using recycled water it could act as a concession for a good old 9L (2 gal) cistern. If your religion or lack of personal hygiene means you don't produce enough grey water to fill the toilet cisterns, then being able to open a valve and let in mains water has got to be an option to maintain sanitation. Likewise if you produce too much, an overflow from the storage tank to the drains has got to exist. With mains water being metered, this will save you money as well as helping the environment.

It bothers me a little that reusing water means that it must be pumped back out of the ground tank into the building or garden – pumps run on electricity and wear out pretty quickly – but apart from that, this has got to be the way forward. If you are on a bank and can use a gravity-fed system, then you have the perfect solution.

Foul-water disposal has for many years been restricted to mains drainage, public sewers, cesspools and septic tanks. The latter leach water, left over from the biological breakdown, back into the ground through irrigation drains and hence is not permitted in water catchment areas. Now, however, it seems that reed beds do an amazing filtration job quite naturally, and these are being used increasingly for the purpose.

Just how many reeds you need to treat any amount of foul water I'm not exactly sure, but research is going on all the time. In Kent, the Stodmarsh nature reserve, managed by the water authority, has constructed acres of new reed beds, which as well as filtering foul water to the river Stour, has also extended a wildlife habitat for many rare species like the bittern. This natural filtering is known in some quarters as water polishing.

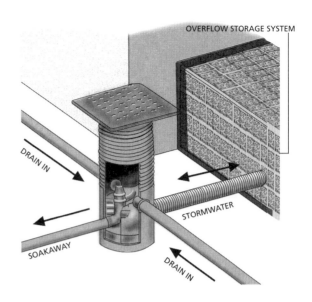

OVERFLOW STORAGE SYSTEM

DRAIN IN

STORMWATER

SOAKAWAY

DRAIN IN

Your home needn't polish foul water; it could gather rainwater from its roof and surroundings, clean it and recycle it for use. Large underground tanks will feed water on through a series of filters before finally exposing it to UV lamps to make it potable, not entirely unlike the way water is treated by large public aquariums. With tanks able to store 25,000L, stored water could last for half the year, coping with long periods of drought.

▲ This proprietary rainwater storage system also controls flooding by controlling the release of water to the soakaway.

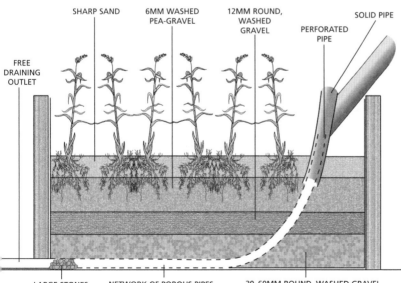

FEED DOSED INTERMITTENTLY OVER WHOLE SURFACE

SHARP SAND   6MM WASHED PEA-GRAVEL   12MM ROUND, WASHED GRAVEL   PERFORATED PIPE   SOLID PIPE

FREE DRAINING OUTLET

LARGE STONES   NETWORK OF POROUS PIPES   30–60MM ROUND, WASHED GRAVEL

◀ Typical vertical flow reed bed treatment system.

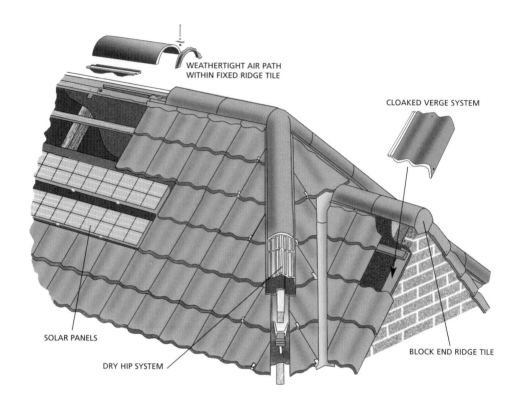

WEATHERTIGHT AIR PATH
WITHIN FIXED RIDGE TILE

CLOAKED VERGE SYSTEM

SOLAR PANELS

DRY HIP SYSTEM

BLOCK END RIDGE TILE

▲ Photo-voltaic roof tiles can be used to form solar panels.

Solar power

Solar panels have been around for a long time, but only a few eccentric buildings sport them. They just haven't taken off at all, and I don't really know why, because they do work: perhaps because some of the almost DIY-conversion kits look a bit, well, DIYish – akin to those secondary-glazing units you could buy made of polythene at a time when double-glazing was coming in but quite expensive, or those grow-your-own-mushroom kits for airing cupboards.

Traditional solar panels are thick glass-based affairs that generate up to 150W per square metre of power, but a new generation of thinner and lighter panels has been developed in recent years. These don't provide such a high power output, but they are cheaper, as in half the price, and they weigh a great deal less, making them more versatile. One other improvement is, because they aren't made of glass they do not have a habit of guiding aircraft down or blinding people in neighbouring buildings with the reflective glare. Finished in 1998, Sunderland's Doxford Solar Office has a raked-back V of a front elevation with tinted glazing panels interspersed with photovoltaic panels. With a steel-blue glint to both the building cuts and impressive façade, it is a stealth bomber of construction, and at 60m long, it is technically Europe's longest solar-panelled wall. It sports nearly half a million solar cells which provide the building with up to a third of its own electricity.

Solar panels or roof slates will harvest the heat from the sun and store it, and the UV light collected will be converted into electricity, fuelling among other things an air-to-water heat pump. This device could also help to provide domestic hot water on very dull days when UV light levels are too low for solar power.

Waste

 You might think that we as a nation are at the top end of the field when it comes to green issues; in fact we are struggling to leave our own half.

Take the recycled waste issue, where in the First World we run second from bottom, only beaten by the Japanese, who throw their TVs away when a new model comes out. At best we recycle only 6 per cent of our household waste. Finland tops the list. When you consider how small our country is and how full the landfill sites already are, you would think that we would be doing everything possible to reuse waste. Some local authorities that have tried to supply separate bins for people and divided up the trash have been thwarted when they found that the small market for recycling paper and glass was already flooded and unable to take any more – the waste ended up in the ground, along with all the rest.

Radiation

Apart from building next to a nuclear power station, and that perennial favourite the mobile phone base station, we don't think much about radiation. In Britain our levels of exposure to the radiation from the latter are said to be a hundred times greater than in other countries. Australia and New Zealand have recognised a health risk from long-term exposure to these emissions, but in Britain the jury is still out.

In Canada, for example, you can't site a new house with an electricity pylon in the garden; here, there are homes everywhere occupying the same plot that gently hum with electro-magnetic energy. And yes, many studies have been carried out by the electricity industry, and all to date have concluded that there are no health risks. You might also have seen reported in the media cases where cot deaths and sickness in children have been attributed by their parents to nearby electrical installations.

In Germany, a Dr Bachler has researched the effects of natural radiation from the Earth. Pulsing out from the Earth's core miles beneath our feet, great waves of electro-magnetic energy rise to the surface and carry on harmlessly out into space, where they form, so I am led to believe, the magnetosphere. So what has the magnetosphere ever done for us, you say? Well, I've looked it up, and apparently it saves your sorry self from being swept off the planet by supersonic solar winds. This is fine, says Dr Bachler, but what happens when underground watercourses distort the radiation and channel it? Geopathic stress is what happens, and buildings that find themselves on the line of geopathic stress are potentially sick buildings.

It is said that the way to discover whether your home is affected by electro-magnetic energy is to hold a bent hazel stick between the thumb and fore-finger of each hand and walk around in straight lines.

The results are plotted onto a plan of your home, which has been overmarked with a grid of squares roughly 3.5 x 3.5m. This is known as the Hartmann Grid and represents the natural and harmless emissions. The harmful line, if there is one, will occur sort of diagonally across the grid, and along it bad spots of intense energy may occur – you may wish to avoid standing the goldfish bowl here, for example.

Assuming that you are not a naturally gifted dowser and the Royal Institute of Chartered Surveyors has not yet trained up their members to do surveys, then there is one other method. Some species are attracted to the 'bad stuff' and others are repelled by it. Oak trees love it and cats love it. Dogs hate it, so it isn't all bad news, unless of course it causes them to bark pointlessly and relentlessly.

So why is placing your home inadvertently across a line of harmful radiation believed by some to be as bad for your health as building it next to a motorway?

The Hartmann Grid was said to be validated by medical research carried out in relation to geographical location. A cross-

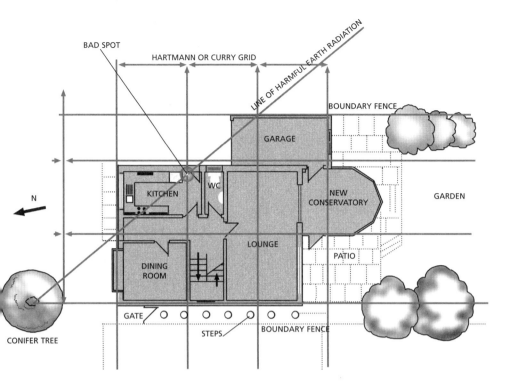

Labels in figure:
BAD SPOT
HARTMANN OR CURRY GRID
LINE OF HARMFUL EARTH RADIATION
BOUNDARY FENCE
GARAGE
N
KITCHEN
WC
NEW CONSERVATORY
GARDEN
LOUNGE
PATIO
DINING ROOM
GATE
STEPS
BOUNDARY FENCE
CONIFER TREE

▲ Hartmann grid applied to a house plan.

referencing between serious illness and mapping, the Grid is comprised of squares running on a north–south axis in line with the Earth's polarity. Proponents of the theory believe that the grid is distorted by refraction of the energy and that this may be more harmful to us than radon gas, affecting our body's bioelectrical balance. Personally I'm not convinced, and neither is the scientific world, but if you'd rather not take the chance of siting your bedroom on a radiation hot spot, then draw a grid and start measuring. Radiation can be measured with a Geiger counter if you don't trust a dowsing rod.

If you do decide to try the exercise, start the grid from the bottom left-hand corner with one axis heading north–south and the other east–west. From your site detection, draw the diagonal, if you have one, across the plan and see where it intersects the grid lines inside your home. These are said to be the bad spots, and if you have only one or two you're doing pretty well. You can relate the same lines on to the floor above.

Faced with the consequences of not being able to redesign the layout of your home but with some serious doubts on this front, you can always resort to devices that employ your ring main as a line of defence against natural radiation, presumably in the same way that stepping inside a circle drawn in salt is supposed to protect you from witches.

You may by now have realized that there are plenty of books on electro-pollution, but that this isn't one of them. The problem with this kind of thing is that it all sounds a bit too New Age. In a world where Feng Shui can state that a carelessly placed sofa can cause you great mental stress, scientists seem driven to go to other extremes of rationality and logic.

Recycled materials

The use of recycled materials in the building industry is a bit underplayed, to say the least. I can't personally think of a better move towards sustainable and green construction than using recycled materials.

The use of hardcore from demolished buildings in our oversites and soakaways is perhaps the one exception, but the quality of the hardcore can be variable, to say the least. It really is essential that it has been sifted and graded to a maximum size of a half-brick and separated from the other detritus that it came with. It isn't uncommon to see bricks not only still backed with plaster but also wallpaper. Avoid blackened bricks that are likely to have come from a sooted chimney. A more recent development is the sale of concrete crusher fines, the residue from the batching plant; this is available for bulk purchase and is affordable and ideal for compaction in oversites. It has the very minor drawback of being the same colour as topsoil, and so it is wise not to spread it around the site because you may lose it. Have it delivered straight into the area of use, and you won't get it invisibly contaminated by rehandling.

The Building Research Establishment is encouraging, through a waste and resources action programme, the use of products of a recycled nature, aimed at reducing the amount of landfill waste. Plastics are a particular worry, and any product that uses recycled plastic must be encouraged, since plastics are seldom biodegradable and will thus remain buried in the ground of landfill indefinitely.

The main aim of the programme is to certify products using recycled materials as fit for use to overcome the industry's, and the public's scepticism over their quality. By 2006, 55,000,000 tonnes of recycled aggregates and materials should be in use in the building industry if the Government's targets are to be achieved.

Greening your home

I am told that a healthy environment has about 1,000 negative ions to every 1,200 positive ones per cubic centimetre of air, with the balance of power being on the positive side, so to speak. Electricity via appliances like computers and telephones can upset the balance, taking our health with it.

Take the computer VDU that I'm sitting in front of right now; the oxygen between me and it is currently being converted to ozone. Those of you who have been pregnant will know that a filter screen placed in front of your VDU will (if correctly fitted) reduce the radiation. But it isn't just electronic equipment, the materials we build into out homes can contain toxic gases – even harmless-looking chipboard flooring, for example, is laced with formaldehyde and vinyl chloride that continues to be emitted into our homes long after we move in.

What saves us is good ventilation, air circulation from outside through the house and out again to restore the balance of ions, and passive whole-house ventilation systems which do this 24/7 are good at this.

Plants with huge green leaves are good for the same purpose, as they stimulate the production of negative ions and clean the air. Ferns, bananas and philodendrons are the best at doing this, but I've also had major success with *Scindapsus* (Devil's Ivy), which has taken over my office; although it is said to be difficult to grow indoors, given light and shade away from direct sun and a deep enough pot, it will travel across the ceiling if you support it.

 A truly green home will need plants to balance the air and act as indicators of the quality of your home's environment.

Energy Performance Certificates

Your new home will, on completion, require an Energy Performance Certificate declaring its efficiency in conserving fuel and power. The rating can only be improved by employing renewable fuels such as solar, wind or geothermal. Integrated into your design, any of these can improve the value of your home, save on fuel bills and reduce carbon emissions.

CHAPTER 10

Water and Heating

WATER **has to be one of the first things to bring to your site. You are going to need it from the start, or at least from the point where you start laying bricks on the foundations. A temporary supply can normally be arranged with the water authority, and at this stage no metering is needed. It makes sense to erect a standpipe on the existing main where a hose can be attached, running to the work.**

The new and permanent water supply pipe will need to be laid in a service trench and into the home at a later stage. For this a blue alkathene flexible pipe is buried at least 750mm below ground level to avoid accidental damage and freezing. To this end the pipes are often laid in ducts or insulated and brought up inside the house the same distance away from the outer face of the wall. If you are proposing to run them through the foundations, a duct cast will accommodate the pipes later and allow them to be drawn out in the future if a leak occurs.

If you can arrange to lay your water supply in the same trench as your drainage, all well and good. Just bear in mind the depth requirement, as it might mean overdigging the drainage trench and laying the services in bedding at the bottom before following over with the drains later, but this is still more economical than digging separate trenches.

Your water supply is often directed straight to the kitchen sink first because it is necessary to provide supply water for drinking purposes before any softening or treating equipment is installed. Any artificial treatment of the water has to take place after a drinking tap of supply-quality water is provided. The kitchen sink is normally the place for this. The local water supply company may want to test the quality of the drinking water at this tap from time to time.

A stop valve before the sink, at the point of entry to the home gives you a place from which to turn off the water supply entirely inside your home for maintenance and when leaks occur. Leaks back between this valve and the main can only be turned off at

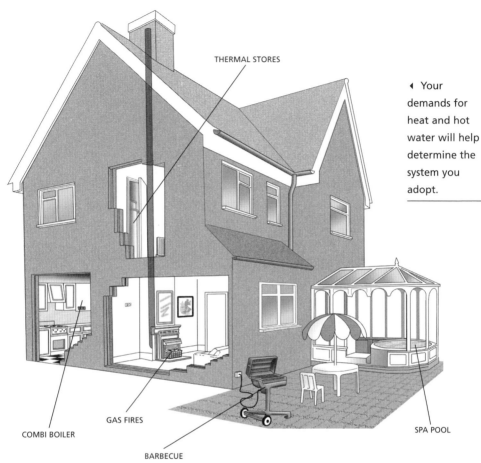

THERMAL STORES

◀ Your demands for heat and hot water will help determine the system you adopt.

COMBI BOILER

GAS FIRES

BARBECUE

SPA POOL

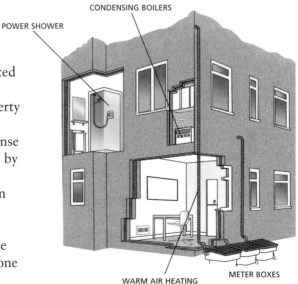

POWER SHOWER

CONDENSING BOILERS

WARM AIR HEATING

METER BOXES

the stopcock that will be located on the boundary of your plot. From herein this is your property and the supply is your responsibility, and it makes sense to avoid the risk of leaks here by using a continuous unjointed length of pipework. Record on your plans the position of the supply through for future reference; it may save someone digging up the whole garden one day looking for it.

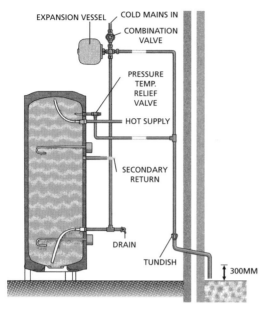

EXPANSION VESSEL
COLD MAINS IN
COMBINATION VALVE
PRESSURE TEMP. RELIEF VALVE
HOT SUPPLY
SECONDARY RETURN
DRAIN
TUNDISH
300MM

▲ A sealed system thermal store.

Hard water

Much of Britain is affected by hard water that can gradually reduce the effectiveness of your system through the build-up of limescale damage. Even service warranties on heating or hot-water systems may be excluded from limescale damage in hard water areas. Combi boilers and thermal stores where the water is heated to high temperatures are particularly prone to damage by hard water. Anything above 40°C tends to result in limescale encrustation, so it occurs pretty much everywhere in the heating and hot-water systems. Your choice is either to soften the water or just reduce the scale in it, which isn't exactly the same thing.

The benefits of softer water really only come from washing. Less soap and detergents are needed to lather it, and softening equipment looks desirable to many of us, but given the difference in size and nature of the plants you can install, what is the best?

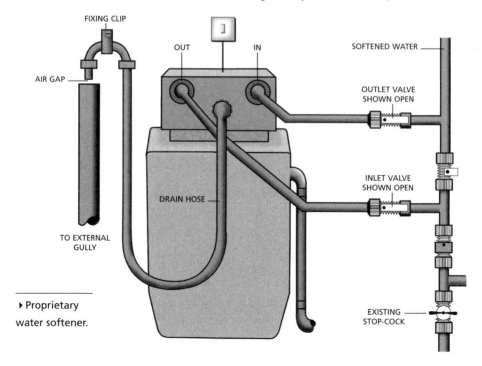

FIXING CLIP
OUT
IN
SOFTENED WATER
AIR GAP
OUTLET VALVE SHOWN OPEN
INLET VALVE SHOWN OPEN
DRAIN HOSE
TO EXTERNAL GULLY
EXISTING STOP-COCK

▶ Proprietary water softener.

The most common water softeners installed in new homes are the salt ones that are about the size of a large kitchen bin and need periodic refilling with salt-based chemicals that change the water by removing the nasty minerals. They take up space and you need to be able to get at them, so they are more popular in new builds than in existing homes.

You need to think about what it is you are trying to achieve first of all, because some treatment equipment tackles hard water only by agitating it and reducing the risk of limescale building up, rather than actually softening the water.

The electronic scale-reducers on the market, which agitate the water particles by electricity, effectively stop limescale from building up but still leave the water hard. They are, however, very cheap to run, do not require any maintenance, and are easy to install – you simply plug them in and wind the wire around the water supply pipe (rising cold main) before it reaches any of your household appliances.

The ionization limescale reducers mentioned above also have a competitor in another form. Polyphosphate compound is an anti-scaling agent that chemically keeps the mineral ions in permanent suspension, like the ionizer type, and in this way retains the minerals and their associated health benefits. Although they need to be topped up once or twice a year, these fittings are plumbed into the water supply after the stop valve or the inlet supply to the boiler. The compound added to the water is classified, in some cases, as 'food grade' under World Health Organization requirements, and in this respect is safe for drinking water. Again, because you have to refill the unit from time to time you have to be able to get at it, so the desire to hide it behind or tucked away in kitchen units should be resisted.

Water tanks

One of the cheapest elements of your self-build, water tanks have been made from plastic for so long that they are cheap and easy to install. The problems with them really came from poor-fitting, thin plastic lids and their awkwardness to insulate.

The water supply has to be kept clean and free from the risk of contamination up there in your loft. Insects dropping in, let alone mice or birds, are not desirable! A tank with a cover that secures down and has any air inlets covered by fine mesh should be used.

The way water tanks are insulated today somewhat disguises them, but is essential. The overflow pipe ought to have a clear finish as a warning device that it is being used (meaning the ball valve may be defective and need replacing), then you have avoided the need to stand outside on cold evenings to see if anything drips out of the fascia outlet.

Lagging the tank in with the inlet and outlet pipes is essential, but now many people have taken to extending the insulation up from the ceiling lagging to form a continuous layer, omitting the lagging beneath the tank so that it is included within the heated envelope of your home. Yes, it's a horrible job, and you may well be the only person interested in doing it properly but the combination of good insulation and access is a tricky one to achieve if you're in a hurry or on a price.

Remember that as well as frost protection, because lofts can get seriously cold with the cross-ventilation you have to build in, you are trying to keep the heat in your pipes and expansion tank.

If poorly sealed and lagged, the immediate consequence will be condensation from the hot water vaporizing in the cold air and condensing on the roofing felt, meaning that a visit to the loft on a cold winter day may have to be accompanied by an umbrella.

Servicing valves

All float-operated valves, like the ball valves of cisterns and water tanks, should have a service valve in front of them. Maintenance again: these valves have a life expectancy or need adjusting from time to time, and you need to isolate them, hence the valve, which on your water storage tank should also occur at the outlet as well as the inlet.

Valves can appear ugly – the old-fashioned brass tap ones are really ugly and shouldn't be allowed outside of a loft or a dark cupboard in a new home. Instead, the in-line chrome valves have no tap as such and aren't much wider than the pipe they are located in. Instead, you have a slot for a screwdriver, and a quarter-turn on will close off the supply to the appliance. I suggest you stick them everywhere – in front of the WC cistern, ahead of the sink and basin taps, bath taps, the shower supply, everywhere. They are discreet and wonderful, and I wish I had invented them almost as much as I wish I had instructed my kitchen fitters to use them before the mixer tap that continually leaks.

The lesson to be learned here is that plumbers and tradesmen can't be relied upon to make life easier for you or think of creative solutions to problems – only you can do that for yourself and instruct them. If necessary, go and buy a bucketful of these valves and make sure they use them.

Mains pressure

Water

You can find out what the water pressure will be from your water company. 4-bar is about normal. This information may be relevant in deciding what plumbing equipment to buy. Some cylinders, for example, can only cope with a certain pressure if they aren't to continually overfill and send hot water to the expansion tank. Cylinders, like all appliances, come with conditions of use and installation warnings of the product's limitations. If the pressure is too high for it, an expansion vessel and pressure-reducing valve can be built into the system at negligible expense to resolve the problem. Very few combi boilers are designed to operate in low-pressure situations.

Gas

Most combis also require a 22mm gas supply pipe rather than a 15mm one. If the boiler is located away from the meter, then make sure your plumber is aware of the boiler's requirements before he runs the gas supply through the house to it, particularly if it is built in through the structure. The flow should always be measured at the appliance inlet to check against the boiler's requirements.

Choosing fuel

To begin with, you need to know what your options are. If you are building on a rural site where mains gas, for example, is not available, you may feel limited, but you still have a choice to make, and an important choice because your decision will affect the running costs of your new home.

There are six types of fuel to select from: mains gas, electricity, heating oil class 2 (kerosene), heating oil class D (gas oil), solid fuel (coal, wood, etc) and LPG (liquefied petroleum gas).

Along with the running costs, the initial costs of the appliances need to be considered, and these vary more than anything with fuel type. Of course the cost of any fuel is likely to fluctuate and it's impossible to predict what it will be at the time of your decision, but it should not be too difficult to find out. You may also be interested in the environmental aspects of each fuel.

Oil has been the cheapest of all fuels, but it is prone to the vagrancies of the international market – a war in the Middle East, for example, can send the cost rocketing. Having said that, in the mid-1980s the price had dropped to less than $10 a barrel, and at something like 7 or 8p per litre it was far cheaper to buy than bottled water.

Because of these low prices and the fact that the gas grid had not expanded at all, the 1990s saw a massive increase in the number of new homes with oil, so that by 2002 some 1,300,000–1,400,000 homes were fuelled by heating oil.

The table below indicates the units in which each type of fuel is delivered to your home, and how many kilowatt hours there are in each unit. The table should help you work out the running cost of each and compare them with each other. You should be quoted a price per delivery unit, which if you note down in pence and divide it by the number of kWh per unit will be the price that you should compare.

Fuel	Unit of delivery	kWh per unit of delivery
Gas	kWh	1
Electric	kWh	1
Heating oil class C2 (kerosene)	litre	10.35
Heating oil class D (gas oil)	litre	10.85
Solid fuel	50kg	420–480
LPG (propane)	litre	7.11

Which is the 'greenest' fuel?

The 'Energy Performance Certificate' which all new homes will require under the Building Regulations and the type of fuel used, will affect the rate of carbon emissions, and possibly the value of the home. Renewable fuels like wind and solar power (even when integrated with fossil fuels) will perform the highest.

Because there are no exhaust gases produced as a by-product of using electricity and there are from all the other fuels, you might be forgiven for believing it to be the greenest of all fuels. Certainly it's the cleanest to use, but of course there are some environmental implications from the production of electricity at the power station which should affect its 'green' status. Improvements have been made by decommissioning coal-fuelled power stations, which as recently as 1990 supplied 67 per cent of our electricity. Switching to Natural Gas fuel reduced that figure to 33 per cent in 1998.

With forest stewardship, wood for solid fuel can be harvested naturally, reducing harm to the environment, but it does smoke somewhat when burned, causing the worst pollution in terms of combustion by-products.

Modern state-of-the-art boilers are exceptionally clean-burning, particularly gas ones, but the burning of all fossil fuels has been responsible for a large percentage of the carbon emissions to our atmosphere, and so if you truly want to be green you are going to have to step away from fossil fuels and find an alternative energy, such as solar or wind power.

Different fuels release different amounts of carbon when burned, and the table below may help you to decide which you would prefer on an environmental basis.

Fuel	Carbon emissions (kg/kWh)
Gas	0.19
Electricity	0.51
Heating oils	0.27
Solid fuels	0.29 to 0.39

Storing and accessing fuel

Two other issues will also affect your choice of fuel: space for storage on your plot and access for refuelling deliveries.

There are regulations that restrict the positioning of stored fuels such as oil and LPG, and if you simply don't have the space available to meet these requirements you need to know before designing your system.

Heating oil has controls under the Building Regulations and sometimes under the Control of Pollution (Oil Storage) Regulations 2001 if you store more than 3,500L. Tank sizes range from around 1,000–5,000L. Invariably the tanks today are plastic and fall into one of two categories – either single-skin or bunded. Bunded means they have a double skin which serves to prevent leakage should the inner skin leak for any reason, acting as a safety catch against oil spillage and pollution. Given the present ethos of 'the polluter pays', it is advisable to choose a bunded tank in any case. In certain environmentally sensitive sites, the Environment Agency may not wish you to store oil at all.

As I'm sure you know, oil is toxic to plants and animals, and if it reaches a watercourse it can spread to a thin film and cause tremendous environmental damage. Even when oil is spilt on the ground it can leach through to underground waterways and contaminate them, and so oil stores close to boreholes, wells and watercourses are thought of as significant risks. You'll be pleased to know that the installer is required to carry out a 'risk assessment' on all installations and therefore take liability for their work. The assessment should take account of where the tank is to go, whether it needs a fire wall to protect a nearby boundary or your home, and so on. The laws relating to building services at least place accountability on those you employ to carry out the job.

Oil safety

Installers of oil appliances and tanks can choose to be registered with OFTEC, the designated 'competent persons' association for this fuel. This is to oil what CORGI is to gas and HETAS is to solid fuel, the only difference being that with CORGI registration is mandatory, and with the others it's voluntary.

The significance of registration enables installers to do work which by itself would normally warrant a Building Regulation Application, but in their case can be self-certified. Of course, as you are building a complete home, the work will be included in your building control service anyway, but you'll gain some protection from the fact that the installer is qualified. They will also issue you with a certificate of commissioning, without which the boiler may not be covered by the manufacturer's warranty.

Oil storage tanks that are close to boundaries need protecting with firewalls, if not an actual masonry boundary wall itself. Since a firewall has to extend beyond the sides and the top of the tank, it makes sense to build a boundary wall that can offer the needed fire protection as well. Freestanding garden walls have to be built from stable foundations and constructed in thicknesses that respect their height, if they are to remain stable and safe (see page 257).

One of the most important safety features of an oil tank installation is the remote sensing fire valve, which isolates the supply if a fire is detected in the appliance. The valve is therefore fitted to the oil supply pipe outside the building itself but with a fire detector inside the boiler casing. There is no limit to the extent of the fire detector's remoteness, since if it can't be connected by a line, wireless versions are available, so do not be dissuaded from installing this essential precaution. I know of one oil tank that exploded in a fireball, engulfing the nearby timber garage and burning it to the ground – all because a fire valve wasn't fitted. Oil tends not to smoulder harmlessly when ignited.

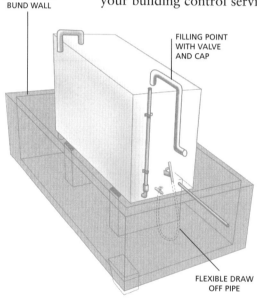

IMPERMEABLE BUND WALL

FILLING POINT WITH VALVE AND CAP

FLEXIBLE DRAW OFF PIPE

▲ Bunded oil tank with bund wall built on site.

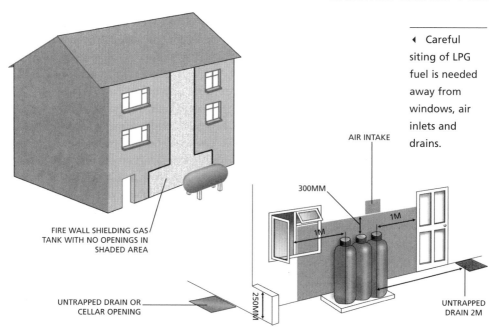

◀ Careful siting of LPG fuel is needed away from windows, air inlets and drains.

AIR INTAKE

300MM

1M

1M

FIRE WALL SHIELDING GAS TANK WITH NO OPENINGS IN SHADED AREA

UNTRAPPED DRAIN OR CELLAR OPENING

250MM

UNTRAPPED DRAIN 2M

LOCATION OF LIQUEFIED PETROLEUM GAS CYLINDERS

LPG

LPG can be stored in either cylinders or bulk storage tanks. I'd recommend the latter, in the same way that I would recommend you position it away from the house and boundary in a discrete position – discrete but accessible – because the tankers that will deliver your gas will need to be able to get within 25m of it.

The table below gives a very rough guide to the size of tanks you need in relation to your boiler output, for an average home:

Boiler output kW	Minimum storage capacity of LPG
Up to 15 kW	360L
15–25 kW	1200L
25–45 kW	1800L

One final point to make is that if you are building in a basement to your new home, you should not fit any appliance to it that uses LPG fuel. I mention this because basements are often ideal places for boilers to be sited – but not for this fuel.

Open fires

It seems a long time ago now when people needed a fire in the house to keep warm. Yet we still seem to miss the dancing flames – central heating may be convenient, but it does little to instil in us a sense of comfort and safety that our instincts have given us

SIMPLE RECESS
SUITABLE FOR
CLOSED APPLIANCES

STRUCTURAL
OPENING PREPARED
TO RECEIVE A FREE
STANDING FIRE
BASKET

STRUCTURAL
OPENING LINED TO
RECEIVE AN INSET
OPEN FIRE

▲ Fireplace
recesses.

▶ These
diagrams show
the position of
DPCs in a typical
brick chimney.

from a fire over millennia. It's more than just a focal point in the lounge – it protects us from beastly things. The new age of fires we like today are more for effect than heat, but real flame is still popular, even if we have a remote control to turn it up.

It seems that not many of us can be bothered with the mess and work that goes with a real fireplace, in fuelling it, lighting it and then cleaning up afterwards. Now we prefer the 'hole-in-the-wall' or a multi-fuel burner that looks like a miniature Aga. Not for the heat – who needs it in our super-efficient insulated homes – but for something to look at other than the TV. Even so, if the fireplace burns fuel it is going to need a flue, whatever its size, and chimneys are popular for aesthetic reasons as well.

Building chimneys

Chimneys add character to the design of any home and are intrinsic to a traditional style. They can turn a box of a house into something that is interesting to look at, whether they work or not. In fact, a fair percentage of chimneys seem only to be aesthetic and provide the home with a feature and a focal point fireplace rather than a working one. The harder thing is to build a working chimney that doesn't smoke or leak.

Bricks are the best materials, but a medium-density block is just as good; in fact, an externally rendered chimney is the best way of avoiding damp problems from driving rain. The really wet winters

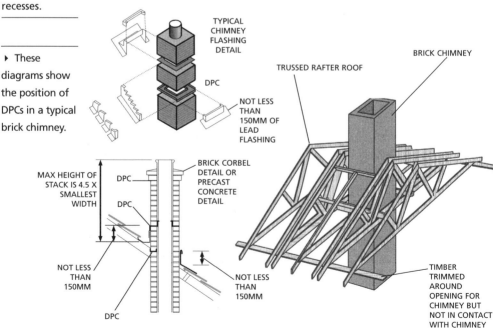

we occasionally have (in between the really wet summers) have revealed chimneys to be a weak point in the weather resistance of homes. Once the rain has penetrated the brick skin it has the flue linings to channel it down into the fireplace surround and the walls.

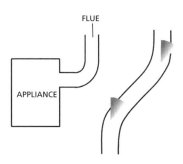

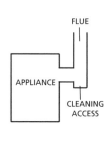

▲ Flues should be installed as near to vertical as possible with bends no more than 45 degrees from vertical.

Maintaining a cavity wall structure for the chimney is something we just haven't been doing – for one thing, when enclosing a 200mm-diameter flue pipe with a 260mm wall, we would have an oversized chimney above roof line. So the cavity wall usually stops at the roof level on an external chimney. Up until then, kicking the wall out in the same construction to accommodate the chimney makes good sense, so long as you can protect the top of it with good lead flashings and a cavity tray where the brickwork converts to solid construction. The only way to stop the water running down the flue face for sure is to take the DPC tray into a joint in the flue liner; a preformed remedial style tray that simply rests up against it might not be good enough.

Sockets and spigots occur at the end of factory-made flue blocks to lock them together. It is easy to build them in upside down and regret it. The sockets, or rebates if you like, should be uppermost so that any moisture from condensation is kept inside the flue. The joints are sealed with fire cement, not ordinary Portland cement; and the gap around the circular flue lining and the square brickwork should not be filled with ordinary mortar. Instead, concrete mixes using vermiculite or perlite should be used as insulants mixed with cement.

Straight up is the best way to build a flue; bends just don't help and are prohibited at angles of more than 45 degrees off the vertical. For another thing, bends make chimneys difficult to clean, and chimney flues have to be swept from end to end periodically if they aren't to get sooted up and become a fire risk. In the old days chimney fires could be relied upon to burn homes to the ground on a regular basis. A cleaning point can be installed with covers as factory-made components to fit the flue linings and maintain their integrity.

Flues have to be checked over by a suitably qualified person and certified as safe and fit for use. Spillage tests are carried out to ensure that they don't leak under the worst conditions, and core-balling tests are done to check that the flue is free from obstructions. You can probably imagine what a core-balling test goes like, but if you can't visualize it, it involves a ball of given diameter, an attached line and a person with a ladder – technology at its best.

From an interior-design angle, you get to choose how to finish your open fireplace, and there are only a few regulations that restrict you dimensions-wise.

Fireplace openings, especially inglenook openings, can be wide, much wider than the flue opening, and so the smoke has to be gathered up and funnelled to the flue. We call this bit the 'gather' – I wish there were more descriptive names in building. You can buy gathers of all designs, shapes and materials, or you can just build your own from corbelled brickwork. The preformed lintel at the bottom of the flue supporting it is usually known as the 'throat', because it is shaped with chamfered sides to draw the smoke into the flue.

The beam across the front is the bressumer or breastsummer, in the case of 'ye olde worlde inglenook' fireplace, and traditionally is made of a whopping great lump of oak in farmhouse-style design. Oak of good size is the best material, since although fundamentally wood and hence combustible, it burns very slowly with a charring rate that would mean that if it did catch fire it would be a very long time if at all before it became structurally unsafe. Bressumers tend to only support a gather or, in most inglenooks, a single storey of corbelled bricks that stops at the very first convenient point, which is often the ceiling. Unless you have money to burn, it makes sense to reduce a chimney to its minimum size when you can't benefit from its fireplace anymore.

▾ Hearth construction.

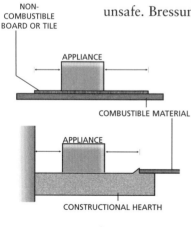

NON-COMBUSTIBLE BOARD OR TILE

APPLIANCE

COMBUSTIBLE MATERIAL

APPLIANCE

CONSTRUCTIONAL HEARTH

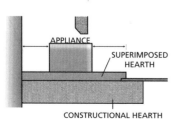

APPLIANCE

SUPERIMPOSED HEARTH

CONSTRUCTIONAL HEARTH

Hearths

Any solid fuel fire or appliance has to be built on a constructional hearth of non-combustible material. This can be concrete, stone or brick, but it should be at least 125mm thick. If you have a solid concrete floor, you already have some of that thickness and a non-combustible finish may be all that is needed. One thing, though, the weight of a chimney and the appliance could be several tonnes, and a foundation is likely to be needed to support that weight. The size of the hearth in area and how

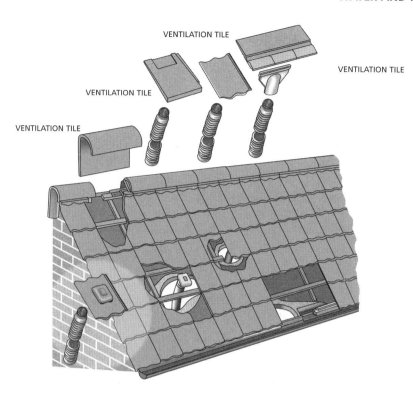

VENTILATION TILE

VENTILATION TILE

VENTILATION TILE

VENTILATION TILE

VENTILATION TILE

◀ Flexible flue liners can terminate at proprietary vents incorporated in the roof tiling.

far it projects into and around the fire is also covered by the Building Regulations with the aim of making sure that combusted fuel doesn't spill out and set alight to floor furnishings, etc.

You also need a gap of at least 300mm between floor and fire or appliance front in the case of appliances (burners) that can be operated with the doors open. If they have to be shut to work, then the distance can be reduced to 225mm.

Balanced–flue appliances and air

What did we do before we had balanced flues, an invention superior to sliced bread? These double tubes, no more than 100mm in diameter, suck in combustion air through the outer tube and push out the exhaust gas through the inner, making them room-sealed. All you need is an outside wall or a roof to position them near, and they are self-contained. No extractor fan will affect them, and so they can be installed in kitchens, bathrooms, cupboards, and so on. In the latest condensing boilers twin plastic tubes provide the balanced flue function, as the heat is exchanged on the way out leaving the exhaust vents cooler. With extension kits it is now possible to extend flues serving fanned boilers for several metres, in so doing, liberating your options for positioning the boiler.

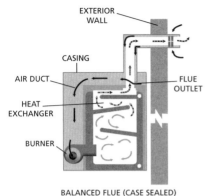

BALANCED FLUE (CASE SEALED)

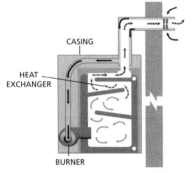

BALANCED FLUE (DUCTED)

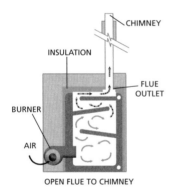

OPEN FLUE TO CHIMNEY

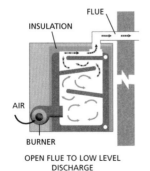

OPEN FLUE TO LOW LEVEL
DISCHARGE

Boilers

I could write a book on construction acronyms, so much has the building industry taken them to heart. SEDBUK is the one printed all over your boiler packaging when it arrives, followed by a letter denoting the boiler's energy efficiency. Since all appliances seem to carry ratings these days, it would have been nice to have had the same system for everything; but the triple A of your dishwasher or washing machine is nothing to do with the A of your boiler – which might have caused people to understand the system. Instead, each type of appliance seems to have its own. By the way, SEDBUK stands for 'Seasonal Efficiency of a Domestic Boiler in the UK'.

Boilers are tested and awarded ratings from A to G, with A being the most efficient. These efficiencies are measured as a percentage with A being somewhere between 90 and 94 per cent, and G being somewhere between 50 and 70 per cent. A, however, is the minimum allowed for new boilers in dwellings under the Building Regulations 2000. The scheme is reportedly only temporary until such time as a European directive for labelling is introduced, so try not to get too excited about it.

What will not change is the fact that condensing boilers with built-in heat exchangers are the most efficient of all, receiving the top banding. This exchanger, made from rustproof material, allows the flue gases to cool and condense on its surfaces and be discharged via a condensing drainpipe. Normal boilers have to run at higher temperatures to avoid this condensation, which would normally cause corrosion in them. With a condensing boiler, the way you run it will affect its efficiency to some extent, but probably not enough to worry about it. Running them with a lower return water temperature and heating large radiators will keep them operating in condensing mode and to maximum efficiency.

The most efficient fuel for these boilers is currently gas, which can gain as much as 20 per

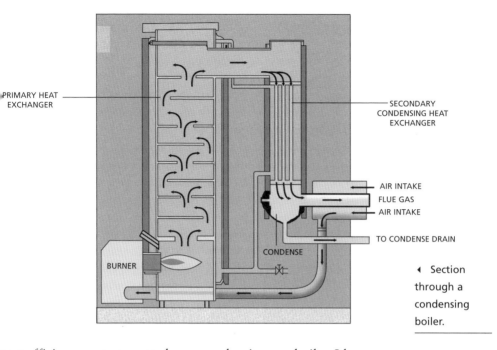

PRIMARY HEAT
EXCHANGER

SECONDARY
CONDENSING HEAT
EXCHANGER

AIR INTAKE
FLUE GAS
AIR INTAKE

TO CONDENSE DRAIN

CONDENSE

BURNER

◀ Section
through a
condensing
boiler.

cent efficiency over a normal non-condensing gas boiler. I have no
idea whether condensing models require higher maintenance or
are more prone to failure; technology seems to be improving all
the time, and certainly some boilers are being produced much
smaller than previously, with the intention of housing them in
kitchen units. They do rely on the condensate drain being kept
clear at all times, but only time will tell on their longevity.

Deciding on the type of hot-water system

I think there are really only three questions to ask yourself when
deciding on the type of system you want for your new home:

◆ What volume of hot water do I need?
◆ What pressure or flow-rate do I need it to be delivered at?
◆ What space do I want to give over to any cylinders or vessels?

The answer to the first question is really dependent on the size of
your family. A three- or four-bedroom home with one bathroom
could be supplied by a 145L cylinder capacity or more, but one
with a shower will need at least 175L. Four bedrooms with
bathroom and en-suite, and you are looking to at least 225L.
Tanks are available up to about 500L capacity, but their size
makes them unplaceable in the average home. With pressure up to
3 bars, copper cylinders are used, but beyond this up to 6 bars,

steel tanks are the order of the day.

The second question comes down to how much water you need at any one time – whether you are likely to be running the bath, dishwasher and washing machine simultaneously. Combis are particularly bad at keeping up with high-flow demands, and I've heard many plumbers say that if you have more than one bathroom to supply, don't install one. That might be a bit of a generalization, as some have flow rates of 14 L/min and above (9 L/min is standard) and can cope much better.

The third question comes down to whether you want water tanks to occupy your loft space, or whether you want a dry loft. It also questions whether you have space in airing cupboards for cylinders and so on. Do not be dissuaded by thinking an airing cupboard must have a cylinder to air dry clothes; all you need is to provide it with a short length of hot water pipe uninsulated, and you can turn any cupboard into an airing cupboard.

Your cold-water supply should never get warmer than 25°C, and it shouldn't be more than 3°C warmer at the taps than it is at the tank. Warm water for drinking can be a problem, to say the least – *Legionellis* (Legionnaire's Disease) breeds in water of a certain temperature somewhere between 25 and 45°C, and for this reason alone hot water should be stored in cylinders at around 60°C.

This is a bit too hot to be delivered to the taps without risk of scalding, so where children will be using the taps, and perhaps not mixing the water and sampling it before plunging their limbs in, thermostatic taps are a good idea. Mostly they are pre-set to 43°C and will prevent water in excess of this from being delivered.

In shower units, mixers with thermostats are essential. Because of the risk of bacteria multiplying at this temperature, though, water that has been mixed to this temperature can't run through pipes longer than 2m, and this governs the length of the shower head pipe, just in case you were thinking of creating your own self-plumbed advanced-deluge shower head. I totally understand if you are – I am amazed at how much can be charged for what is basically a piece of bent pipe with a watering can rose at one end on the grounds that is Victorian-style.

Vented or unvented?

This decision is a fundamental but important one: do you want a traditional open-vented system or a sealed system? Knowing just what the difference between the two is might be useful in making this choice.

Vented systems

Traditionally and until the late 1980s or thereabouts, all our domestic-heating and hot-water systems were open-vented. Water tanks in the loft, indirect or direct cylinders, air in the unpressurized system being pumped around and diverted by separate fittings – you can design your system along these traditional designs if you prefer. The drawbacks come from hot-water demand more than anything else – having to wait for the cylinder to reheat before you can run the bath, or limiting your time in the shower. Like our demands on electricity, our demands on water have increased, with dishwashers and multiple bathrooms becoming standard. To meet those demands for instant and limitless hot water, you have to look towards a sealed system.

Sealed systems

When they first appeared, combis seemed only to fill a specific niche in the market, namely flats. Why else would you buy an unnecessarily complicated package of a boiler that could run the heating and hot water supply without all the gubbins in the attic, unless it was because you actually didn't have an attic?

Like everybody else, I couldn't really see the point of having one in a house. Since then they have become rather more commonplace, with improved technology, reduced size and better supply rates. But unless you desperately want the space for something else, I still wouldn't install one in a new home. There are better options. Ordinary balanced-flue condensing boilers can be much more efficient (SEDBUK A) and are less likely to fail. They can also be incredibly quiet-running, especially the cast-iron ones, which run so silently that you struggle to know if they are on or not.

Combis come under the heading of sealed systems, which means they are not open-vented but still contain an expansion vessel for dealing with the expanded volume of water when it heats up. The vessel has to cope with the expansion that would occur from a 100°C increase in water temperature up to 10°C above boiling.

To run, combis must be charged with an adequate amount of water pressure, usually around 1 bar. They tend not to run at all if the pressure drops too low, although some have been specifically designed for use in low-water-pressure areas.

If the pressure drops the system must be topped up by way of a filling loop, a flexible pipe that you, the owner, can attach and detach to the boiler, then open a valve and charge the system to its optimum running pressure. Most come with a filling loop,

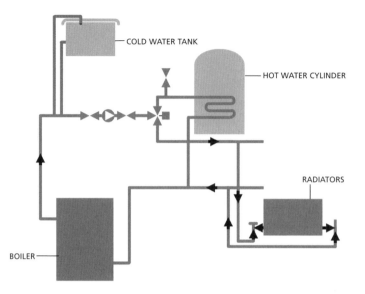

COLD WATER TANK

HOT WATER CYLINDER

RADIATORS

BOILER

▶ Conventional
open-vented
system.

some don't, and as you are going to need one, check which yours
is. Since water in a sealed system cannot evaporate, you can only
get air in and hence reduced pressure after refilling it following
installation or maintenance, so the pressure shouldn't drop in any
other circumstance. This lack of air in a sealed-system has
benefits: corrosion should all but be eliminated, and because you
don't have tanks and pipes in the loft, you will have less
condensation up there and no chance of water pipes freezing up in
the winter from all that roof ventilation you have to build in.

You don't have to have a combi boiler to have a sealed system;
all those components squashed inside a combi can be located
outside with a large unvented hot-water cylinder that stores plenty
of hot water to meet your needs. These thermal stores are
becoming popular.

Thermal stores and unvented hot-water cylinders

Thermal stores are large cylinders that provide mains-fed hot
water without the need for a cold-water storage tank in the loft.
Unlike the indirect heating systems of the past, where we heated
our hot water cylinders with a coil (rather slowly), these stores are
directly connected to the primary heating circuit. The heat is
passed on to the cold-water mains through an efficient heat
exchanger, and in this way high flow rates can be achieved. When
you look at the 10L/min from a combi, the flow rate here can be
twice or three times that. If you have two showers to feed, you
will really need the 30L/min flow rate.

Thermal stores aim to do the same thing by providing hot

water on demand, either by firing up themselves or by supply from a separate boiler. They can be used to provide space-heating water in addition to hot tap water, and in this instance they are referred to as integrated thermal stores. If you have the space for one – and they do need some space – they are worth considering seriously.

Unvented cylinders are especially good for running showers given their pressure balance with the mains supply. Since their introduction, however, they have been covered by the Building Regulations because of their inherent safety requirements – incorrectly installed, and you more or less have the potential for a hot-water bomb. Qualified installers are essential for these, and the cylinder itself needs to be approved by the British Board of Agrément.

▲ Plan your layout and consider where best to site tanks and appliances.

Unvented hot-water cylinders have been available to buy here since the late 1980s, but only since the turn of the century have they really become a popular choice. You have the option of heating them directly off an immersion heater, but most are indirectly heated by your boiler. With the pressure and temperature of the supply maintained even when other taps draw off water, they are often used in preference to combi boilers. Two showers can be fed, for example, one to an en-suite and one to the main bathroom or where high-pressure mixer showers don't need pumping externally.

The one major drawback is where to put them, because the side effect of having a large capacity of hot water is a large volume of tank and finding somewhere to stick it. Garages and roof spaces are the best options, but you might consider the airing cupboard if you do not actually want to use it for anything else. I have seen cylinders occupy the entire 2m-high larder cupboard in a flat, leaving nowhere for food storage.

Pipework

Traditionally our water pipes have always been copper, 15mm and 22mm being the common metric sizes, with soldered joints and compression fittings. Now, however, you have yet another decision to make, that could save you quite a bit. Plastic pipes

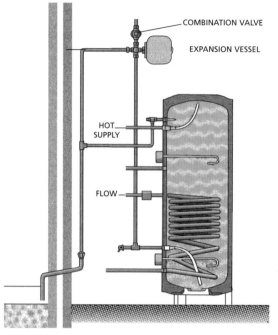

COMBINATION VALVE

EXPANSION VESSEL

HOT SUPPLY

FLOW

INDIRECTLY HEATED SCHEMATIC

available for heating and hot-water systems have simple push-fit connectors to join them. No special tools are required, and you can bend them around corners, gradually of course, but this does save time and money on buying and fitting bends.

There are not many shortfalls to using the plastic pipe system, which might as well have been invented for self-builders wishing to do their own plumbing, but the major one is radiator tails – the bits of pipe that surface above the floor and go into the radiators. These are traditionally straight short bits of pipe that can be painted. It doesn't sound like a problem until you see the plastic pipe equivalent to this, which is never straight and looks decidedly plasticy, which is where many people revert to copper via a suitable connector.

▲ ▾ Sealed hot water cylinders deliver on demand from the taps.

Of course you need to know enough about the layout of your system to install the flow and return pipework and fittings

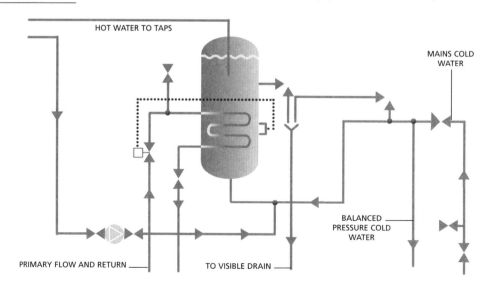

HOT WATER TO TAPS

MAINS COLD WATER

BALANCED PRESSURE COLD WATER

PRIMARY FLOW AND RETURN

TO VISIBLE DRAIN

correctly, but it could be a useful saving to have a system designed and later commissioned by a qualified plumber, leaving you to install it in between.

Pipe sizing comes into the design since the radiators will need enough of a flow of hot water to reach their designed rated output, and obviously the pipes themselves offer resistance to that flow, along with the other fittings and the boiler itself.

Accessibility of pipes

 Pipes aren't pretty, and our desire to hide them has meant that wherever possible they are run through floors or roofs, and until the early 1990s that also included burying them in floor screed.

Around then water bylaws were introduced to prevent the latter without access ducts being formed. Today, wherever possible, pipes should be accessible for maintenance and repair. You can purchase ducting for the purpose, or you can make your own. I have known of homemade floor ducts that obviously weren't deep enough, and much damage and accusation resulted from a carpet layer's gripper rod being nailed through the cover into the pipe.

The prefabricated service ducts, formed from galvanized steel, allow you to screed up to them and run the water pipes inside unsleeved, because they run the entire length of the pipe through the floor. A screwed-down access cover the length of the duct means that once you've had the carpet or whatever else up, you can lift the cover and repair the pipe. I know what you're thinking – tiling or laminated flooring or even carpet: to rip up the whole floor seems a little extreme. I agree, the damage from a leaking pipe might not seem any worse. The option they give you isn't quite so bad, however: instead of running the whole pipe in a duct, wrap the pipe in a round plastic duct and bury that in the floor screed, with removable access panels at the bends, elbows, tees and valves so that you can get to them; if you have to, disconnect or saw through the pipe and pull it out from its duct. This is easier with a plastic water pipe, which is sufficiently flexible, than with copper.

With screeded floors, my advice is to lay this stuff in ducts of slightly larger diameter and include accessible covers where you absolutely have to; because you can bend the stuff around corners, that tends to be less frequent than it would in the case of copper.

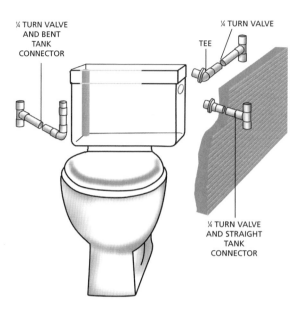

¼ TURN VALVE AND BENT TANK CONNECTOR

TEE

¼ TURN VALVE

¼ TURN VALVE AND STRAIGHT TANK CONNECTOR

In a floating floor, the insulation can easily be trimmed to accommodate pipes, even if this means you then have to use pipe lagging to make up for it. Boarding or flooring can then be laid over the top. At those tees where you may want to convert to copper for the radiator upstands, stick an access panel. I have yet to meet anybody who uses plastic pipe right up to the radiator; even painted, it appears like a piece of bendy plastic tubing that could easily be damaged in connecting it to a solid-looking steel radiator. The massive and noticeable difference in materials is too much to bear, so most convert to copper tubing at floor finish level.

▲ Include in-line valves at appliance connections.

I am amazed that even in prestigious (read, expensive) developments builders do not go to the trouble of encasing their vertical pipes in ducts to walls. Surface-drop pipes to radiators and rising water mains are left clipped on the wall and painted with white gloss so frequently that you could be forgiven for thinking that they had to be. To some extent, that is true. Because of this maintenance issue, they can't be built into the cavity of your cavity wall, as most homebuyers would probably like. But they can be tucked away in ducting that is chased into the wall, leaving it flush, so long as you have a screwed removable access plate at the bottom for the bend or over any fitting.

▶ Standard plastic water tank (cover not shown).

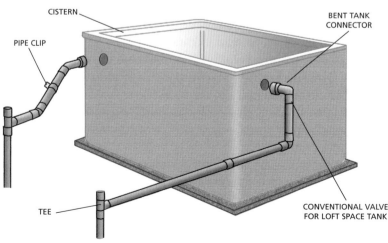

CISTERN

PIPE CLIP

BENT TANK CONNECTOR

TEE

CONVENTIONAL VALVE FOR LOFT SPACE TANK

In an internal stud wall, with some prethinking (that will be you again) the pipework can be dropped through holes drilled through the noggins between the studs, so long as it is a continuous pipe length. For your own piece of mind as well as the regulations, make sure you have more than enough cover for your pipework, and record where pipes run on your plans. Access covers that run continuously over proprietary pipe ducting are ideal if they can be decorated in with the room.

Controls

For your system to comply with the Building Regulations it must include a boiler interlock. I first assumed this to be some device you could pick up from plumbers merchants, but in fact it isn't a part at all but a function of the system that shuts down the boiler when it isn't in demand by virtue of the controls. For example, a combi boiler could be shut down by a roomstat when the room temperature is reached.

Programmers and timers have become quite advanced now, but they are essentially clocks that switch the system on and off automatically. Most will allow you to programme three or four sequences a day, with options for weekends to suit your lifestyle. I always liked the holiday switch on mine, which allowed you to shut down the system when you go away but programme it to spring back into action on the day you come home (or indeed, the day before in winter). However, the programmable roomstat combines two functions in one.

If roomstats switch off the heating when your pre-entered target temperature is reached, programmable roomstats allow you to enter different target temperatures at different times on different days of the week, controlling the room temperature accordingly. You may want the room temperature cooler when you are in and out of the house during the day, then higher in the evenings and lower again later around bedtime, for example.

Look around for one that is compact and neat as well as functional; they usually should be located about 1500mm above floor level on the wall of your coolest living room, so they have to be visible and not hidden behind furniture or tucked into a corner. I think that the digital ones do look better than the old-style annular clocks, which I have known be removed at the next round of wallpapering and never put back. You can also get weather compensator controls that adjust the heating by monitoring the outside air temperature. The weather in Britain can fluctuate dramatically over any given day, let alone a week, and this outside temperature has a dramatic effect on whether the house becomes too cold or too warm. A device such as this must be worth every penny.

Frost sensors can be installed in ventilated roof spaces or garages where you have water services located that will switch on the heating system, overriding any other control, when the temperature becomes dangerously low and the risk of freezing occurs. Thermostatic radiator valves (TRVs) are the most common of all controls for heating systems and have been since the mid-1980s. They enable each radiator to have its own optimum temperature by pre-setting the flow of water through it, in effect letting you control the heat room by room.

Underfloor heating

This has become extremely popular with self-builders since the late 1990s, and is now even being used in home extensions. Instead of a system of surface radiators heating the home, you run a series of water-filled plastic pipes in loops beneath the floor. Because each loop has its own thermostatic control, you can, if you wish, monitor the temperature in each room individually.

Under a solid ground floor the pipes should be laid over the insulation (pinned to it), which is placed on top of the concrete floor slab and then screeded in. Frightening, isn't it, burying all

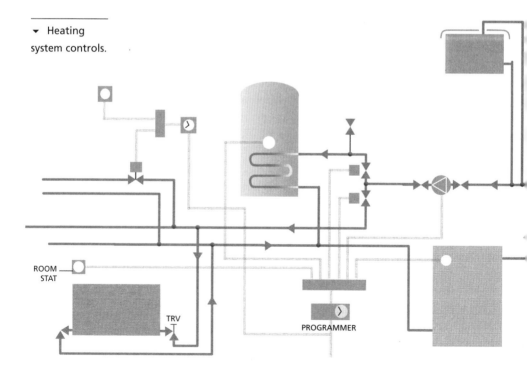

▼ Heating system controls.

ROOM STAT

TRV

PROGRAMMER

that pipework in cement and sand – but the pipes are joint-free and pressure-tested before this happens, so there should only be a problem if you puncture the screed with fixings later on.

With timber floors, the pipes are supported in clips that also set the spacing of the loops, and these are fixed to the underside of the floorboards. 22mm thick flooring is required here to reduce the risk of the pipes being nailed through when fitting carpet.

In practice the work of laying these loops out, covering the entire floor, looks more akin to electrical work than plumbing. Perhaps this is why some people have found it hard to find a plumber to do the work, and the fact that they can't solder joints, bend copper tube over their knee or make a mess. This work is clean and thoughtful and requires a degree of concentration (which eliminates me for one from doing it) and can be carried out by the unskilled self-builder. The suppliers provide a detailed layout plan for you to follow and an installation manual. Starting with the outer loops and gradually working inwards, you might complete one or two rooms in a day.

If the water in your area is quite hard and limey, you should fit a limescale reducer to the system.

You can get in-line cartridge filled ones that require a new cartridge every 12 months and are small enough to plumb in beneath a kitchen cupboard.

As you won't be adding any rust inhibitor to the water, unless you specifically wanted to turn it into a sprinkler system, any towel radiators that you add in the bathroom will have to be made of solid brass rather than steel. Thoughtfully, underfloor heating suppliers can also provide these expensive extras.

If you imagine the small surface area of even a double panel radiator heating a room, it needs to operate at a high temperature if it is to do its job. Underfloor heating is different, because the entire floor is your radiator; the temperature at which it operates is much lower, typically only 2–3°C above the room temperature required. No longer will you be walking past a hot convecting current of air on one wall of the room; instead, the entire room is warmed gently and more slowly to an even temperature. For maximum efficiency, the heating system should be served by a condensing boiler with a low-temperature output.

Bear in mind that not only will the ground floor be insulated beneath the pipes, but also any upper floors that you run heating through. Of course you wouldn't normally stick thermal insulation in internal floors, but it will help to make sure that the heat radiates up from between the joists and not down to give you the warmest ceiling in the country.

 ## If your home has high or vaulted ceilings, then heating the rooms from floor level is the ideal way.

Many people choose this form of heating simply to rid themselves of the clutter of pipes and radiators and allow total freedom with furniture and decorating.

In terms of floor finishings it is advisable to find materials that will not shrink when heated. Timber blocks are not ideal, given their thickness, but other forms of timber flooring can be used. Perhaps the real problem comes from laying timber boarding that arrives on site with a given moisture content and is laid almost immediately and then heated by the underfloor system. Inevitably this course of events will lead to the boards cupping (curling up at the edges).

If you do decide on a timber floor finish, your best options lie with floating floors that aren't actually fixed down but simply glued together laterally, because these will accommodate some thermal expansion without splitting or buckling. For the same reason, if you are planning on laying your floated timber over a screed finish, then make sure the screed has been laid several weeks before and has thoroughly dried out. There is no point in paying for kiln-dried flooring with a low moisture content if you lay it on a damp floor or in a damp room to absorb the moisture. Have the heating on and make the home dry first.

Designing the system

Some manufacturers of boilers and radiators provide a free design service for the entire system if you commit to using their product within it. You sometimes have the benefit of professional indemnity insurance in respect of the design work, and they are usually efficient at preparing it and returning your plans. 1:50 floor layout plans are usually all that they require, along with the specification.

CHAPTER 11

Fitting Out

Electrical Installation

A fact I've brought up before is worth mentioning again here: one of the biggest grievances new homeowners have is that there weren't enough power points built in. Essentially this is because our demand on electricity is always increasing. A decade or two ago, we might have just had a TV set in the corner – now we have a TV set, VCR, DVD player, game-play machine, and a satellite or digital box. Then of course there are the hi-fi and personal computer – and just how many power points do you need for a computer workstation?

So before you engage an electrician in quoting, you need to mark up your plans with your requirements. Start with the socket outlets and assume you are only going to install double outlets – I have no idea why they bother to make single ones! The labour cost is the same, the material cost only marginal. To avoid your plans becoming confused use coloured pens, one colour for the ring main power supply and another for the light circuits later.

Accessibility requirements under the Building Regulations mean that plug points have to be located slightly higher than you may be used to. They can no longer be run along at just above skirting level, but instead have to be located in a more easily reached zone higher above floor level. Like all new rules, when this one was introduced it was unpopular because power points are utilities that we aren't used to seeing in our eye-line, and now they are. Perhaps the manufacturers will make them available in a much wider variety of colours or a plastic that can be painted into your colour scheme.

Most of your power sockets will be located on ring circuits, which, as the name suggests, run out from your consumer unit (fused distribution board) around part of the house – with plug points along the way – and back to the unit. A small home would

▸ This ring
main layout
shows two
separately
fused circuits.

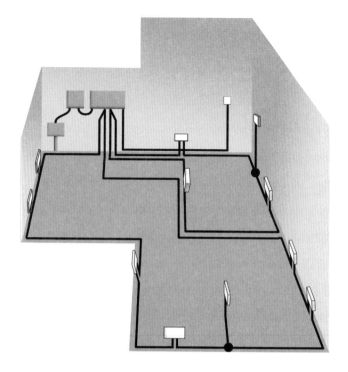

have a minimum of two ring circuits, perhaps one on each floor, but it has become more common to isolate the kitchen with its own since there is likely to be so much demand now from appliances in this room – dishwasher, washing machine, dryer, cooker, etc – although that could mean kitchen/utility room in your case.

With your drawing marked up with the locations of your socket outlets and wiring routes linked between them, it is worth drawing up a schedule of the sockets numbered, their room location and fuse rating on a computer spreadsheet. If you do this on paper, use a pencil because undoubtedly you will revise it.

Safety fittings

Typically these are 13-amp circuits protected with RCDs at the distribution board where miniature circuit breakers (MCBs) have replaced fuses. These breakers pop out when a short occurs and are reset once the problem is resolved. RCDs are residual circuit breakers that immediately trip out the supply if an earth leakage is detected anywhere in the circuits, reducing the risk of anyone being electrocuted. They became essential items for garden or outdoor circuits some time ago, but have now become common for internal wiring and are included on distribution boards.

Fused connection units are those that contain a fuse, to reduce the current to the appliance. This might be done to supply a light,

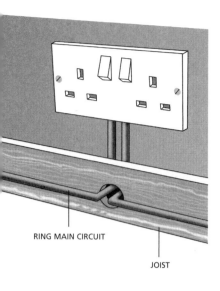

RING MAIN CIRCUIT

JOIST

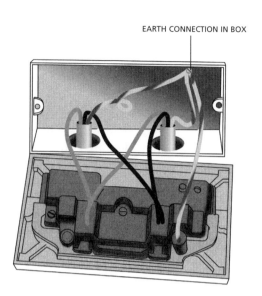

EARTH CONNECTION IN BOX

SOCKET CONNECTIONS IN STANDARD RING MAIN

for example, in an understair cupboard where the lighting circuit cannot reach. Because lighting circuits are rated to only 5 amps, a fused connection unit will be needed to reduce the current down from 13 to 5 amps.

The only common domestic appliances requiring higher current installations are cooker units (commonly 45 amps) and some direct hot-water cylinders with immersion heaters (15 amps or more). But obviously if you are going to install some arc-welding equipment in your garage or a lift or something, your electrician will advise you what is needed to cope with the load.

Apart from the ring circuits looping around your home, dead-ended circuits known as radial circuits can be spurred off them to pick up remote places – the garage outside, for example - but wherever they run off to, they end there.

Cable rating

Circuits need ratings and calculations of the load (power output) from the appliances on them to establish what type of cable is required. Cables are rated by the thickness of the copper wire inside and its resistance, but also by the fact that they may be partially buried in insulation, where they run through a roof void, for instance. Because this can assist towards them overheating, which is what happens when cables are not rated high enough for the load placed on them, they have to be downrated to

▲ Double socket outlets are preferable to single.

compensate. This is done by halving the rating of the cable, or in other words installing a 30-amp cable to a 15-amp circuit where it is going to be totally surrounded by insulation.

Lighting circuits are commonly in 1–1.5mm twin and earth cable depending on the length and load to the circuit (1.5mm sq cable will add about 50 per cent to the maximum length of the circuit over 1mm sq cable), and ring mains are 2.5mm sq.

Lighting circuits are generally sized to cover no more than about eight lights, given the uncertainty over the wattage of the lamps that are going to be fitted to the circuit. This number could be significantly increased if lamps of no more than 100W, for example, were to be assumed.

Loop-in circuits that pick up each light fitting as they go around the circuit are usually adopted, with four terminals in each fitting (including the earth terminal) allowing wires to run in from the switching, as well as supplying the electricity and loop-in to the next fitting on the circuit. Although cabling is universal in colour, red for live and black for neutral, the switch live wire becomes unexpectedly sleeved in black but is actually a live when in operation. To overcome this a piece of red duct tape should be wrapped around it at the connections to identify its true nature.

When it comes to locating the switches for lights, finding the right position on the wall is essential. Walking into a dark room, you are going to need to find that switch instinctively by touch rather than sight. From the plans, you can mark the wall with the approximate position, but I would strongly recommend waiting for the electrical first fix (running out the cables) to begin before you chalk the final switch position on the wall. The best way is to close your eyes and reach out to the wall as you enter the room. Without your internal doors hung at this stage you are going to need to know which way the door is to open, so you don't want to locate the switch behind it or too far ahead of it. Switches should also be located within the accessible zone required by the Building Regulations, so your electrician may have to lower your chosen position a little if it is too high – 1200mm above floor level to the top of the plate is becoming the standard.

Give some thought to wall lights in rooms (and outside) as well as the position of ceiling lights. Wall lamps are not easily repositioned if you change your mind, since the cabling will be buried in a conduit within the wall finishings and therefore inaccessible by the time the second fixing (connecting the light fittings) is done. If your wall lamps include picture lights, then their positioning is even more critical.

Earth bonding

Because of the danger that comes from the combination of wet rooms in your home and electricity, cross-bonding is required for all exposed metalwork. Earthing clamps are used to attach the cables to the conductive parts (and labels identifying they are for safety and not to be removed are secured nearby the connection). Earth bonding is usually insulated in green and yellow sleeving and the connection should be made to bare metal, not painted or decorated metal, so make sure whoever does the decorating knows this.

Supply equipment

I hear more complaints from self-builders about electricity supply companies than any other trade or body. It seems that some have achieved the ultimate level in bureaucracy when it comes to arranging a connection to your new home. It is generally necessary to make arrangements months ahead, obtaining job codes that you can quote at every opportunity and reconfirming them regularly. Among other things, enquire about test certificates and even how much excess cabling you should leave in the meter box for them, as it may cost you if it has to be extended because there isn't enough.

Meter boxes themselves are of a standard format and have to be located on an accessible outside wall, so they can be got at for any maintenance or meter reading. The supply into your home passes through some serious conduit through the wall construction to the distribution board or consumer unit inside. Again, you can decide where you want this board to be positioned, since they aren't pretty, but you will need to get at them from time to time. I say they aren't pretty, but I have heard

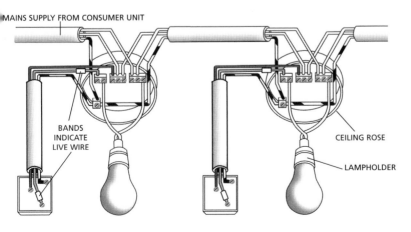

MAINS SUPPLY FROM CONSUMER UNIT

BANDS INDICATE LIVE WIRE

CEILING ROSE

LAMPHOLDER

◀ Looped-in lighting circuits use ceiling rose connections.

▸ Earth bonding in bathroom.

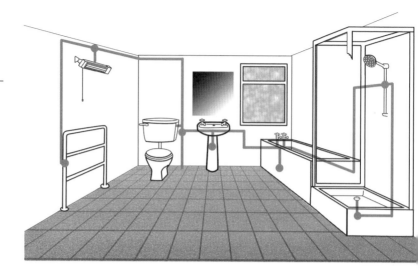

of one make that is produced to take paint, which can be decorated in with the wall.

Smoke alarms

When research showed that only 45 per cent of battery-powered smoke alarms went off in a fire, the case for installing mains-powered units was set.

Since 2000 the Building Regulations have required that all new homes, whether they be bungalows, houses or flats, are fitted with mains-powered smoke alarms; at least one on each level, but inter-linked so that when one of the detectors is activated it triggers the alarm in the others and they all sound off together.

A greater coverage of detectors is now required, and given that the price of mains-operated smoke detectors has come down since their introduction to the housing market, it makes good sense to install as many as you feel comfortable with. Certainly all the bedrooms should be equipped with their own, as they have done in the United States for some time.

Providing that you buy all your smoke alarms from the same manufacturer, it should be possible to interlink them and use concealed wiring. Adding extra units later, for example after you have been in for a year or two, might mean that surface wiring is necessary, and even that compatible alarms are no longer available.

Assuming that you want to go the whole hog and provide protection throughout your home, where and what type of units should you install?

Where is easy: all habitable rooms, with the exception of bathrooms and WCs, can be protected, even those spaces such as attached garages and attics, where fires can start unnoticed.

Generically speaking there are two types of smoke alarms, ionization and optical, to choose from. Ionization ones are more suited to detecting fast-growing, flaming fires and optical ones to slow, smouldering fires. For this reason ionization detectors are recommended for use in habitable rooms where soft furnishings, curtains and the like can rapidly ignite. Bedrooms and living and dining rooms all fall into this category, but if you plan on stuffing your loft full of Christmas decorations and perennial junk (like mine) you should include this space as well.

Optical (aka photoelectric) smoke alarms suit landings and hallways which are usually free from inflammable furnishings and more at risk of smoke logging. Since these areas are your vital escape routes, you need to know when smoke is entering them to receive an early warning. Smoke is what kills people in home fires, usually while they are asleep, as it can creep up and overcome us. Smoke alarms detect the vast majority of fires in the first few minutes, when escape is still possible.

Kitchens and garages should only be protected by heat detectors that activate when a certain temperature is reached. If you fit a smoke alarm in a kitchen, it going off every time you burn the toast is only going to add to the annoyance. Heat detectors activate the unit at around 57°C, which is quickly reached by a burning chip pan, for example, but not by conventional cooking.

▼ Earth bonding of electricity supply.

Most of these mains-operated units are equipped with batteries for a back-up supply should the electrics be knocked out during a fire. This type can be wired in from the lighting circuit if you don't wish to install a separate fire alarm circuit from the distribution board.

Qualified electricians

Electrical work may be carried out by yourself but you should be aware that it is now covered by the building regulations and you may have to pay additional fees in order to

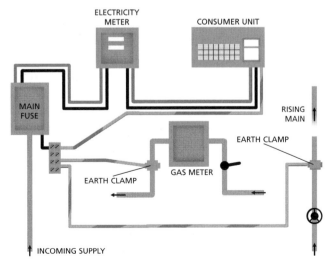

ELECTRICITY METER

CONSUMER UNIT

MAIN FUSE

RISING MAIN

EARTH CLAMP

GAS METER

EARTH CLAMP

INCOMING SUPPLY

have it checked and certified by a qualified electrician.
Electricians who are registered to self-certify their work
under the Building Regulations (Part P in England and Wales)
will provide certification on satisfactory completion and
testing of the system. Electricity supply companies always
reserve the right not to connect the supply (or alter it from
temporary to permanent) to your home if they believe the
installation is not safe, but you will have to comply with the
IEE wiring regulations. You can find registered electricians on
the websites referred to in the Useful Contacts (see page 262).

The registration of electricians, voluntary as it is, falls to
membership of one of two bodies, the Electrical Contractors
Association (ECA) and the National Inspection Council
(NICEIC), and both of these do contain full registers of
their members.

Members are usually required to have three years or more of

**One of the many benefits of employing registered
electricians is that their work is usually guaranteed
to be in compliance with the codes, in addition to
it being covered against the company's insolvency
during the contract by an independent warranty.**

audited accounts to establish their financial acumen before they
can register in the first place.

Even if an electrician isn't registered, there is a legal
obligation for them to issue you with a certificate once the
work is complete, verifying (or rather taking responsibility for)
the installation. If you decide to carry out the installation
yourself, the certificate isn't obligatory, but you'll obviously be
keen to meet the requirements of the IEE Regulations and any
Building Regulation requirements in any case. If you were
thinking of having your own installation tested and inspected
by a registered electrician, then you can expect to be charged
for around 30 minutes of time per sub-circuit and final circuit.
Certificates are issued under BS:7671.

Extractor fans

Assuming your home isn't being provided with a whole-house
ventilation system to remove condensation from wet rooms, you
will have to install extractor fans. I loathe them personally, but

they are effective. In kitchens by far the most effective are the cooker hob extractors that suck out the steam from your cooking direct from the source and expel it to the outside air. Extractors located here can be 50 per cent less powerful than those stuck on the wall across the room because of this, but they must be ducted to an outer wall. The charcoal-filter varieties are not acceptable alternatives; you are looking for the condensation to be expelled from your home, and this means out through the wall or roof.

If your cooker isn't located on an outside wall, flattish rectangular ducting can be run along the top of kitchen wall units and concealed by the cornicing.

Fans that are fitted with timers to allow them to overrun after switching off (to complete an air change) should also be isolated by a three-pole switch that switches them off from both the switch live and mains live current, enabling maintenance to take place or the complete isolation of the fan in a short-circuit situation. These three pole switches are placed at high level (usually over the bathroom door, but on the outside) and should be identified with

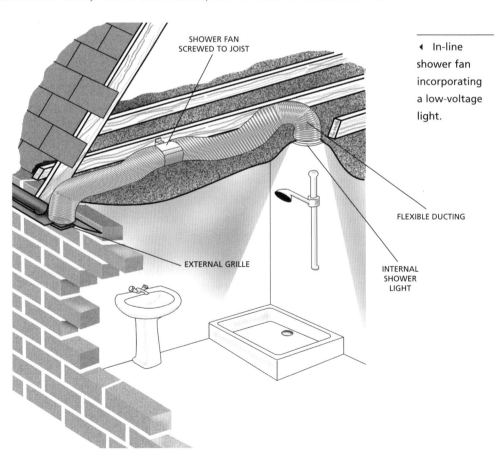

SHOWER FAN
SCREWED TO JOIST

◀ In-line shower fan incorporating a low-voltage light.

FLEXIBLE DUCTING

EXTERNAL GRILLE

INTERNAL
SHOWER
LIGHT

regard to their purpose, the point being that they shouldn't be used to control the operation of the fan.

It isn't unusual for fans to suffer from shorting out, particularly when the duct has been run through a cold roof void. In this situation the warm moist air being sucked out can easily condense in the duct and run back into the fan motor. To avoid this, fan ducts are best laid level or with condensation traps built in. Running them vertically through a cold roof void to a tile vent for example will only lead to continuous problems.

It is possible to design a mechanical extraction system that caters for up to five rooms in one unit. This is sufficient for most new homes with a kitchen, utility room, bathroom, ensuite and internal WC cloakroom. These systems duct all the rooms to one extractor unit located in the loft space and expel the waste air via the roof in one external vent. Instead of five holes in your house you only get the one, reducing the damage on the design appearance of the property. The powerful extractor unit may have different running speeds that on the fastest setting can deal with the steam from cooking or showering.

The choice with fans always ran along the lines of centrifugal or co-axial, followed by wall-mounted or ceiling-mounted and timer or no timer. It has become a little bit more evolved now with the advent of in-line fans that let you place the motor in the middle of the duct rather than in the room, because, let's face it, nobody wants to see the thing and certainly nobody wants to hear it. Switching has also become a bit more advanced, with humidstats now built into many models that switch them on automatically when the humidity reaches a critical level – usually this is defined around 65 per cent (the border RH from which mould can start to grow). I am constantly amazed by the number of home-builders who fail to invest in either.

Start with the in-line fans. If you have a loft void above the ceiling, then all you need to actually see on the ceiling itself is the duct opening or the duct opening with a low-voltage halogen lamp in the middle of it. The latter has been developed for showers, and having just installed one myself, I can tell you they are superb. The fans are mounted to the side or top of the joists in the loft, from which you should still run a fused connection unit to act as an isolator switch, and the flexible ducting is run in and out of it to the eaves vent. You have the added benefit of sound insulation from the ceiling and loft insulation above with these, but they are fairly quiet to begin with. It is important to appreciate the direction of airflow, and the fans usually have an arrow stuck on the side to point the way.

Invariably a lower current is required, and a switched fused connector unit is needed instead of the usual triple-pole isolator switch to reduce the current to the motor and light transformer. The switched live can be connected to your bathroom light with most other fans. To have the fan operated by the room's light switch is fair enough in a windowless room, but where you have plenty of daylight, an extractor that only runs when the light is on seems like a waste of power. By using a fan with an integral electronic thermostat you can forget the light switch and rely on it coming on only when it actually is needed, such as when you're running a bath or taking a shower.

I've seen a few fans on the market with built-in delay switches that wait for a couple of adjustable minutes to see if you are going to switch off the light and leave. In this way the unit is trying to discover whether you just popped in to use the toilet and really won't appreciate the fan motor whirring away for the next 15 minutes or have actually come in to generate some serious steam. Some even have a trickle-vent facility where they tick over very slowly in rooms where no windows exist.

Bathroom fans typically need to extract at least 15L of air per second, whereas kitchens need at least two to four times that amount to cope with the condensation from cooking.

 If you loathe the idea of having any fans at all in your new home, then your only choice is to install a passive whole-house ventilation system.

These are installed as stack pipes that allow the warm moist air from your wet rooms to rise up naturally into the roof void and out through vents in the roof. To do this convincingly, a low-rated fan is often needed to draw the air up and help it on its way, because you never know in summer if the air outside your home is going to be even warmer. For more information on these systems, see Chapter 9, pages 180-181.

Intruder alarms

As much or as little protection as you want can be wired in with a burglar alarm system. Most of the manufacturers offer add-on PIRs or contact breakers that can be added to rooms later if you would rather start off with a minimum installation, particularly easy if they are wireless and rely on sending a high-frequency signal to the control panel when broken.

The hard part comes from locating the control panel in a discreet but accessible position where you can set it as you are leaving home. The popular choice lately seems to be the downstairs cloakroom WC, which is often close to the front door – a bit less obtrusive, perhaps, than in the hall itself, where a panel looks like a second distribution board. From the panel the wiring (even in a wireless system) must run out to the alarm sounder outside, and this is not always easily placed. It should be inaccessible with little (if any) exposed wires for the burglar to cut. Sounders should also be highly visible as a deterrent. Up tight beneath the eaves where the wiring can run in through the roof void is best.

Surround-sound systems

Hi-fi wiring traipsing across our lounges to speakers is just as annoying as any other surface wiring. It is easy to include speaker points that provide for your TV or hi-fi or, more increasingly, both in one hard-wired service. All that is required is to plug in your speakers as and when they are needed, sit back and enjoy.

If you still think that that is a bit of a bind, you can install the speakers as well, flush-fitting to ceilings in as many rooms as you want, for channelling the entertainment to specific rooms.

Waste-water plumbing

Plumbing in waste-water drainage is becoming more and more suited for DIY work, largely due to the advent of push-fit pipe systems that complement the original solvent weld and compression-fitting products we are so used to. Solvent-welding or gluing the joints of waste plumbing may have put off some self-builders from installing their own system, but it shouldn't have. The trick with solvent welding is to make sure everything is fitted together as it should be and as you want it, with the appliances connected up before you take each joint apart for gluing.

Solvent weld doesn't come apart without a saw once it's set, and is not very forgiving.

Compression joints, on the other hand, are easily removed and refitted. They require only hand tightening to be waterproof so long as the chamfered rubber seals are not pinched or misshaped. The fittings, such as elbows and T-pieces, are a bit bulkier than the other types and you do need fairly good access to get at them, so they can't be fitted tight against walls so easily. For this reason

I've always thought a combination of compression fittings and push-fit ones to be best.

Push-fit pipes have a thinner wall than the rest and aren't compatible with solvent-weld pipes; the difference between their outside diameter may only be minor, but it's enough to mean you can't join the two together. Compression fittings by their nature will accommodate both and can be used therefore as adapters between the two if need be.

Push-fit pipes are accidentally bendable, which I find a little troubling. They will spring back if collapsed, but the pipe will be kinked a bit and their lack of robustness must mean they need plenty of support if hot water is to be flowing through them without deformation.

Limits for waste pipe runs and fittings

Appliance	Waste pipe size	Max length of waste	Trap size	Standard fall
WC	100mm	6m	50mm	20mm
Bath	40mm	3m	50mm	20–40mm
Shower	40mm	3m	50mm	20–40mm
Basin	32mm	1.7m	75mm	20mm
Combined	50mm	4m	–	20–40mm

The fall on waste pipes of 32–50mm diameter should be somewhere between 18mm and 90mm per metre run. Outside these limits, problems may occur.

With 100mm pipes for WC pans, the fall should be at the lower gradient of 18mm per metre for a single WC, but if you have long runs of waste and more than one pan connected, you could reduce this to 9mm per metre.

All appliances connected to the foul drainage have to be protected by water seal traps (although some waterless traps are now on the market and may be used) to protect them from the smell of foul drainage.

To stop the water seals being broken (pulled out) by the air pressures that can exist in the system, maximum lengths apply. You can exceed these lengths by ventilating the branch waste runs, either by introducing a vent pipe to them, or more commonly, by fitting air admittance valves (AAV) to the pipes. These devices draw air into the system when it's needed to aid the flow of water and protect the traps. You can buy them as 100mm fittings to go on top of stub stacks (shortened SVPs) or as smaller diameters to go on bath and basin waste pipes.

▲ Push-fit (top) and compression (below) wash pipe fittings.

If you have a WC that needs to be connected further than 6m away from the soil vent stack pipe, then a stub stack terminated with an AAV is what you need.

These products have a rubber seal inside them which could freeze up if fitted outside, so you are restricted to internal stacks with them. They can go in the loft space, but either way the stack must be taken up inside the home.

Access is important to waste drainage at changes of direction, and boxing them in is fine if you include removable covers at spots where you need to get at. Stub stacks and AAVs can be boxed in, but bear in mind that they need to draw air in so leave some gaps or include a vent grill.

Try to avoid waste pipes connecting into stacks directly opposite each other, a staggered connection or a proprietary boss connector should be used to make sure you don't get foul water from one running at maximum flow into the other.

Since the year 2000 we have seen quite a few changes in plumbing fittings: flexible pan connectors that bend to any angle, 90-degree pan connectors with small pipe inlets to take basin wastes, and so on, all designed to make plumbing easier.

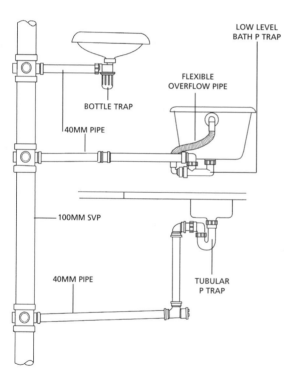

LOW LEVEL BATH P TRAP

FLEXIBLE OVERFLOW PIPE

BOTTLE TRAP

40MM PIPE

100MM SVP

40MM PIPE

TUBULAR P TRAP

▲ Above ground plumbing system.

Testing

Once all the pipes are connected up and appliances are fitted, the system should be air-tested to check for any leaks. Plumbers will have the equipment needed for this, and you need to ensure that they test their own work and notify the building control officer to witness the test. This is one of those statutory inspection stages that are vital to you receiving your Completion Certificate later.

If you've carried out the plumbing work yourself, you can hire the equipment. You will need at least two 100mm adjustable bungs to seal off the stack at the top and bottom (in the first manhole), and possibly a manometer to measure the air pressure in the system. With all the traps full of water and nothing left open or unconnected (such as washing machine or dishwasher waste points), it should be possible to push up the gauge gently with air to at least 38mm and hold it there for three minutes or more.

Bags that can be inflated in pipes are an alternative to bungs, and air tests can be successfully measured without gauges. Instead, the WC pan can be filled with water and a level should be found without it disappearing into the system if air pressure is present. It is entirely possible to flood your home by doing this, particularly if you use an upstairs WC and the pressure forces water out downstairs, or if you have open appliance wastes in the kitchen. So don't blame me if you trash your floor finishings.

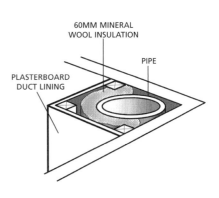

▲ Fire and sound insulation of service ducts.

Sanitaryware

On the whole, you can describe our preference in sanitaryware as conservative. It hasn't really changed much over the years. From high-level WC cisterns to low-level, from porcelain to vitrified china, the WC has always been the WC. Yes, we experimented with colours in the 1970s, but now the pampas green suites are being skipped and white is back. The cistern has shrunk by a third in size in the name of water conservation, but otherwise it has remained timeless.

Not so in other countries – take Japan for instance. Their high-tec toilets have been described as something out of *The Hitchhiker's Guide to the Galaxy*, with selection panels that offer you a choice of extras ranging from water sprays of varying intensity to blow-drying and even massaging – although I can't bring myself to think about the latter. In 2000, only about 3 per cent of their sales were overseas, but if you don't mind shopping on the Internet I'm sure you could get one. It will, I'm sure, widen your circle of close friends.

A bit less radical are wall-hung WCs, which will look the business in any contemporary-style bathroom. If your taste is for hidden plumbing and minimalism, they might be just what you're looking for. A glass bowl basin with stainless steel trap and waste will complement this style, which frees up the floor and makes the bathroom look a lot more spacious than it actually is.

The wall-hung toilet cantilevers off a structural bracket concealed behind a wall panel or partition, and only the pan and its seat project – no pedestal exists – so to begin with, an act of faith is required, but once you've got your confidence there will be no stopping you and you'll be sat there, swinging your feet in no time at all.

Apart from glass, vitrified china is the material we are stuck with. Stainless steel would be a choice if you wanted to make the place look like a public convenience, although baths are commonly available in enamelled steel and cast-iron. They have a solid feel to them that you don't get with fibreglass, although it has to be said that you get what you pay for with fibreglass – the price can vary hugely, and so can quality and thickness.

Glass and steel baths are a good deal more durable and never likely to split as fibreglass ones can. They do feel a little cold to the touch if you don't run the hot water first to heat them up, but otherwise I unreservedly recommend them.

For the opulent Victorian style, the roll-top cast-iron bath is the *pièce de resistance*.

It needs to be placed in the middle of the floor rather than up against a wall, with its legs firmly supported by a structural strengthened floor because these things weigh. I have known them have to be crane-lifted into place.

Corner baths, usually kidney-shaped, are proving popular and so are those with massaging jets or spa facilities built in that turn them into jacuzzis at the press of a button. Showers have developed in much the same way. For years we bought electric showers that trickled out water until they packed up from limescale build-up. Now, thanks to combis and unvented hot-water vessels, we have mixer showers that can be fed with a huge supply of hot water at pressure. This has widened the choice of showers significantly. Power showers until recently needed pumps to boost the water pressure, but now it is possible to get convincing water pressure from the system without pumping the water anymore. The pumps were difficult to locate, given their noise, and many of them seemed to make the house shake from the vibration.

Since waterproofing showers is a perpetual problem, you might want to expand on your options for the enclosure lining. Tiles don't have to be used; you can buy preformed glass-fibre panels or use high-gloss finished PVCu cladding. The latter is now available in wider tongue-and-groove 'boards' in a wide variety of finishes for wet areas, and all you need is a good-quality silicone mastic to finish at the tray.

Ceilings

There are only so many things you can do to a ceiling, and most of them have surely been tried already. Over the years polystyrene tiles must rank as one of the all-time lows in ceiling finishing, but I'm not sure now whether to place next the stained wood boarding in that log cabin/sauna style that was popular in the 1980s, or the DIY plastic painting. I think the timber boarding – plastic paint, or Artexing to give a trade-name, can still look good when done by professionals, but plaster is where we are today. Not exactly novel is it. A smooth plaster finish applied to plasterboard and painted white, clean and uncluttered – nothing fancy, apart from optional coving around the edge with the walls to conceal any shrinkage cracks that dare to appear. Plastering is a definite skill and one that you can't acquire overnight, so a good plasterer is a valued tradesman in this skill-deprived industry.

The level or out of level where plasterboarding and plastering become unacceptable is around plus or minus 10mm over 5m. Surface planeness is going to look wrong beyond this tolerance.

Because our ceilings at least have to resist the spread of fire across their surfaces, plaster is the material of choice and doesn't need any treatment. It is inherently fire-resistant, and its thickness determines how much fire resistance you get out of it. Available in two standard sizes of 9.5 and 12.5mm, the right board has to be selected both for the joist centres to which it is being fixed and the resistance needed.

Board thickness	Board width	Max. joist centres	Nail length	Nail diameter	Nail head diameter
9.5mm	900mm	450mm	30mm	2.5mm	7mm
9.5mm	1200mm	450mm	30mm	2.5mm	7mm
12.5mm	900mm	600mm	40mm	2.5mm	7mm
12.5mm	1200mm	600mm	40mm	2.5mm	7mm

19mm thick boards are available as a special order, and for these 50mm nails are necessary. But it does get a bit difficult when lagging materials like polyurethane foam board or mineral-fibre sheets are used under insulated ceilings to underdraw joists and bring the thermal resistance up by negating the cold bridging. In these cases nailing the plasterboard through the insulation into the joist is a good deal more trying, and helical fixings should be used instead, which may well have to be 75mm long.

Because the edges of plasterboard sheets have to be supported and fixed, noggins are used between the joists at strategic centres. These timber cross-pieces are first needed close to the walls so

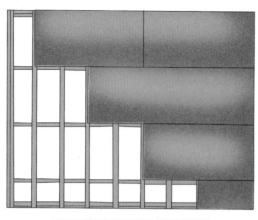

PLASTERBOARD CELING FOR DIRECT FINISH

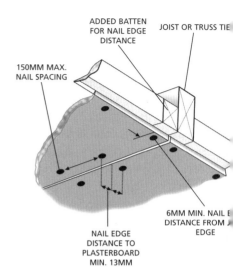

ADDED BATTEN FOR NAIL EDGE DISTANCE

JOIST OR TRUSS TIE

150MM MAX. NAIL SPACING

6MM MIN. NAIL E DISTANCE FROM J EDGE

NAIL EDGE DISTANCE TO PLASTERBOARD MIN. 13MM

▲ Plasterboard sheets should be staggered and fixed to joists.

that the boards don't have to oversail more than 50mm to the edge. Noggins are best kept the same size as the joists in width, but could be reduced to as much as 38mm wide. Missing fixings at the board ends will result in cracks and improperly supported ceilings where tapered edge boards are used for direct joint filling and decorating. If a two-coat plaster finish is to be adopted, you can avoid having to support all of the board joints, but I still think it makes good practice to do so, even if it is one of those jobs that you have to do yourself because nobody else will.

Ceiling	Min. joist width	Max. joint spacing	Floor decking	Fire resistance
12.5mm	38mm	600mm	sq. edge board or 15mm T&G	20min
12.5mm	38mm	600mm	21mm T&G wood or 18mm T&G chipboard	30min

The above figures all rely upon the joints to the plasterboard being taped and filled, or a skim finish of plaster at least 5mm thick being applied to the soffits generally.

The 20 minutes is also known as a modified half-hour, acceptable for most two-storey homes (but not integral garage ceilings), although the use of tongue-and-groove flooring is now standard practice for new construction, where you don't need to come along with a circular saw and cut it up to lay pipework.

Boards are always staggered to avoid long straight cracks appearing across the ceiling or beneath the Artexing, and nails need to be carefully located in from the board edges to avoid chopping them off, and about 150mm apart. Running down, the joist abutting boards can be nailed at least 13mm away from the edges, but they also need to be located into the joist or noggin by at least 6mm to get a proper fixing, and if this means adding batten on to the side, then so be it.

The good thing about plasterboard is that it can be scored pretty easily with a sharp knife and then bent to snap. The drawbacks are that it hates getting wet, upon which it sags and has to be chucked away. For this reason the ceilings can't be drawn until the home is weathered in – if your windows aren't ready and you just have to absolutely get on with the lining work, then make sure you polythene over the openings to keep out the rain until they arrive.

Timber floor finishes

Chipboard has been, and in all fairness remains, the most common floor deck material. But only because it's cheap. At 22mm thick it will span 600mm between joists, and factory-made sheets that are tongued-and-grooved fit neatly together, but that's about it. It isn't particularly strong, damages easily when wet, and actually seems to rot when it gets damp frequently. For quite a while a moisture-resistant 'green' sheet for floors has been made, originally to allow its use in bathrooms, but now for general use. Fixing down has been its real bugbear: nails just pull out as the joists dry out, leaving the boards to creak as you walk around.

▼ Floating timber floor finish laid over concrete slab.

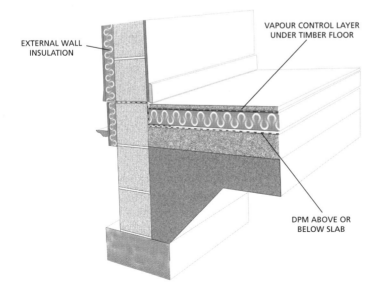

EXTERNAL WALL INSULATION

VAPOUR CONTROL LAYER UNDER TIMBER FLOOR

DPM ABOVE OR BELOW SLAB

Even screws haven't proved that effective, and so now the conscientious carpenter beds the sheets on a thin line of mastic sealant as well as screwing them down.

Floorboarding, in traditional softwood tongue-and-groove board form, has the unique advantage of being accessible for maintenance. You can pull up individual boards to get at pipes and wiring in the floor without having to raise the floor across an entire room. Solid floorboards with a finish that you can admire are popular and come in a variety of species, from softwood to American oak and chestnut. At something like 25mm thick, the boards are dense and very strong and intended to be laid with joints glued, or simply locked together to form a floating floor. Be aware that although the material is sold kiln-dried, if introduced to the damp air of a newly built home it will still cup after being laid if it isn't left to acclimatize first.

If you want or need a structural deck of a floor, plywood is the material of choice. It has known strength and can be used to transmit lateral forces like a webbed structure or diaphragm. It is ideal for bracing floors together around stairwell openings, for example in room-in-the-roof designs, where the floor joists are needed to act as ties to the rafters. You can't do this with chipboard, but ply sheets screwed down are rigid and strong. Grades with phenolic resin bonding are weather and even boilproof, so ply is an ideal product for timber-framed house construction where the floor is decked out before the roof is covered. In this situation chipboard does not fare well if the weather turns wet. The boards will dry out afterwards, but not necessarily in the same shape as they were before! If you do use it, make sure you buy the type with removable protective film.

Laminated flooring with a finished top layer lacquered with acrylic for cleaning is still very popular, and you can buy artificially faced chipboard laminate for less than carpet underlay. These products at the top end are available as natural wood, albeit laminated wood, to provide the cleanest and healthiest of floors. We have discovered that carpets harbour dirt and dust and dead skin that hoovering just seems to send airborne. With a finished laminated floor that can be swept or wiped clean, the rest of the room needs less dusting. If you suffer from asthma, hard floor surfaces like this are a godsend.

With the advent of flexible tile adhesive, ceramic tiles can now be laid over timber floors. Even so, given the amount of drying out new joists have to do, I wouldn't recommend it.

CHAPTER 12

Externals

Cladding

IF face stone or brickwork isn't your choice of wall finish, another form of cladding must be. Cladding is about appearance but also about weather resistance, and your choice of finishings must reflect on both. Render, boarding and tile-hanging make the three options, although there are also sheet cladding materials on the market more commonly used in commercial buildings. Even small areas of cladding help to enhance the external appearance of a home and distinguish it from others. On severely exposed elevations, cladding can prove to be the only guaranteed barrier against rain penetrating, and nothing does this better than render.

Render

A wet-applied process, trowelled or sprayed on and essential for outdoor plastering, traditional render is done with a mix of cement and sand, although lime can be added to improve its flexibility. It is applied in two coats to a total thickness of around 20mm and requires a surface that it can adhere to, and fine-weather conditions for application. Winter is usually out for rendering – the risk of frost following the work is enough to discourage most plasterers. If frost attacks the render before it is fully cured, it will blow it away and leave you with nothing but the job of hacking it off and preparing the surface to start again. An expensive mistake.

From late May to early October the chances of frost are negligible, and rendering can be done during dry weather. Attempting it during a rainy spell isn't really a good idea; those that have tried have seen the finish pitted and even the mix washed out. In the latter case, with the cement content degraded, the hardened render is left with a sandy quality that can be removed with gentle abrasion and is not likely to last for very long.

EXTERNALS

Below is a table giving some advice on suitable mixes for render. The proportions stated are of Portland cement (OPC):lime:sand, and masonry cement:sand. Sand used for rendering needs to be kept in the 1-tonne bags, clean and uncontaminated by other sand or materials.

Use	Designation	Mix	
		OPC:lime:sand	Masonry cement:sand
First/scratch coat for base. Highly shrinkable.	I	1:0.25:3	–
Standard mix range for both	II	1:0.25:4–4.5	1:2.5–3.5
coats. Less	III	1:1:5–6	1:4-5
shrinkable than I	IV	1:2:8-9	1:5.5–6.5
Permeable and only usable in sheltered locations on weak backgrounds	V	1:3:10–12	–

With timber-frame construction you may be rendering to an expanded metal-lathing background over the sheathing material. It's important in these situations to maintain a cavity behind the render on the timber framing for drainage and ventilation purposes. This is usually achieved by vertical battens on stud centres over which the expanded metal lathing can be fixed.

Not all renders are traditional. Modern polymer renders are much thinner and offer a flexible alternative to cement and sand. Often they are spray-applied in two thin coats and achieve a decoration-free finish that is as pure as the driven snow and guaranteed to last.

Breathable homes

You might have seen in recent years a trend towards outdoor clothing being breathable – materials that are windproof and water-resistant but peppered with microporous holes that allow our sweat to be released through the fabric, keeping us not only warm but comfortable. Our homes sweat even more than we do; just by living in them we create gallons of moisture from bathing, cooking and laundry, and even from breathing and perspiring. To avoid all this water vapour condensing and damaging the building, we need to remove it. From the worst areas, bathrooms and kitchens for example, we can do this by installing extractor fans that drag out the warm, moisture-laden air. But that won't remove all of it; heating will help to dry out the air, and good

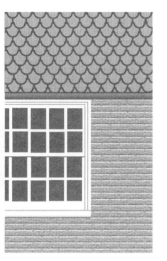

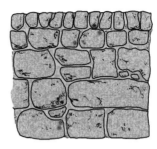

STONE

VERTICAL TILE HANGING   BOARDING

ventilation will also help. The problem is that our desire to keep the heat in with sealed double-glazed windows and insulated floors, walls and roofs makes it difficult for vapour to escape. What we really need is breathable walls.

You can achieve this quite easily by following basic steps in the way your walls are clad:

◆ A breathable membrane (not polythene) behind the weatherboard or tile cladding.
◆ A counter-batten between the breather membrane and the cladding to create a drainage space.
◆ A vapour check (like polythene) on the warm face of the insulation, that prevents air leakage. Your home may have to be pressure-tested to show compliance with air-tightness standards.
◆ Materials of increasing permeability towards the outer face of the wall.

▲ Variation in external cladding can improve the appearance of your home.

Tile hanging

Vertical tiling or tile hanging uses standard plain roofing tiles in the same way as they would be used in roofing. At about 60 to the square metre, the tiles are nailed to battens dressed over breathable felt – perforated, non-tearable underlay felts are great for this. The tiles themselves can be concrete or clay, or even cement fibre, and can make an interesting aspect to any elevation, although cladding always works best when helping to protect a severely exposed wall. Clay tiles when mixed in their autumn colours can really enhance the appearance of a home and

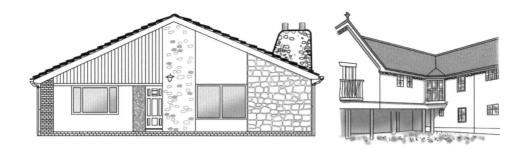

complement red clay bricks beautifully. All tile hanging has the advantage of offering some fire resistance and can normally be used in any boundary situation, but you should bear in mind access for maintenance if any should slip or need to be replaced in the future.

Boarding

Nailed direct to timber battens, PVCu boarding is usually ship-lapped and totally impervious to the extremes of weather if the joints are sealed. Plastic is maintenance-free, but isn't a sustainable material environmentally, in any language. It also only comes with Class 1 surface spread of fire rating at best, which means you can line surfaces with it inside and out everywhere except within 1m of the boundary. Class O is needed here to restrict fire spread from one property. In these situations cement-fibre cladding boards can be used; some are available with timber-effect finishes and very lengthy guarantees in terms of their durability.

Timber is the only sustainable material for boarding, and of course has the same fire-spread problems as plastic, but it's the only choice for a truly natural finish. Western red cedar, for example, requires no treatment at all.

Choosing timber

Timber is perhaps the greenest of all building materials. It is reuseable and can be obtained from renewable sources without causing environmental damage through deforesting or excessive energy use in producing sheets and boards.

The quality of the timber is the prime consideration, together with its treatment. For increased life expectancy, any timber that has been pressure-treated will outlive paint-treated wood by many years. This is because the preservative has been applied under vacuum and has impregnated the timber throughout, rather than ust soaked in a bit from the surface.

The quality of the timber itself will also determine its appearance and durability. The weight of dry timber is an indication of its density and strength. Scandinavian redwood and spruce are popular choices because of their rich warm colour and tight grain, but as with red cedar they may look and smell wonderful when new, but you need to be aware that they don't stay that way – as they age, they dry and split and take on a shiny grey patina. You can help delay the ageing process by applying an oil-based preservative every year, but you'll never stop it.

If a natural look to your timber building is essential to you – and bare timber has become increasingly popular to finish all kinds of buildings – then there are only three softwoods to choose from: Western red cedar, Douglas fir and European larch, all of which can be used externally without any treatment. Hardwoods can also be used, at greater expense, untreated: in Europe the most popular are oak and imported tropical iroko.

Western red cedar has a life-span of up to 60 years, but because it is rather soft in the early years and becomes somewhat brittle in time, it might not be ideal for uses or locations where it could be damaged by impact. It does have a rather unique cellular structure which gives it an improved resistance to fire spread that other species don't have. European larch is a softwood of particularly high strength; tightly grained, it can be used for cladding without treating. Because it is much stronger and tougher than Western red cedar it can stand up to impact damage as well as general wear and tear much better – which is perhaps why it is so expensive in most countries.

Most softwoods available will be white and more knotty than redwoods, but in either case they make excellent cladding material when painted or stained with preservative. If you really want to push the boat out for a durable timber finish, or if you need to sympathize with a Conservation Area or Area of Outstanding Natural Beauty, then you can't beat European oak. Yes, it will twist and warp as it dries out and yes it will adopt that silver-grey patina that cedarwood takes on with age, but the sun-bleached look can add character to the building, and oak is about as tough and durable as any wood can get – so much so that nailing oak boarding to a timber-framed building can be tough work, particularly if you use annular ring shank nails to prevent the boards from creeping off later.

For a less natural but more preserved timber appearance, wood stains come in a variety of colours and finishes that can be applied to ordinary whitewood or redwood. The most efficient timber

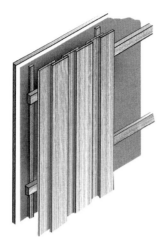

OVERLAPPING VERTICAL BOARDING

T&G VERTICAL BOARDING

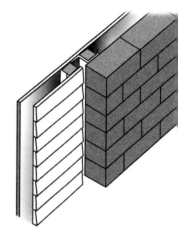

WEATHERBOARDING

▲ Variation in style and finish of boarding.

preservatives are highly toxic and require some protective clothing when applied, but with increasing environmental awareness, new water-based products are available that are free of solvents and will not harm pets, plants or people. Look for the low VOC (volatile organic compounds) content on the tin.

Timber that has been labelled with the FSC mark will be from sustainable forests where logging is not causing environmental damage. The temperate rainforests of British Columbia were badly deforested in the 1990s, thanks partly to the European garden shed market, and only by consumer awareness can this be prevented in the future.

If you choose a tropical hardwood such as iroko, you will need to look for the FSC mark to ensure that it has come from a sustainable plantation.

Hard landscaping

Vehicle access and sight lines

Before you can occupy your home, your vehicle access needs to be safe and in accordance with the details approved as part of your Planning Consent. The finished surfacing can wait if need be until later, if your funds have been stretched and you can only afford to lay the sub-base material for your driveway. So long as it is clean, compacted and hard enough to take the weight of your car and possibly a fire engine, it can suffice for the time being.

What is more important is establishing the lines of sight at the junction with the road. Sight lines enable you to see and be seen as you emerge to and from your driveway, and should never be reduced to a level where road safety is compromised.

Unobstructed visibility through a splay as shown in the diagram on page 249 should exist from a distance of 2m back from the highway edge. Just how far you need to see down the road from this position depends on the class of road and the speed limit for it.

An example of what sight line distances may be necessary is given in the table below, although each case can be different and subject to planning approval.

Speed limit (mph)	'Y' distance along road (metres)
20	*45*
30	*90*
40	120
50	160
60	215
70	295

Where the *bold italic* figures occur (20 and 30mph limits) an allowance has been made for speeding motorists travelling at 6mph over the limit. The 'Y' distances can be reduced to 33m and 60m respectively, where traffic-calming measures exist to prevent speeding.

Vertically, sight lines need to reflect the seated driver position, and so an eye level of between 1.05 and 2m is usually given to an object height of 0.6–2m. This can have a bearing on where you position the access, but more commonly what you plant within the splayed zone. Low-level shrubs that won't grow over 600mm are fine, as are some fine-trunked trees like silver birches that bush out above 2m.

Driveway design

A few figures control the design of driveways, but outside these you are free to introduce whatever design you like. We tend not to be over-imaginative with this feature of our self-build because funds may have become a bit short by now, and there is little benefit in making the drive anything but functional.

Single driveways are at least 3m wide, but if yours doubles as your pedestrian access 3.2m is considered the minimum. Double drives should be at least 5.4m.

If your parking area or garage is at right angles to the road, then it becomes necessary for it to be set back a minimum

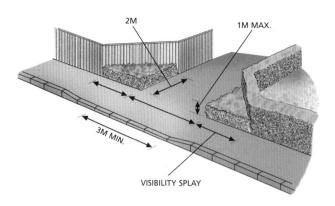

VISIBILITY SPLAY

▲ Keep planting in the visibility splay below 1m.

distance to enable turning; 6m is the preferred minimum for this. If your garage or space faces the road, the nature of the road has a bearing on the distance between the front face of the garage/space and the back edge of the highway – 4m minimum for access onto urban roads, country lanes, minor access roads and residential shared surfaces. In the case of major access or faster roads, 7m is considered the minimum.

It is usually considered essential to pull out of your driveway in a forward position on anything but shared residential roads and small cul-de-sacs. To achieve this a turning head is needed, or possibly at the last resort, a 'vehicle turntable'. These motorized platforms have been used on small urban plots where space would otherwise have prohibited building.

Gravel is seldom thought of as a suitable material for drives now, unless it is bonded, as loose material can be spread onto the highway and people with disabilities find it difficult to traverse. Brick pavers, tarmac and concrete remain popular choices, although the later needs forming in small enough sections with movement joints if it is to remain crack-free.

Dropped kerbs

If your access depends on crossing a path, a vehicle crossover will need to be constructed by suitably qualified and insured contractors. The path will need to be excavated and re-formed over a concrete sub-base to a given specification agreed by the Highways Authority. Four dropped kerbs across a 3m-wide drive width are usually needed, with one on either side reducing to the dropped level.

▶ Lines of sight along main roads vary with vehicle types.

FULL ZONE OF VISIBILITY

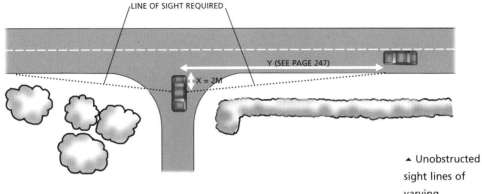

LINE OF SIGHT REQUIRED

Y (SEE PAGE 247)

X = 2M

▲ Unobstructed sight lines of varying distance are needed. Refer to table on page 247.

Garden buildings

It seems that only recently have we begun to realize that garden buildings can be put up that actually enhance the garden as well as serving a basic need. Indeed, gardens themselves are now considered to sell houses, and structures within them of quality can only add interest and value to the home.

🏠 It's all too easy to think of garden buildings as simply utilitarian structures.

Structures that serve a basic need for storage – whether a car, a lawnmower or a spade – but that needn't mean they should look unattractive or be badly constructed. A garden building can be solidly built to last, and, designed with imagination and style, it can complete the garden and enhance the value of your home.

Garages and workshops

If you are planning on building a detached garage to complement your home at some point, you should include it within the planning and Building Regulations applications. You will get consent for it and it won't cost you any more, fee-wise. Leaving it until later may attract an application and problems.

Detached garages can sometimes be treated as permitted development and be exempt from Planning Permission, but the same volumetric rules apply. In Building Regulation terms most single detached garages are exempt, as they are less than 30sq m in floor area. Larger double garages and those with useable loft areas in the roof are controlled under the Building Regulations, as are those constructed with combustible materials that are near the boundary (within 1m).

Design

If space allows, most of us would build a garage of more generous proportions than mass-house-builders do. The standard 2.4m parking width that can have you squeezing out of the barely open doors of most cars is less than desirable. Make sure you measure your vehicle (with the doors sufficiently open and room at the back to get the shopping out) before the plans are finalized.

Unless you are proposing to heat the garage, there is little point in constructing it with cavity walls.

It is usually sufficient to use a half-brick (112mm) construction with solid (215mm) brick piers internally to strengthen it. The position of these one-brick-thick piers is important. To start with, the wall either side of the garage doors, short though it may be, should be constructed with them if the action of the doors isn't to damage the wall.

The corners of the walls should also be formed by solid piers and the walls themselves split up by a central pier or at least one every 3m, which is about as far as a half-brick wall can run before the wind gets the better of it.

Gable end walls to the roof apex can be built the same, but lateral restraint straps should be used at the ceiling and rafter levels to secure the wall back across the joists. This allows the roof structure to help support the wall against wind pressure.

Pitched roofs are always more attractive, but there is no reason why a flat roof for a garage cannot be formed and covered with a roof sheeting material; providing it is adequately secured and the joints are well lapped, it will last for many years.

Sectional garages are still available and have been since at least the 1950s. The difference these days is that they are no longer supplied as asbestos sheet panels to fit to an iron frame, but as either timber-frame or precast concrete panel kits. The latter can be purchased in a variety of finishes, from pebbledash render to a brick appearance, and the former as either modern timber-frame construction or as a heritage 'barn-style' building formed with oak beams traditionally jointed. These make for very striking buildings, weatherboarded on the outside and with roofs covered in traditional clay peg tiles, and can often outshine the house.

To maximize the use of a garage, the roof space can be constructed to allow the loft void to be used, either as a workshop or, more ambitiously, as a habitable room. Workshops may need a stronger floor if they are to house heavy benches or store weighty materials. They do, however, have the advantage of being accessed by an open stair from within the garage, an option that isn't available if a habitable room is formed above. In these instances, the stair should be either external or enclosed with fire-resisting construction – the garage would also need a ceiling below for the same reason.

You are rather spoilt for choice when it comes to garage doors, from the simple open-out double timber doors, to metal or fibreglass up-and-over and even roller shutter doors that disappear into a neat barrel above the door opening. Electronic devices are also available so that you needn't leave the car to open the doors when you arrive home; the press of a key fob button will do it automatically.

Off-the-shelf sheds

Having self-built your own home, you may feel you have done enough construction work for the time being. On the other hand, you may be wondering why you want to buy a garden shed made of matchwood to complement it, when you can build your own decent one.

The vast majority of kit sheds sold are made of simple larch lap-panelled walls of thin, warpable timber. They can be erected in an afternoon simply by standing the walls up and nailing them together, and they look great when they're new, but usually within a few years they start to twist, the roof bows and the door ceases to fit the opening. At a push they may last ten years in a serviceable condition.

You can always upgrade a shop-bought shed to increase its strength and longevity, but better still, you could self-build one.

Self-built sheds

It is possible to build a shed yourself from raw materials that will last much much longer and provide a solid and safe storage space for everything you don't want in the house. Even a standard 2.4 x 2m shed can be solidly built at minimal cost.

Weatherboarded wall panels can be framed on timber plates and posts of 50 x 50mm in cross section instead of the shed industry standard of 25 x 19mm, and the weatherboarding can be fixed on with galvanized nails instead of staples or pins. The roof panels can be formed with 75 x 50mm rafters and sheeted with external-grade plywood so that it never bows. The door can be sheeted with plywood on the inside and boarding outside so that it won't twist or warp. In short, a whole host of benefits come from building your own garden shed that are simply unavailable from the mass-produced models that are on offer in garden centres and superstores.

The following step-by step guide to designing and building your own garden shed will enable you to achieve what you want at the price you want.

Design

The great thing about garden buildings is that you can liberate yourself when it comes to their design. Taste is only an option. Look at it this way, when you start from the basic design principles of the DIY-store potting shed things can't get any worse.

Whatever you do is going to be an improvement, but there are some basic rules that will help.

◆ Use a masonry plinth around the base of the building before starting the timber frame and timber cladding. It will prevent the wood from rotting prematurely and also keep out rodents such as rats, which have a habit of eating through wood.

◆ Use a concrete floor; again it will keep out rats and other rodents, and it will also last longer, as well as allowing you to place higher loads in the building such as heavy furniture, storage or equipment like gym machines, etc.

◆ Use galvanized nails or even stainless steel screws; they will last so much longer than ordinary bright nails, which will soon rust. Hardwood boards are best screwed or nailed into position with annular ring shank nails.

◆ Paint the backs of boards with preservative, or at least primer, to help prevent them from rotting through lack of ventilation when insulation and internal linings are being used.

◆ Use boards that are no greater than 150mm wide or 3m long. The timber will move through moisture changes, and larger sections will be more prone to splitting. Not only this, but anything larger is likely to look out of scale.

◆ Treat the back of the boards with a preservative stain to increase their longevity.

◆ Add a ventilated cavity behind the boards by fixing them to timber battens nailed to the studwork frame.

◆ You can also create a more individual style by fixing the boarding diagonally or vertically rather than horizontally.

Garden studios

I built mine with a large rooflight, window and French doors to maximize daylight for painting and drawing. You can leave a wet painting overnight on the easel without fear of the smell of oils reeking the house out or the cat walking over it. For writing, the solitude is perfect, all I can hear is the birdsong from the wood outside. Roald Dahl wrote all his books in his studio shed, in a comfy armchair with a rug over his legs; George Bernard Shaw had a shed that revolved on a turntable to track the sun as it arced across the sky; even the TV gardener Alan Titchmarsh built one to write in, when he already had who knows how many potting sheds and greenhouses.

 From a creative point of view, an isolated space like this can really be uplifting.

Design

A skylight is almost essential, but it will heat the place to oven-like temperatures very quickly if it isn't shaded or north-facing. A north light is perfect for artwork since it doesn't vary with the sun arcing across the sky, remaining constant and free from direct sunlight and strong shadows. But if you want the benefit of a south-facing rooflight for the winter months, you will need an efficient shade and plenty of ventilation for the summer. My rooflight window measures 1.2 x 1.2m, and even when the temperature outside barely reaches 12°C, the sun through this window and the insulation I've built in raise the studio temperature to 25°C.

Planning Permission

For many garden structures it will not be necessary to obtain planning permission, but you should always check with your local authority planning department first to obtain a definitive answer, since the conditions for exemption can be quite complex and prone to change. At time of publication, under the Town and Country Planning Act 1990 if your garden building fits into the following categories it will not require planning permission in England or Wales.

◆ It is a detached building that is at least 5m away from any house.
◆ It is less than 4m high to the apex of the roof (in the case of a pitched roof).
◆ The walls are less than 3m high in the case of a pitched-roof building, or the roof is less than 3m high in the case of a flat-roof building.
◆ It is sited at least 20m away from any public highway (public road, footpath or bridleway).

◆ It does not amount to more than 50 per cent of your garden being covered by buildings.
◆ It is not sited in a Conservation Area, Special Landscape Area, National Park or Area of Outstanding Natural Beauty.
◆ It is not sited in the grounds of a Listed Building (or Ancient Monument).
◆ The building's use is ancillary to the residential use of the home (i.e. ancillary to a single-family dwelling).

If any of the above apply, you are best to include them in with your full Planning Permission application, since to do so later will require a separate fee and plans.

Building Regulations

In England and Wales the majority of garden buildings and garages are exempt from control under the Building Regulations 2000. The checklist below sets out the current requirements for exemption, and if you plan on building during work or after you have finished, the building won't need to be controlled in this respect so long as:

◆ It is sited at least 1m away from the boundary if it is built from timber and is over 15sq m in floor area.
◆ It is a garage or detached garden building of less than 30m sq in floor area.
◆ It provides no sleeping accommodation.
◆ It is less than 15sq m of floor area.

The exemptions cover single to small double garages with controls over material combustibility when less than 1m to the boundary of the property and small (under 15m sq) buildings irrespective of boundary proximity or materials. Any garden building, no matter how small, that is proposed to be attached to the dwelling is not currently exempt under the Building Regulations 2000, so if you plan a lean-to, for example, make sure you include it with the application and building of your home. In this way you will avoid unwelcome fees or problems later.

Outdoor lighting

I am a big fan of outdoor lighting when it is done right – not the blanket floodlighting of our back yards with 500W halogen lamps that we saw so much of in the 1990s, but creative lighting that picks out a particular part of a building or its surroundings and lights it efficiently and cleanly. Surrounding our homes and the neighbourhood in light may improve security, but at the cost of energy consumption and light pollution. There is an argument that 500W lamps create so much glare that they actually reduce security. 150W so-called mini-floodlights are more than adequate if they are thoughtfully positioned, and should only be used with a PIR detector that is also photoelectric-sensitive and only operates during darkness.

If the lights are properly adjusted, they should not strike neighbouring homes. Although there are no specific light-pollution laws, nuisance lighting can be antisocial and generate much complaint. I don't believe that domestic lights need be a problem at all; street lighting, with its ubiquitous orange glow over our towns' skies, is much much worse. Headlamps from cars at night and public buildings that have their lights on all night are the real villains here. The glow from my town's International Railway Station at night is phenomenal, and globally our artificial lighting is such that satellites in space can produce images that illustrate population levels around the world by it.

Landscaping

It isn't unusual for Planning Permission to come with conditions attached regarding landscaping. A plan of the plot with the species and positions of trees and shrubs may have to be provided and approved before the works are started or finished. This is more likely to be the case in rural areas than urban, but it could occur anywhere where the planning authority have an interest in protecting the environment or screening the landscape from the visual impact of your home.

Indigenous species are what they tend to look for in these circumstances, rather than ornamental garden species. If your plot is large and has boundaries to countryside, then hedging may be sought or the occasional tree. Field maples and oaks make for good individual species dotted along boundaries, but hawthorns, blackthorns and the like can be planted as hedging, with the occasional ash or sycamore tree included.

On average-sized plots, selecting tree species and their positions needs considerable care because of the effect of their roots and growth on the ground and your home's foundations. Silver birch trees are one of the few species that can be planted close to paved surfaces and visibility splays. Their slender trunks are seldom a problem in blocking sight lines, the leaves offer light and dappled shade for plants below, and their roots systems aren't invasive. Some species have surface-rooting habits that prevent them from being used near roads and pathways; cherry trees are primary culprits and can cause damage by lifting the surface material over a number of years.

Lime trees seem to damage car paintwork with their sap and are highly attractive to aphids, so I really wouldn't recommend them close to your driveway or home. Willows, weeping or otherwise, as pretty as they are by a brook side, are the thirstiest of all trees and can dehydrate a clay soil for up to 25m away. Willows, oak and beech have to be avoided anywhere within clay, as their high water demand desiccates the soil and brings a significant risk of subsidence to conventional foundations.

Planting trees

It's important to set trees in planting pits where the soil in the bottom has been well and truly dug to at least 150mm depth, if not more. This will give their roots a chance to get started. The pit needs to be big enough to get the roots spread out and still have some clearance around the sides. It ought to be able to take at least 0.5cu m of topsoil in with the tree.

Topsoil with some added peat-free compost and slow release fertilizer (about 200g per tree) is by far the best planting medium for trees.

The important thing with planting young trees or saplings is to stake them, so they start off upright, even if they bend and do their own thing later. Stakes can be driven in diagonally to avoid the spike damaging the tree roots. They need to be stout, that is to say, thick and strong, and with an adjustable cable tie to the tree that can be let out to accommodate its growth as it becomes thicker. Stakes made from chestnut are ideal since they need only the minimum of preservative and are strong and durable.

Shrubs

With a new garden it is nice to try and reach a landscaped stage early on. Shrubs can do that for you. You can buy them established and semi-mature, or you can plant fast-growing species that will in a couple of years provide you with sizeable plants bringing a structural element to your garden. With these in place, you can always add herbaceous perennials, annuals and flowery things later on to fill the gaps. Having been exposed to instant gardening on television now for many years, we have grown accustomed to the creation of a landscape in a weekend. Shrubs, certain species at least, can do that for you.

Conifers like juniper, cypress and thuya are excellent structure plants, providing year-round colour in shades of gold through to greens and blues. Some are painfully slow, and others grow at

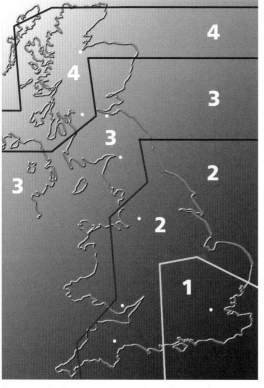

Map of wind zones

1. Ratio H/W = 8.5
2. Ratio H/W = 7.5
3. Ratio H/W = 6.5
4. Ratio H/W = 6

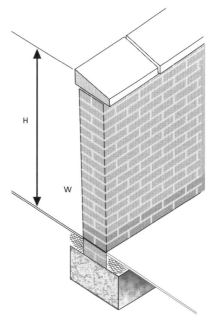

FREESTANDING GARDEN WALL

▲ Height of garden walls should be restricted by their thickness and location i.e. in zone 4, the height should not exceed 6 x the width.

tremendous speed. Clay seems to favour their feet, and they never seem to mind whether they are in shade or sun. Look for species that are frost-resistant, tough and don't mind getting knocked about a bit. A mature height in ten years is often quoted in gardening books, and I've made the mistake of thinking this was the final mature height, only to discover that it is just a marker on the way up. Not all coniferous shrubs are compact; some, like Lawson's cypress, can grow to 25m.

You can plant certain shrubs along boundaries, to act as a deterrent to intruders or for screening in some privacy. Pyracantha and hawthorn can be grown into hedging, but with sharp thorns on stout branches they become difficult, if not impossible, to pass through. These species have the benefit of providing flowers in the spring and a wealth of red and orange berries in the autumn, making them popular with birdlife.

Turfing

To seed or to sod, that is the question. And by now, having reached the end of your self-build, you may know what you'd like to do. Developers go for the instant lawn with turf sods, even if they shrink away from each other in summer like halitosis sufferers in a lift. Grass does have a habit of recovering, long after you've given it up for dead. Seeded grass doesn't tend to brown off so readily, but you may have to wait much longer before you can cut it and generally believe that it's a lawn.

With either method, what makes all the difference is preparation. Topsoil at least 100mm thick levelled and rolled out will pay dividends in years to come. In clay soil, the drainage or lack of it could mean that your grass will be boggy and intraversable for half the year, or cracked and scorched for the other half. If you add drainage now, you might give yourself a year-round lawn that is usable in all seasons.

A reduced level, if you don't already have one, is what's needed to allow you to spread a layer of crushed stone across the site and cover it with landscaping geotextile material. There was a time when this was only used on road building, but the domestic building industry now uses it too. Tear-resistant and perforated with lots of tiny holes, it allows water to filter through for drainage while stopping soil from doing the same. It means that when covered with topsoil, your grass should grow uncontaminated and free-draining. True, you'll still have to weed it and mow it, but that's all part of the fun, isn't it?

▼ Good landscaping will enhance the appearance of your new home.

House naming or numbering

I don't know of anybody who isn't challenged by the prospect of naming their new home. If you haven't already agreed on it, you need to get thinking now. You are required by law to either name it or number it with an accepted postal address, so you can't avoid the issue for too long. Working in your local authority's highway section is somebody responsible for street naming and numbering, and it is with them that you must discuss and eventually lodge your new address.

There are scores of published books on baby names, but are there any on house names? If you can't bring yourself to create a house name from your and your partner's Christian names – and I wish more people couldn't – or call it after the tree out the back, you might settle for a number. This isn't always easy, either: I have seen infill plot after infill plot developed on some streets with the result of 2, 2A, 2B, 2C and number 5 being half a mile down the street; it must drive postmen mad. Your local authority's street-numbering person will do all they can to help you, but even they may not be able to make a cryptic name out of Marjorie and Roger.

Enjoy your new home – you deserve it.

Glossary

Air-admittance valve An anti-vacuum valve that allows air into, but not out of, a plumbing system.

Balanced flue A room-sealed flue that lets in the air supply and lets out the exhaust gases.

Bargeboard A timber fascia that runs along the verge of a gable wall.

Benchmark The title given to a known datum.

Bill of quantities A detailed, item by item account of the building work, measured and priced.

Bonding (*plaster*) Lightweight plaster with vermiculite added for two-coat plastering.

Bonding (*electrical*) The earthing of metal pipes and fittings by connecting them to earth wiring to prevent electrical shock.

Breathable construction Vapour permeable construction that allows moisture as vapour to pass through rather than condense on.

Casement The hinged and opening part of a window.

CDM Regs. The Construction (Design and Management) Regulations 1994.

Combi boilers Combination boilers heat water on demand in pressure systems, without the need for storage tanks.

Condensing boilers High energy efficiency boilers that run at lower temperatures with built-in heat exchangers to cool and condense the exhaust gases.

Consumer unit Panel that holds MCBs or fuses for the home's electrical supply. Also called distribution board.

Contingency sum A sum of money retained for unforseen work.

DPC Damp Proof Course incorporated in walls to resist rising damp.

DPM Damp Proof Membrane built in to a concrete floor. Usually polythene but can be liquid bitumen.

Fascia The board at the eaves of a roof (fixed to the rafter feet) and to which the guttering is fixed.

Flashing A sheet cut and fitted around joints in construction to weatherproof them.

Flitch beam A site-formed beam comprising of two timbers and a steel plate between, all bolted together.

Geotextile membrane A permeable fabric that can be buried without degrading, to allow water but not soil particles through, allowing free drainage without clogging.

JCT The Joint Contracts Tribunal produces standard forms of contracts, guidance notes and other standard documentation for use in the construction industry.

Joist Horizontal structural timber making up a floor or ceiling.

LTV (*Loan To Value*) How much towards the total sum a lender is prepared to loan you.

Mesh reinforcement Fabric steel mesh in sheets for reinforcing concrete slabs.

Newel The post at the top or bottom of a staircase fixing the handrail.

Noggins (dwangs in Scotland) Cut pieces of timber packing between joists or rafters to stop them twisting.

Option The right to buy land or property at an agreed price within a given time.

Oversite The hardcore preparation beneath a ground floor slab (a.k.a. sub-base).

PAR Acronym for planed timber (Prepared All Round).

PC sums Prime Cost sums are the material element of the building costs, not the labour.

Pressure system A sealed heating and hot water system with a pressure valve instead of a vent in the header tank. See Combi boilers.

Pitch The angle of the roof or rafters.

Purlin The horizontal structural timber in a roof, often halfway up, supporting the rafters.

PV *(Photo-Voltaic)* **tiles** Solar energy roof tiles that harness UV light.

Radial circuit A type of electrical circuit; like a ring circuit but fed from one end only.

Rafter The sloping structural timbers of a roof supporting the tile battens.

Racking The name given to the movement of an element due to wind loads.

Ring circuit Electrical circuit for power sockets that runs around part of the home, joining up socket outlets and back to the distribution board.

RCD *(Residual Current Device)* Electrical contact breaker that monitors the earth wiring and switches the power off instantly if live current crosses to it.

Reed bed drainage A natural means of cleaning foul water by filtration through reeds, the rhizomes of certain species (including yellow-flag irises and sedge) are able to remove the bacteria and ammonia.

Render External or internal base coat plaster.

Riser The uprights between the step (tread) of a stair.

Sarking A roofing felt also used behind wall cladding for extra weather-resistance.

Screed The level floor finish of cement and sand, between 50 and 75 mm thick applied to concrete floors.

Set The finishing coat of plaster.

Shim A wedge-shaped packing piece for levelling windows, doors and wall plates.

Skim The thin finishing coat of plaster applied over plasterboard.

Snagging The term given to all the little bits and pieces that need sorting out at the end of a job.

Soffit The board under-drawing the eaves of a roof beneath the rafter feet.

Solar gains Internal heat generated by the sun through glazing.

String The side board of a stair supporting the treads and balusters.

TJI® joists Tradename for webbed floor joist system.

Tread The step part of a stair.

Trussed rafter A factory-manufactured roof member jointed with metal plates in a web of triangular shape. The members of each truss act holistically and not in isolation so they cannot be cut or altered without damaging the truss.

TRV A Thermostatic Radiator Valve fitted to a radiator to switch off at a pre-set but adjustable temperature.

Verge The edge of a roof at the gable end.

VO Variation Orders are documented changes to quotations and contract sums.

Winder A turning tread in the stair.

Wind post A structural post used where the buttressing masonry return is insufficient.

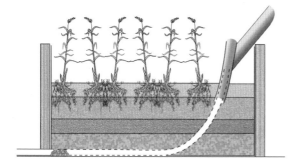

REED BED DRAINAGE

Useful Contacts

ARBORICULTURE
ASSOCIATION
Ampfield House
Ampfield
Romsey
Hampshire
SO51 9PA
01794 368717
www.trees.org.uk

ASSOCIATION OF BUILDING
ENGINEERS (ABE)
01604 404121
www.abe.org.uk

ASSOCIATION OF PLUMBING
AND HEATING
CONTRACTORS
14–15 Ensign House
Ensign Business Centre
Westwood Way
Coventry CV4 8JA
0800 5426060
www.licensedplumber.co.uk

BATHROOM
MANUFACTURERS
ASSOCIATION
Federation House
Station Road
Stoke-on-Trent
ST4 2RT
01782 747123
www.bathroom-
association.org

BRITISH INTERIOR DESIGN
ASSOCIATION
1–4 Chelsea Harbour
Design Centre
Chelsea Harbour
London
SW10 0XE
020 7349 0800
www.bida.org

BRITISH WOOD PRESERVING
AND DAMP-PROOFING
ASSOCIATION
1 Gleneagles House
Vernon Gate
Derby
DE1 1UP
01332 225100
www.bwpda.co.uk

CONSTRUCTION
CONFEDERATION
020 7608 5000
www.theCC.org.uk

THE COUNCIL FOR
REGISTERED GAS INSTALLERS
(CORGI)
1 Elmwood
Chineham Business Park
Crockford Lane
Basingstoke
Hampshire RG24 8WG
01256 372200
www.corgi-gas.com

ELECTRICAL CONTRACTORS
ASSOCIATION
34 Palace Court
London
W2 4HY
020 7313 4800
www.eca.co.uk

ENERGY SAVING TRUST
www.est.org.uk

ENVIRONMENT AGENCY
www.environment-
agency.gov.uk

FEDERATION OF MASTER
BUILDERS
Register of members
www.findabuilder.co.uk

GLASS AND GLAZING
FEDERATION
44–48 Borough High Street
London
SE1 1XB
020 7403 7177
www.ggf.org.uk

GREEN BUILDING
www.greenbuilder.co.uk

HETAS (HEATING
EQUIPMENT TESTING AND
APPROVAL SCHEME)
PO Box 37
Bishops Cleeve
Gloucestershire
GL52 9TB
01242 673257
www.hetas.co.uk

HM CUSTOMS AND EXCISE
0845 010 9000
www.hmce.gov.uk

INSTITUTE OF ELECTRICAL
AND ELECTRONIC ENGINEERS
(IEEE)
www.ieee.org.uk

THE INSTITUTE OF PLUMBING
64 Station Lane
Hornchurch
Essex
RM12 6NB
01708 472791
www.plumbers.org.uk

INSTITUTE OF STRUCTURAL
ENGINEERS
020 7235 4535
www.istructe.org.uk

INSTITUTION OF CIVIL
ENGINEERS
020 72227722
www.ice.org.uk

KITCHEN BATHROOM
BEDROOM SPECIALISTS
ASSOCIATION
12 Top Barn Business
Centre
Holt Heath
Worcester
WR6 6NH
01905 621787
www.ksa.co.uk

THE MORTGAGE CODE
COMPLIANCE BOARD
01785 218200
www.mortgagecode.org.uk

NATIONAL ASSOCIATION OF
SCAFFOLDING CONTRACTORS
(NASC)
020 7608 5090

NATIONAL FIREPLACE
ASSOCIATION
6th Floor McLaren
Building
35 Dale End
Birmingham B4 7LN
0121 200 1310
www.nationalfireplace
association.org.uk

NATIONAL HOUSE-BUILDING
COUNCIL
Buildmark House
Chiltern Avenue
Amersham
HP6 5AP
www.nhbc.co.uk

NATIONAL INSPECTION
COUNCIL FOR ELECTRICAL
INSTALLATION CONTRACTING

Vintage House
37 Albert Embankment
London SE1 7UJ
020 7564 2323
www.niceic.org.uk

OFFICE OF THE DEPUTY
PRIME MINISTER
www.odpm.gov.uk

OFTEC
Oil firing technical
association for advice
on oil boilers and
storage
0845 65 85 080
www.oftec.org.uk

PLANNING PORTAL
www.planningportal.co.uk

PLASTIC WINDOW
FEDERATION
Construction House
85–87 Wellington Street
Luton
Beds LU1 5AF
01582 456147
www.pwfed.co.uk

THE PYRAMUS & THISBE
CLUB
028 4063 2082
www.partywalls.org.uk

ROYAL INSTITUTE OF
CHARTERED SURVEYORS
0870 333 1600
www.rics.org.uk

SOLID FUEL ASSOCIATION
0845 601 4406
www.solidfuel.co.uk

SPON
www.pricebooks.co.uk

TIMBER RESEARCH AND
DEVELOPMENT
ASSOCIATION
01494 569600
www.trada.co.uk

ZURICH FINANCIAL
SERVICES
UK Life Centre
Swindon SN1 1EL
08000 966233
www.zurich.co.uk

Index